BEYOND SCHENKERISM

EUGENE NARMOUR is associate professor in the Department of Music at the University of Pennsylvania. He is also a performing musician and is now conductor of the University of Pennsylvania Symphony Orchestra.

NARMOUR, Eugene. Beyond Schenkerism: the need for alternatives in music analysis. Chicago, 1977. 238p ill bibl index 76-25632. 20.00 ISBN 0-226-56847-4. C.I.P.

Performers and composers who still write for conventional instruments and audiences have long suspected the faults inherent in Schenkerian analysis. As a teaching tool, Schenker's system has limited value, about on a par with parsing sentences as compared with a study of literature. In the wrong hands it ignores elements of rhythm and the stylistic ornamentation that make melody and harmony both interesting and functional. The philosophy of Schenker's system has been thoroughly explored (cf. *Readings in Schenker analysis,* ed. by Maury Yeston, CHOICE, Jan. 1978), with a fascinating variety of conclusions stemming from the basic ambiguity of its premises. Narmour has challenged the system with courage and insight, and attempts to offer an analytical alternative based on the aesthetic principles of Leonard Meyer. Unfortunately Narmour's system is still divorced from the details of music, itself. His final footnote gives us hope that his forth-coming "The melodic structure of tonal music" will "make explicit the principles of the implication-realization model." Highly recommended for music theorists.

CHOICE   MA
Performing Arts
Music

BEYOND SCHENKERISM

The Need for Alternatives in Music Analysis

EUGENE NARMOUR

The University of Chicago Press

CHICAGO AND LONDON

EUGENE NARMOUR is associate professor in the
Department of Music at the University of Pennsylvania.
He is also a performing musician and is now
conductor of the University of Pennsylvania Symphony Orchestra.

The University of Chicago Press, Chicago 60637
The University of Chicago Press, Ltd., London
© 1977 by The University of Chicago
All rights reserved. Published 1977.
Printed in the United States of America
81 80 79 78 77   987654321

Library of Congress Cataloging in Publication Data
Narmour, Eugene, 1939–
  Beyond Schenkerism.
  Bibliography: p.
  1.   Schenker, Heinrich, 1868–1935.   2.   Music—
Theory—20th century.   3.   Music—Analysis,
appreciation.   I.   Title.
ML423.S33N4   780'.15   76-25632
ISBN 0-226-56847-4

For my mother

CONTENTS

PREFACE

This book attempts to refute the principal beliefs of Schenkerian theory and to dispute many of the analytical practices of its followers. Since the late 1950s, Schenkerism has had an enormous influence on music theory (witness the growing number of derivative studies); yet no extended criticism has appeared. Thus the present study is long overdue—though it is offered only as a first step.

Schenker has never been without his critics, of course. But they have been concerned mostly with the metaphysics of the *Ursatz*, largely overlooking the analytical importance of the voice-leading principles (*Stimmführung*). It is the analytical operation of these principles on many levels that has been the prime attraction for Schenker's followers, who today probably constitute the most influential school of music theorists in this country.

But if Schenker's critics have disregarded the contrapuntal aspect of the theory, it must also be pointed out that, in espousing Schenker's dictum of voice leading as the "only real given" in music (*Der Freie Satz*, p. 46), the disciples have often ignored the manifold problems created by his giving "spiritual" status to the harmonic scale step (*Harmony*, p. 294) and melodic apriority to the second progression (*Der Freie Satz*, p. 153). Since all recent Schenkerian work still relies implicitly or explicitly on the theory of the *Ursatz*, chapter 2 of this book thus considers the whole matter anew. But the main concern of my argument throughout is to demonstrate that Schenkerian voice-leading principles produce analytical results that are patently indefensible.

It is naturally incumbent upon any critical study to present alternatives to the practices being criticized. Since the analytical alternatives submitted here are framed within a concept of implication, a second major concern of this book is thus to explore the conceptual basis of an implication-realization model. Toward that end, all the analytical alternatives presented in the first part (chaps. 5–8) are designed to prepare the reader for a parameter-by-parameter analysis of implication and realization in the examples in chapter 10. The analysis there in turn raises important questions about matters of style theory and analytical criticism—yet a third major area of discussion (chap. 11).

One other subject of debate in this book is the relationship of the theorist to history. Many present-day scholars see music theory as a field similar to linguistics. The Schenkerians particularly have been attracted to Chomsky's theory of transformational grammar as a possible model for constructing a synchronic theory of tonal music. Chapter 9 argues against the merits of this view and by implication places it within the intellectual tradition of classical Schenkerism criticized in chapter 3 (Gestalt theories of psychology, Hegelian theories of history, Lamarckian theories of evolution, and so forth). Essentially, I will maintain that the nature of music demands that all theorists involve themselves with diachrony in a real sense. A Hegelian (or Marxist) attitude toward history will not do. The temporal aspect within a piece of music has to be treated as a virtual characteristic, untrammeled by rationalism. In my view, Hegelianism in history, Gestaltism in psychology, Lamarckism in evolutionary theory, Chomskyism in linguistics, and Schenkerism in music theory are all similarly defective.

A word about the examples. Those to be criticized have been chosen mostly from the work of Schenker and his most productive disciple, Felix Salzer. This may seem narrow to some, considering the number of Schenkerian scholars working in the field, but owing to considerations of space and economy of presentation, I found it necessary. I have, however, endeavored to point out only those problems common to the whole field, and in the case of Schenker's work I have tried, moreover, to pick examples from various periods of his life so that the reader may get some sense of Schenker's development as a theorist and of the consistency of his thought.

I have been helped both intellectually and personally in the writing of this book by my friend and colleague Leonard B. Meyer. It was Meyer who first directed my attention to the importance of the implication-realization concept, and I have learned much from our discussions about Schenkerism. In addition, Professor Meyer read the original manuscript twice, offering many suggestions for improvement. It goes without saying that I am indebted to him in ways that cannot be repaid.

It is also a pleasure to record my thanks to professors Lawrence F. Bernstein, Barbara Herrnstein Smith, Constant Vauclain, Richard Wernick, and Eugene K. Wolf for advice and criticism. And gratitude is due the University of Pennsylvania for a fellowship grant during the summer of 1975 when this book was written.

Since that time I have often marveled at the selfless help my wife Kathryn has given in typing and proofreading the many revisions of the manuscript. There are, of course, no words that can express my feelings of gratitude for her help and her unceasing encouragement during the writing of this book.

One
INTRODUCTION

I N THE PAST THIRTY YEARS OR SO WE HAVE WITNESSED THE BEGINNING of a revolution in the theory and analysis of tonal music. Although the changes taking place have for the most part not yet reached the mainstream of American musicology—analytical practices and theoretical concepts die hard—there seems to be a recognition that many of the concepts and methods commonly employed are seriously inadequate. Dissatisfaction with the misleading results of the old descriptive procedures—the naive associationism inherent in the roman-numeral analysis of harmonic function, the lifelessness of symbolizing form by letters or numbers (ABA, 4 + 4), the trivial results of analyzing melodic "climax" according to curvilinear graphs (symmetrical vs. skewed shapes, etc.)—has resulted in a growing appreciation of the work of Heinrich Schenker. Although Schenker's theoretical stance is not without contradictions, his recognition of the importance of harmonic process in tonal music, his symbolization of it through the formulation of the *Ursatz* and the *Urlinie*, and particularly his concept of harmonic transformations on various levels all clearly remain among the most consequential achievements of music theory in this century. Even though the work of scholars like Tovey and Kurth testifies to an increasing awareness of the importance of hierarchical processes in the realization of harmonic and tonal structures, in our time only Schenker can claim to have created an entirely new system of analysis. What other theorist's work so consistently occupies a place in the curricula of our graduate students? More important, who else has produced so devoted a following, a veritable cadre of reformers whose efforts to articulate his thought

I

have resulted in a constant and distinguished expansion of the theoretical literature?[1]

The importance allotted Schenker's theory and the enthusiasm surrounding his work seem justified. For if one is willing to contend with his rather turgid German and has faith to follow (via the theory of the *Ursatz*) the meaning of his complex analytical graphs, Schenker's hierarchical reductions of functional processes seem to offer great possibilities to musical scholarship. For example, such reductions might someday enable us to write a history of syntactic pitch structures; they might make it possible to formalize the analytical rules governing diatonic tonality; or they might enable us to offer substantive deductive arguments in analytical criticism rather than vague intuitions.

Tantalizing as such prospects are, I must argue that they can never be attained through Schenkerian theory. Indeed, I will argue that despite its importance in our current wholesale revision of tonal theory Schenkerism is fatally defective in several crucial ways and eventually

1. The chief studies that come to mind are Felix Salzer, *Structural Hearing* (New York: Dover Publications, 1962); Oswald Jonas, *Einführung in die Lehre Heinrich Schenkers* (Vienna: Universal Edition, 1972); and Adele T. Katz, *Challenge to Musical Tradition* (New York: Alfred Knopf, 1945). Specialized studies attempting to elaborate and refine Schenkerian theory have also appeared, the most recent being Arthur J. Komar, *Theory of Suspensions* (Princeton: Princeton University Press, 1971), and Maury Yeston, *The Stratification of Musical Rhythm* (New Haven: Yale University Press, 1976). For a bibliography of articles devoted to Schenkerian theory—now somewhat out of date—see David Beach, "A Schenker Bibliography," *Journal of Music Theory* 13 (Spring 1969): 3–37. The bibliography lists some seventy items (not counting Schenker's works). *The Music Forum*, ed. William J. Mitchell and Felix Salzer, 3 vols. to date (New York: Columbia University Press, 1967-) has devoted considerable space to the dissemination and development of Schenker's ideas. Although the material published so far in *The Music Forum* deals with a variety of subjects, according to its editors Schenker's ideas remain the unifying point of view (vol. 1, p. viii). Schenker's ideas have also found their way into undergraduate theory texts: for example, William J. Mitchell, *Elementary Harmony* (Englewood Cliffs, N.J.: Prentice-Hall, 1964); Allen Forte, *Tonal Harmony in Concept and Practice* (New York: Holt, Rinehart and Winston, 1962); Felix Salzer and Carl Schachter, *Counterpoint in Composition* (New York: McGraw-Hill, 1969); and most recently Peter Westergaard, *An Introduction to Tonal Theory* (New York: W. W. Norton, 1975), and Gerald Warfield, *Layer Analysis* (New York: David McKay, 1976).

must give way to something more powerful—a theory based on what I will call the implication-realization model. Although I believe that my criticisms are valid regardless of whether the reader accepts an implication-realization model, they will often be made from this viewpoint, since competing theories must ultimately be evaluated on the basis of analytical results. Before considering the inadequacies of Schenkerian theory, however, let us briefly review its major premises.

Schenker based his analysis of tonal processes on the epistemological concept of the *Ursatz*, one version of which is shown in example 1.[2]

Example 1. After Schenker, Der Freie Satz *(rev. ed.), appendix, p. 1*

Ontologically, he conceived of the *Ursatz* as an elaboration of a single tone (the tonic) together with the first five overtones (*Klang in der Natur*), making a triad. As he points out, "The human ear can follow

2. *Ursatz* has been given various translations: "primordial structure" (Katz), "fundamental harmonic progression" (Salzer), "fundamental structure" (Forte and Zuckerkandl), and "proto-structure" (Krueger). For an introduction to Schenker's ideas written in English see: Adele T. Katz, "Heinrich Schenker's Method of Analysis," *Musical Quarterly* 21 (July 1935): 311–29, or Allen Forte, "Schenker's Conception of Musical Structure," *Journal of Music Theory* 4 (April 1959): 1–30. The article by Victor Zuckerkandl entitled "Schenker System" in the *Harvard Dictionary of Music*, ed. Willi Apel, 2d ed. (Cambridge: Belknap Press, 1969) is useful, as is Sonia Slatin's "The Theories of Heinrich Schenker in Perspective" (Ph.D. diss. in musicology, Columbia University, 1967). (Slatin discusses the various translations of *Ursatz* and *Urlinie* on pp. 170–72.) Other good discussions of Schenker are found in Oswald Jonas's introduction to his edition of Schenker's *Harmony*, trans. E. M. Borgese (Chicago: University of Chicago Press, 1954) and Sylvan Kalib's "Thirteen Essays from the Three Yearbooks '*Das Meisterwerk in der Musik*' by Heinrich Schenker: An Annotated Translation," (Ph.D. diss. in musicology, Northwestern University, 1973). The standard source in German is Oswald Jonas's *Einführung in die Lehre Heinrich Schenkers*.

Nature as manifested to us in the overtone series only up to the major third as the ultimate limit; in other words, up to that overtone which results from the fifth division."[3]

Although the idealistic *Klang* is a simultaneous event, in art it becomes arpeggiated (*Brechung*). On the highest level, this arpeggiation takes on specific structural shapes in the various forms of the *Ursätzen*. The *Ursatz* has two theoretically separable aspects, the *Urlinie* (symbolized $\hat{3}-\hat{2}-\hat{1}$ in example 1), which is the goal-defining structure of melodic motion, and the *Grundbrechung* (I–V–I), the goal-defining structure of harmonic motion.[4] In analytical practice, however, the

---

3. Heinrich Schenker, *Harmony*, ed. Oswald Jonas, trans. E. M. Borgese (Chicago: University of Chicago Press, 1954), p. 25. (Five is apparently a magic number for Schenker; in formal analyses, for instance, he recognizes nothing past five parts; see *Der Freie Satz*, p. 218.) Jean-Philippe Rameau, *Treatise on Harmony*, trans. Philip Gossett (New York: Dover Publications, 1971), pp. 5–20, argues also that a single sound is the source of harmony. Thus, some writers have allied Schenker to Rameau—e.g., Michael Mann, "Schenker's Contribution to Music Theory," *The Music Review* 10 (February 1949):19. But this conclusion is mistaken. Although throughout his work Schenker constantly tries to rationalize his concept of organic unity to acoustical phenomena—which is undoubtedly misguided—his use of acoustical theory in the actual formulation of his theory bears only passing resemblance to Rameau's work. In Rameau, tone generation from acoustical phenomena is translated directly into chord generation (musical phenomena); a succession of chords identified by the *basse fondamentale* "explains" the function of the voices. In Schenker, however, the theory is somewhat the opposite: contrapuntal voice-leading principles determine the function of the chords. Thus, Schenker and Rameau explain connections between musical events from essentially different points of view. For Schenker's view of the differences between his theory and Rameau's—essentially, Rameau is Schenker's bête noire—see Schenker's essay on Rameau in the third yearbook of *Das Meisterwerk in der Musik* (Munich: Drei Masken Verlag, 1930). A number of essays from *Das Meisterwerk* (including the one on Rameau) have recently been translated. See Sylvan Kalib, "Thirteen Essays from the Three Yearbooks '*Das Meisterwerk in der Musik*' by Heinrich Schenker: An Annotated Translation" (Ph.D. diss., Northwestern University, 1973). Except where noted otherwise, all footnotes to *Das Meisterwerk* in this book refer to Kalib's translation. For the sake of convenience, I have cross-referenced these to the German for the reader who wishes to compare Kalib's translation with the original source.

4. The *Urlinie* need not be only $\hat{3}-\hat{2}-\hat{1}$. For the various other ways in which it may

Urlinie is not conceived as an independent part of the *Ursatz*: "Neither ... the *Urlinie* nor the arpeggiation of the bass can exist by itself alone; they produce art only by working together, united in a contrapuntal structure."[5] Thus the *Ursatz* as a whole creates a contrapuntal unit of harmonic and melodic, vertical and horizontal dimensions.

Schenker's levels (*Schichten*) are determined primarily by the *Ursatz*; they are displayed in his analyses on three basic layers, called "foreground" (*Vordergrund*), "middleground" (*Mittelgrund*), and "background" (*Hintergrund*), corresponding to lower, middle, and higher levels. But these three strata are only general demarcations, and within any one of them many more hierarchical orderings are found, indicated by note size, type of stem, verbal abbreviations, parentheses, and so forth (see example 2, an analysis of a waltz by Brahms). How a piece evolves or is prolonged (*auskomponieren*)[6] can be seen by employing the concept of the *Ursatz* on each of the three basic levels. Analytically, these are represented from foreground to background in voice-leading graphs. The analysis results in a hierarchical "tree." Looking up the tree, one can see how the overall structure is "achieved"; looking down, one can see how it is "generated"; looking across, we have a kind of "flow chart" of harmonic process.

Melodically, the *Urlinie* fills out the structural harmony in various ways, all of which are related to the original idea that linear motion is ultimately a horizontalization (*Horizontalisierung*) of the vertical *Klang*. As Schenker says, "The harmonic element ... has to be pursued in both directions, the horizontal as well as the vertical."[7] Filling in the space between the harmonies (the *Tonraum*) creates voice-leading

---

appear, see Heinrich Schenker, *Der Freie Satz*, rev. ed. (Vienna: Universal Edition, 1956), appendix; examples 14–19, pp. 3–7.

5. *Der Freie Satz*, p. 40. All translations from *Der Freie Satz* in this book are my own.

6. The word *auskomponieren* may be translated literally as "composing out," but it is best translated in English as "to prolong." Sometimes it has been rendered as "unfolding," but then it becomes confused with *Ausfaltung*, which Schenker uses to refer to horizontal motions which stay within the same chord as opposed to *Auskomponierung*, which occurs contrapuntally between two different chords.

7. Schenker, *Harmony*, p. 134. Unless otherwise noted, all quotations from Schenker's *Harmony* are taken from Borgese's translation.

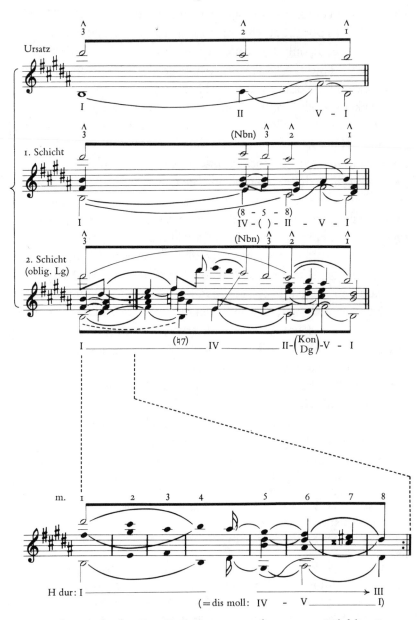

Example 2. Schenker, Der Freie Satz, *appendix, pp. 20, 62* (oblig. Lg = *obligatory register of the* Ursatz; Nbn = *adjacent tone, usually translated as neighboring tone;* Kon Dg = *consonant passing sonority*).

progressions (*Züge*)[8] of thirds, fifths, or octaves—motions which prolong the most functionally important chords (*Stufen*), that is, those harmonies structuring the *Ursatz*.[9] Melodic prolongation may also take place through such compositional procedures as voice exchange and octave transfer.[10] Consequently, the notes of the *Urlinie* do not necessarily appear in the top voice of the music but rather may be found in middle voices—or occasionally not at all. In the last case (*Vertretung*), the pitches are nevertheless included in the analytical graphs, since they are "expected" on the basis of direct voice leading.[11]

Example 2, an analysis of a waltz by Brahms (op. 39, no. 1), is taken from Schenker's most important work, *Der Freie Satz*.[12] (Although

8. Sonia Slatin, "The Theories of Heinrich Schenker in Perspective," p. 182, discusses the various translations of the word *Zug*. She feels that "progression," because of its Rameauean connotations, is a corruption. Kalib, "Thirteen Essays," usually translates the word as "span."

9. The word *Stufe* is also used by Schenker to refer to the seemingly innate function of the scale step. In no way should the term be confused with "chord" in the Rameauean sense, however. Schenker stresses throughout his writings that the vertical aspect is of secondary importance. As he says in *Der Freie Satz*, "the *Tonraum* is to be understood only and always as horizontal" (p. 44).

10. For Schenker's view on exchanging voices (*Stimmentausch*), see *Der Freie Satz*, p. 133; on octave transfer (*Höherlegung* or *Tieferlegung*), see pp. 89–91 and 134–35. Other techniques include "coupling" (*Koppelung*, which implies transfer of register), see p. 135, and "underlapping" (*untergreifen*) and "overlapping" (*übergreifen*), pp. 130–32. These last-mentioned terms are sometimes translated as referring to shifting "inside" or "outside" parts.

11. On *Vertretung*, see *Der Freie Satz*, p. 133. Schenker also occasionally advocates adding to the analysis bass roots which are not present in the actual music. See *Der Freie Satz*, pp. 140–41.

12. *Der Frei Satz*, appendix, pp. 20, 62. The *Ursatz*-level and *Schicht* 1 and 2 come from p. 20, the foreground from p. 62. This compilation results in four levels instead of the customary three. *Der Freie Satz* has been translated into English: T. Howard Krueger, "'Der Freie Satz' by Heinrich Schenker: A Complete Translation and Re-editing" (Ph.D. diss., State University of Iowa, 1960). Owing to copyright difficulties (as I understand it), this translation is no longer available. In any case, it is not trustworthy. Krueger simply takes too many liberties in paraphrasing Schenker's text. Also, the translation is inconsistent. In one place Krueger translates the word *Ganze* in three different ways (p. 37) in the same paragraph (*Der Freie Satz*, p. 28).

Schenker gives the foreground for only the first part—up to the double bar—the middleground and the background analyses of the entire piece are reproduced here to demonstrate the relationship of the first part to the rest of the *Ursatz*.) In order to understand the note reductions, one should compare the first eight measures of Brahms's Waltz (example 3) with Schenker's analysis in example 2.

Example 3. Brahms's Waltz op. 39, no. 1, measures 1–16

The analytical reduction begins by "verticalizing" the horizontal D♯–F♯–D♯ and C♯–G♯–C♯ melodic motion in measures 1–2 and the similar G♯–D♯–G♯ and F♯–A♯–F♯ motion in measures 5–6.[13] These

On p. 71 he renders "Spenderin" as "generator" (p. 48 of *Der Freie Satz*); on p. 101 he translates the same word as "donor" (*Der Freie Satz*, p. 70). Such inconsistencies abound throughout—there is hardly a page without some problem—making it hard for the reader to interpret Schenker's thought accurately. It is my understanding that Professor Ernst Oster is preparing a new translation of *Der Freie Satz*.

13. Schenker leaves out Brahms's upbeat which forms the *Anstieg* (ascent) to the 3̂. Inexplicably, he also does not symbolize an important melodic motion in the bass in measures 7–8.

motions are viewed in the analysis as voices of the harmonies under-neath. Because of Schenker's belief that such horizontalizations can be reduced to the voice leading of harmony, it follows that dissonances should be relegated to an ornamental status as well. Thus, looking from the bottom up, we can reduce the first four bars harmonically to a I–II^6–V–I progression in B—actually the I is a pedal—the whole progression being a prolongation of I (shown by the slur in the bass). The reduction therefore enables measures 1–4 to be analyzed melodi-cally as a third-progression (*Zug*) from D♯ down to B (also shown by a slur). On the second *Schicht* the first four bars, then, simply become a prolongation of the first chord of the *Ursatz*, the $\hat{3}$ (melody) / I (harmony).

In the second four bars (measures 5–8) of Brahms's Waltz, the IV–(I$_4^6$)–V$_2^4$–I^6 progression in D♯ minor (foreground IV–V–I in Schen-ker's analysis) becomes a prolongation of the III in B major. The G♯–A♯–G♯–F♯–D♯ motion in the bass in Brahms's Waltz (low notes) is reduced to a harmonic motion of G♯–A♯–D♯ (the IV–V–I). A low-level, $\hat{3}$–$\hat{2}$–$\hat{1}$ *Urlinie* organizes the melody in the second phrase as well (F♯–E♯–D♯, stemmed notes, measures 6–8 in the analysis) which again prolongs a third-progression (the slurred F♯–D♯). This time, however, the third degree (F♯) in D♯ minor is not preserved as the structural tone, as the third degree (D♯) in B major was at the beginning; rather, the first degree in D♯ minor (D♯) in measure 8 is beamed back to the D♯ at the very beginning to show that, melodically, the whole phrase is a prolongation of the $\hat{3}$ in B on the next level. On *Schicht* 2, then, the III chord underlying the beamed D♯ in measure 8 is analyzed as a harmonic motion connecting to the V^7 after the double bar. Thus, to Schenker all musical connection consists in the prolongation of various *Zügen*.[14] By working through the rest of the waltz, we can easily see the rationale behind the whole reduction.

Several observations are pertinent. First, any roman-numeral sym-bolization carries a significantly different meaning under the paradigm of the *Ursatz*. In Schenkerian analysis the traditional approach to tonal functions is radically changed, since, looking downward from

---

14. *Das Meisterwerk in der Musik*, p. 213 (Schenker, 2:38). See also p. 164 (Schenker, 2:11).

the top of the analytical tree, a lower-level progression is a transformation of a higher-level harmony. That is, the embedding of progressions that takes place is determined from higher levels to lower. The medial harmonic motion in D♯ minor in example 2 is not equal to the initial motion in B major; the former is subsumed under the latter. Melody is also subsumed by higher-level voice leading. Although the high-level *Urlinie* by itself is clearly not a complete representation of the structural tones of the melody, the placement of the *Urlinie* in conjunction with the *Grundbrechung* does determine the types of melodic prolongations—whether passing tones, neighboring tones or whatever—at the middleground and foreground levels, since the *Urlinie* establishes points of departure and goals of motion.[15]

Second, in Schenkerian theory a piece can often be reduced to its harmonic-contrapuntal structure without reference to form, meter, rhythm, or specific register. Consequently, the symbology of the foreground reduction does not reflect clearly the motivic-formal relationships in Brahms's Waltz. Measures 5–8, for instance, are clearly 2 + 2; yet the analysis makes them look like 1 + 3 (note the slurs). The driving eighth-note rhythmic motion in measure 3 to the downbeat of measure 4 plays no part in the choice of the structural tones for those measures. That the melodic eighth-note motion culminates on the downbeat C♯ in measure 4 does not militate against the choice of the more consonant B on the second beat as the structural tone. And the closing tonic in Brahms's piece (in measure 32, not shown in example 3), which becomes the $\hat{1}$ in the *Ursatz*, occurs in the actual music an octave lower.[16] Thus form, meter, rhythm, and specific register in the piece are not explicit factors in making the reduction.

In looking up the tree, all tones are always seen as moving to harmonic processes on ever-higher levels until they reach the *Ursatz*. The eighth notes in measure 3, for instance, become subsumed as A♯, the third degree over the dominant F♯ in the bass. This dominant in turn

---

15. It should be noted here that in certain earlier analyses of Schenker's *Der Tonwille* (Vienna: A. Gutmann Verlag, 1921–24), foreground and middleground *Urlinien* ascend.

16. Obligatory register (*obligate Lage*) in Schenker's theory refers to the register of the *Ursatz*, not necessarily to the register of the music.

becomes part of a melodic-harmonic motion connecting the D♯ over the I in measure 1 (the $\hat{3}$) to the B over the I in measure 4. The D♯ over the I in measure 1 then becomes connected to the III in measure 8, and so on up the analytic tree to the *Ursatz*. The broad outline of the whole piece is $\hat{\frac{3}{1}}$ moving to $\hat{\frac{2}{v}}$. On the highest level, everything before the final $\hat{\frac{1}{1}}$ is in some sense either a prolongation of the initial $\hat{\frac{3}{1}}$ (e.g., the *Nbn* after the double bar) or a preparation for the penultimate $\hat{\frac{2}{v}}$ (e.g., the II).

The structural or nonstructural status of a pitch always depends, therefore, both on the rules of voice leading and on the specific way the *Ursatz* is dispositioned in the analysis.[17] Although according to Schenker voice leading is the "given" (*Gegebene*) in a piece of music,[18] the *Ursatz* nevertheless remains "the only possible focal point" for considering the whole.[19] Thus since all melodic and harmonic structures are eventually assimilated by the *Ursatz*, the *Ursatz* remains the final arbiter in all analytical decisions and the ultimate determiner of the structural weight given any tone. We must therefore consider further the epistemological and methodological status of the *Ursatz*, for from it issue many of the anomalies in the Schenkerian system.

17. The fact that the *Ursatz* can sometimes be dispositioned in various ways in the same piece partially accounts for the analytical differences we find even among Schenkerians.

18. *Der Freie Satz*, p. 46.

19. Ibid., p. 28.

Two
THE LOGICAL PROBLEM

THE *URSATZ* AS AXIOM

ONE IMPORTANT QUESTION TO BE ASKED IS, WHAT KIND OF THEO-
retical system does the Schenker method exemplify? The neo-
Schenkerians attempt to classify Schenkerian theory as an axiomatic
system, since structures are generated from a "base component," the
Ursatz.[1] And indeed a good deal of evidence suggests such a classification. Schenker implies throughout his writings that the *Ursatz* determines the choice of middleground structures and ultimately those of the
foreground also,[2] that prolongations fill the "prescribed chordal spaces
of the third and the fifth,"[3] and that transformations (*Verwandlungen*)
obey the laws of the *Urlinie*, their progressions being completely

---

1. The designation of Schenkerian theory as an axiomatic system is hinted at by
Milton Babbitt in his review of *Structural Hearing* by Felix Salzer in *Journal of the
American Musicological Society* 5 (Fall 1952):260–65. (Babbitt attempts to defend
Schenker from charges of the a priori error.) Eric Regener in his article, "Layered
Music–Theoretic Systems," *Perspectives of New Music* 6 (Fall 1967):52–62, discusses
Schenkerian theory as an axiomatic system, as does Philip Batstone in "Musical
Analysis as Phenomenology," *Perspectives of New Music* 8 (Spring–Summer 1969):94–
110, and Arthur J. Komar in *Theory of Suspensions*. Both Michael Kassler, in the
second essay ("Toward Development of a Constructive Tonality Theory Based on
Writings by Heinrich Schenker") of his "A Trinity of Essays" (Ph.D. diss., Princeton
University, 1967), and Robert P. Morgan, "The Delayed Structural Downbeat and
Its Effect on Tonal and Rhythmic Structure of Sonata Form Recapitulation,"
(Ph.D. diss., Princeton University, 1969), also believe Schenkerian theory can be
classified as an axiomatic system.

2. See, for instance, *Der Freie Satz*, p. 57.

3. *Das Meisterwerk in der Musik*, 1:192 (translation mine).

controlled by it.[4] All this sounds very much like an axiomatic approach.

Moreover, in view of the idealistic conception in Schenker's ontology, it is easy to see philosophically why the axiomatic classification might obtain. Schenker's belief that all complexities and differentiations come from simple things (*Einfachen*)[5] follows from the conception of the *Ursatz* as an externalization of the simple Idea in Nature (the *Klang*). Even "artificial" creations like the *Auskomponierung* of the *Klang*, the minor key, equal temperament, the subdominant, seventh chords, and progressions of seconds reflect this Nature.[6] Harmony itself Schenker regards as a system of "ideally moving forces"[7] in which there are no tonal spaces other than 1–3, 3–5, and 5–8.[8] And, like our concept of geometric space, a composer's feeling for this tonal space is, according to Schenker, innate.[9] Thus we are confronted with a rationalistically based theory.

Despite such rationalistic allusions, Schenkerian theory will not bear serious scrutiny as an axiomatic system. Difficulties exist, for instance, in predicating the very names (the "subject-matter signs") upon which the functional propositions rest. For example, take the names "tonic" and "dominant"—Schenker's *Stufen*. In the harmonic progression of I–VI–II–V, if we try (as most teachers have found themselves trying) to explain why the chord symbolized by the I is the tonic, we find ourselves saying something like "the meaning of I as the tonal center lies in its relation to the V, and the meaning of V as the dominant lies in its relation to the II, and the meaning of the II as the supertonic . . . etc." In other words, in using roman numerals as the symbols of structural chords—and all tonal theorists rely on such symbols in one way or another—we predicate the meaning of one thing on the prior meaning of another. That is, we keep coming back circularly looking

4. *Der Freie Satz*, p. 103.

5. Ibid., p. 49.

6. Schenker makes these points throughout *Harmony*.

7. Schenker, *Harmony*, p. xxv.

8. *Das Meisterwerk in der Musik*, p. 158 (Schenker, 1:203).

9. Ibid., p. 160: "Only the genius is endowed [blessed] with the feeling for tonal space. It is his apriority just as every human being possesses . . . an innate *a priori* concept of space (as an extension of his body) and time (as growth and development of the body)" (Schenker, 1:204).

for the meaning of some chord in the chord whose meaning we originally set out to find. We assume that I is the "core" within the given context, but we cannot find anything single and definite as "context."

The neo-Schenkerians, I suppose, believe that this sort of difficulty in predication can be circumvented in the usual axiomatic way by treating I and V as undefined terms. That is, in an axiom system certain terms always remain undefined (unanalyzable), with the consequence that a "dictionary effect" (defining a term in terms of another term) always obtains. But there is a difficulty in accepting terms like I and V as undefined. For I and V, as theoretical symbols of tonal function, are heavily laden with *prior* semantic meanings of consequence, interpretation, and validity. That is, given any syntactic string of symbols in roman-numeral symbology, I and V function as exceptionally privileged elements. The orderings IV–I and I–V, for instance, are interpreted very differently. But what is the relationship on which an ascription of these symbols rests? Certainly not the fifth-relationship, because *both* pairs of chords involve an ascending fifth-progression; the fifth-relationship thus has to be classified as a simple (nonpredicative) attribute. Or consider the privilege accorded to the dominant: in roman-numeral symbology, we allow the dominant to enter into fifth-relationships with all the other scale steps in the key (by means of the so-called tonicizing, e.g., V/V of IV, V/V of VI, etc.), whereas we do not permit other symbols that right. We do not, for instance, recognize the symbolization III/IV (otherwise named the VI chord) as a valid expression in the system. Thus, the terms I and V scarcely qualify as "primitive," because they are accorded so much prior meaning—a meaning guaranteed by the way we manipulate the symbols.

Observe how different the matter is in symbolic logic and mathematics. If I assert in a formal language L an axiom schema like $(a \rightarrow (b \rightarrow a))$, (where $\rightarrow$ symbolizes "if-then"), or if I assert in a real number system the following axioms of equality,

$$a = a \qquad\qquad \text{(reflexive)}$$
$$a = b \rightarrow b = a \qquad\qquad \text{(symmetric)}$$
$$a = b \ \& \ b = c \rightarrow a = c \qquad\qquad \text{(transitive)},$$

I make no important intellectual commitment in accepting *a*, *b*, and *c* as primitive symbols, for neither the formal language *L* nor the language of mathematics has any connection with the real world. That is, the rules of inference employed in deriving other axioms from the symbols making up a propositional (sentential) logistic system like *L* remain purely syntactic and uninterpreted. Similarly in a real number system: since the symbols used in stating the axioms of equality are so enormously general, whatever certainty we ascribe to their prior conventional use in the language of mathematics is, in an empirical sense, empty. In other words, in both of the above symbolizations the lack of definition of the terms presents no serious impediment in accepting the axioms because the terms are not "about" anything concrete. Even if we state in natural language the axiom "two things equal to a third thing are equal to each other," the proposition is so artificial and rationalistic that we need not be bothered about the lack of definition.

But in music theory this is not the case. For it is clear that to permit I and V to operate as unanalyzable (undefined) terms is to allow certain favored relations to *predetermine* structural features of certain individual works of art—the real world. And it is this sort of fallacious apriorism that prevents Schenkerism from being accepted as a valid axiom system.

All this is by way of saying that in music theory the more meanings a term symbolizes, the more necessary it becomes to know its predication. Such terms cannot be accepted as undefined. As we shall see, Schenker cannot predicate the terms I and V even though such terms determine in important ways the strategies of his analysis and the major hypotheses he uses in his attempt to make valid analytical statements about specific artworks. For the choice of the unpredicated concepts of I and V in Schenkerian theory—a choice that entails the full range of prior semantic meanings attached to them (interpretation, consequence, validity, satisfiability, and so forth)—specifies to a large extent what counts *as system* and what is admissable *as logic* within the system (recall the invalid III/IV). As Weizenbaum points out with regard to computer models in visual perception, "the worker on vision problems will have virtually determined major components of his research strategy the moment he decides on say, edges and corners as elements of his primitive vocabulary."[10] Put another way, because of the prior meanings attached to I and V, the Schenkerian makes too great an intellectual commitment in accepting such terms as undefined— a much greater commitment than either the mathematician or the logician makes in accepting *a*, *b*, or *c* as the undefined terms in mathematics or symbolic logic. And it is this commitment that prevents us from accepting I and V as undefined terms in an axiomatic system. Thus, we are not intellectually justified in accepting axiomatically any statements in Schenkerian theory.

In this connection it is important that we do not confound the concept of predication with "decision procedures." Obviously, in many respects the problem of predicating the terms I and V is closely related to the problem of discovering precise general criteria that will enable us to designate with near certainty the governing tonal center of any given piece. Decision procedures can be given, of course, that will let us consistently call one and only one tone the tonic. We might say about the melody of "God Save the Queen," for instance: "Collect all the tones and arrange them in a sequence of ascending fifths. One interval will not be perfect but instead will be diminished. From the last tone of that interval in the ascending series, project another ascending perfect fifth and name that tone the tonic. Project two perfect fifths from the last tone of the diminished fifth and name that tone the dominant." And so on. But such procedures cannot genuinely be called predicative. The unique position of that tone in the series that we are calling the "tonic" in "God Save the Queen"—the tone a perfect fifth away from the last tone of the diminished fifth in the series— constitutes only one attribute among many and cannot automatically qualify as predicative unless a valid *set of arguments* is given. And clearly these arguments are going to have to be based not on some hypothetical context like a series of fifths but rather on the specific syntactic structural relationships that obtain in "God Save the Queen."[11]

10. Joseph Weizenbaum, *Computer Power and Human Reason: From Judgment to Calculation* (San Francisco: W. H. Freeman and Co., 1976), pp. 185–86.

11. There are other decision procedures used in designating the tonal center. Another, for instance, is the idea that the tonic is determined by the dominant and that

The fact is that, to date, we simply do not know the set of arguments that justifies our accepting "tonicness" in a piece as axiomatic. I am not denying that as a *generalization* a tonic exists in "God Save the Queen," nor am I suggesting that we abandon the notion of tonics or dominants. Nor am I saying that the voice-leading rules of Schenkerian theory are useless in helping to determine the defining attributes of tonality. What I am saying is that the present state of music theory is such that there are no arguments sufficiently compelling to enable us to accept the assertion of the tonic (or the dominant) as a subject-matter sign in an axiomatic system.

There are other basic problems in viewing Schenkerism as an axiomatic system. For instance, even if the I–V–I relationship could be validly predicated in Schenkerian theory, it is common knowledge that in an axiomatic system predicates must not have different meanings.

---

the dominant is the result of either the II–V relationship (a minor triad followed by a major triad an ascending fourth away) or the IV–V relationship (two major triads a second apart). This notion rests upon the fact that these two pairs of relationships are unique in the context of a triadic system built on the steps of the major scale. However, since tonal centers are commonly ascribed in pieces where no such II–V or IV–V occurs, and since such progressions also occur in pieces that are commonly classified as non-tonal, neither relationship can be regarded as an invariant attribute in determining tonality. Thus, the use of the II–V or the IV–V progression is a decision procedure in ascribing tonal function and not really predicative. Moreover, there is the matter of "tonicalization" (Schenker's *Tonikalisierung*). The VI–V/V progression has all the earmarks of the II–V progression; yet often we do not call such a V/V a dominant in a new key. Similarly, the I–V/V progression evinces all the attributes of a IV–V progression, and yet often we do not analyze the I as a IV or the V/V as a V in another key. On the other hand, we might interpret progressions involving such V/V's as belonging to a new key if they were greatly prolonged, or if they recurred continually, or if they were constantly stressed, or if the originally implied tonic was greatly delayed, or if the originally implied tonic never occurred at all, or if . . . The point is that we do not have consistent and precise rules for ascribing tonal centers or assigning roman-numeral symbols. Anyone who doubts the ad hoc nature of our decision procedures in specifying names in harmonic analysis need only examine the most popular textbooks on the subject—or better yet, try formulating a set of coherent rules for undergraduate music majors to apply to the repertory commonly designated as "tonal." We plainly do not know what the universes of discourse are in regard to tonality.

In ordinary language one predicate may have two different meanings. Thus "teaches" in "Tom teaches Greek" is different in meaning from "teaches" in "Tom teaches Dick." And "Tom teaches Dick" with the first meaning of "teaches" is not a sentence at all but a nonsensical expression, just as "Tom teaches point $(1,1)$" is nonsensical. In an axiom-system a predicate must not have different meanings, and the syntactical rules must enable us to know which names can be significantly combined with a given predicate.[12]

Thus the *Ursatz* cannot be asserted as a "true" proposition about the structure of, say, the harmonic progression $\begin{smallmatrix}\hat{3}-2-1-2-3-\hat{2}-\hat{1}\ \text{(melody)}\\ \text{I } \underline{\text{V I}}, \text{V I} \underline{\text{V I}},\text{(harmony)}\end{smallmatrix}$ unless we are able to give the complete set of analytic reasons why the predication of the last $\begin{smallmatrix}\hat{2}-\hat{1}\\ \text{V I}\end{smallmatrix}$ is different from the predication of the other $\begin{smallmatrix}2-1\\ \text{V I}\end{smallmatrix}$. It will not do to declare that in this progression the last $\begin{smallmatrix}\hat{2}-\hat{1}\\ \text{V I}\end{smallmatrix}$ is more closed than the other simply because it *is* the last. That kind of reasoning commits the a priori error—jumping from the empirical generalization to the assertion of a specific law without knowing the structural foundation of, and therefore the logical validity of, the generalization. For the *Ursatz*-proposition is significant only if the subject-matter signs, the terms of the statement, are justified:

> A proposition is not a single entity, but a relation of several; hence a statement in which a proposition appears as subject will only be significant if it can be reduced to a statement about the terms [e.g., I–V–I or $\hat{3}$–$\hat{2}$–$\hat{1}$] which appear in the proposition. A proposition, like such phrases as "the so-and-so," where grammatically it appears as subject, must be broken up into its constituents if we are to find the true subject or subjects.[13]

There is, of course, no question that the predication of the first $\begin{smallmatrix}2-1\\ \text{V I}\end{smallmatrix}$ in the progression *is* different from the last $\begin{smallmatrix}\hat{2}-\hat{1}\\ \text{V I}\end{smallmatrix}$; and there is no question that empirically we accept the last $\begin{smallmatrix}\hat{2}-\hat{1}\\ \text{V I}\end{smallmatrix}$ as being more closed than the first. But what are the sets of arguments according to which the

12. J. H. Woodger, *The Axiomatic Method in Biology* (Cambridge: Cambridge University Press, 1937), p. 3.

13. A. N. Whitehead and Bertrand Russell, *Principia Mathematica*, vol. 1, 2d ed. (Cambridge: Cambridge University Press, 1957), p. 48.

last $\frac{2-\hat{1}}{V\ I}$ in the progression is more closed than the first $\frac{2-1}{V\ I}$? We simply do not know yet, even though the "true subject"—the musical structure—of the V–I signs and their predication manifestly resides in a complete knowledge of just such rules of closure.

To repeat: our inability to predicate the names of tonic and dominant, on which Schenkerian theory rests in particular, renders false the notion that the theory is axiomatically based. And until we are able to give the set of arguments about why a certain tone has the property of a tonic or a dominant thereby justifying the nominal ascription of "I" or "V" or why one $\frac{2-1}{V\ I}$ relationship is predicated differently from all other $\frac{2-1}{V\ I}$ relationships in a given system, any axiomatic approach relying on roman numerals for some of its subject-matter signs of structure will remain a failure. That being the case, there is no reason to accept any statement in Schenkerian theory as axiomatic, since the theory relies throughout on ascribing functional identification to tones according to scale degrees as symbolized in roman-numeral and arabic-numeral names.

Other fundamental reasons why Schenkerian theory cannot qualify as a formal axiomatic system will be examined shortly. But even as an informal axiomatic system where general syntactic and semantic statements about relationships between events would normally be accepted as a preliminary background to axiomatization, Schenkerian theory fails on several counts. First, the *Ursatz* cannot function as an axiom because, as Schenker emphasized throughout his writings, it defines something else, namely, the basic tonality of a piece as evidenced in a single chord. That is, the *Ursatz* "composes out" the main chord; it is not the irreducible minimum. Therefore, if anything has to be asserted as the basic proposition in Schenkerian theory, it is the tonic root position triad. And in this sense, the subject-matter signs have to be the notes by themselves without the names "tonic" and "dominant." But this, of course, leads to an absurdity, because a fundamental chord by itself is not a temporal syntactic pattern but a relational entity. And using a relational entity as the axiomatic base from which to derive the syntactic structure of a composition is like using inert chemical elements to understand the temporal processes of subatomic particles.

But there is perhaps another interpretation of the informal axiomatic view. We might, for instance, posit the *Urlinie* as one axiom and the *Grundbrechung* as another. With these united in the *Ursatz*, structural derivation would proceed via the syntax (i.e., the rules of inference) from this "set of axioms" to the middleground and the concluding foreground. There is some evidence for this view. In *Der Freie Satz*, for instance, the *Urlinie* and the *Bassbrechung* are treated in separate discussions as if they were independent axioms. But again there is a problem: for axiomatic theory stipulates that no undefined axiom should be deducible from another. Yet, according to Schenker, the way to deduce the *Urlinie* is from the *Grundbrechung*—not just in the sense of positing the ontological *Klang* in nature and then going on to generate the epistemological formulation of the *Ursatz* in art, but rather in the sense of specifying the structural nature of the *Urlinie* in any given piece. The *Urlinie* in any well-formed composition must always "come to terms with the two-part *Bassbrechung*."[14] It cannot be independent of it. Thus the analytical methodology where the placement of the *Urlinie* depends on the bass:

> In order to determine more easily the path of the urlinie, I recommend, first of all, the tracing of the large arpeggiation through which the bass unfolds the fundamental chord.[15]

As we shall see, this is partly why Schenkerian analysis involves so many problems. If the *Urlinie* and the *Grundbrechung* were true axioms, of course, each would operate independently within the system. And if their application led to logically consistent consequences, their statistically recurring congruence in tonal works would be a significant indication of an internally coherent repertory. But Schenkerian theory is not formulated to let us objectively establish the consistency of the tonal repertory.

The question whether tonality organizes an internally consistent repertory is by no means trivial; for if it does not, we are not justified

---

14. *Der Freie Satz*, p. 45. Compare Salzer's comment: "A melody may admit of different structural interpretations. It is the bass, and consequently the chords, which can eliminate this possible ambiguity" (*Structural Hearing*, p. 114).

15. *Das Meisterwerk in der Musik*, p. 182 (Schenker, 2:21).

in invoking *any* axiomatic approach on the basis of internal facts alone. Are we willing to believe that we can formulate a complete specification of the rules governing all tonal processes? Are the syntactic rules of inference governing Bach's music the same as those governing the music of Brahms? Can style change and syntax remain the same? Can the foreground and middleground events in, say, the first movement of Beethoven's *Eroica* Symphony be accurately subsumed under the same tonic-dominant-tonic tonal scheme that we assume in the symphonies of Haydn and Mozart? Is the music written between 1700 and 1850 sufficiently homogeneous and systematic in style to be contained within one "tonal" syntax? Can the study of music become an exact theoretical science?

It may be true that the syntax of a spoken language could be systematized and verified under a few initial axioms—though I doubt it—but, as we shall see, music is unlike language in crucial respects. For one thing, music has many more parameters. And since we have no satisfactory theory of rhythm, melody, dynamics, orchestration, or performance, it is doubtful that in our present state of knowledge we can generate the structure of musical works in axiomatic terms. Unlike a work of nature, a great work of art in all its peculiarity is what it is, after all, partly because there is no known specification—no logical model—upon which to reconstruct it. Thus it may be dangerous to attempt to apply to artworks those arguments that are valid for logical models.[16] Notwithstanding the triumphs of the axiomatic approach—the systematic derivation and verification of statements and their logical consequences in successive applications—we can become blinded and misled by its seductive power. For there is no inherent virtue in a perfectly rigorous process of inference if the premises on which we base our inferences are wrong, and no merit in the conclusions drawn from them if the model we use is manifestly inappropriate.[17]

16. On the subject of the applicability of models, see Mary Hesse, "Models and Analogy in Science," *Encyclopedia of Philosophy*, reprint ed. 5:354.

17. Which, incidentally, is the main problem with all formalizations of music: all too often logical models (set theory, group theory, etc.) are grafted onto the music willy-nilly without justifying whether or to what extent the analogue is appropriate.

Finally, if the *Ursatz* were a true axiom, there would be much less disagreement among Schenkerians themselves about analyses of the same piece. Axioms, after all, are supposed not to lead to contradictory results. But the fact that the same *Ursatz* form can be dispositioned in several different ways in the same piece, yielding quite different prolongational derivations, both proves that Schenkerian analysis is not a true axiomatic system and suggests that several analytical inter-pretations may be *equally* valid.[18] That is to say, disagreements among theorists may result not from incorrect inferences but from "inconsis-tencies" inherent in the musical object itself. The "rabbit–duck" phenomenon in visual perception is a psychological truism (example 4).[19] Similarly, we should get used to the idea that musical pieces

Rabbit or duck?

Example 4

can be perceived with equal validity from structurally "incompatible" vantage points.

Melodically, the first four bars of the second trio from Beethoven's Quintet, op. 4, for instance, can be understood both as an axial (en-circling) prolongation of the dominant (E♭) moving to the third degree (C) in measure 5 (example 5a) and as the linear progression of E♭–D♭

18. Compare, for instance, Schenker's analysis of Beethoven's Piano Sonata, op. 10, no. 1 (*Der Freie Satz*, appendix, example 154,7, p. 116) with Salzer's (*Structural Hearing*, vol. 2, example 463, pp. 228–29). Both authors construe the development section of this sonata as a long prolongation of 3̂ to 2̂. Contrast also both authors' analyses of Schubert's Waltz, op. 77, no. 10 (example 68 in *Der Freie Satz*, p. 33, versus example 333 in *Structural Hearing*, p. 124) or their analyses of Beethoven's Piano Sonata, op. 13, second movement (example 155 in *Der Freie Satz*, p. 116, versus example 383 in *Structural Hearing*, pp. 150–51).

19. Taken from E. H. Gombrich, *Art and Illusion* (Princeton: Princeton University Press, 1960), p. 5.

Example 5. Beethoven's Quintet op. 4, Trio II, measures 1–15

moving to C (example 5*b*). The D♮ in measure 3 functions as part of an *ascending* line back to the E♮ in measure 4 (5*a*) *and* as part of a *descending* line to the C in measure 5 (5*b*).

Almost all Schenkerians, it is true, admit the possibility of different analyses of the same piece, seeing such analyses as a way of perceiving pieces from structurally different vantage points. My argument here, however, is not only that two "readings" of the melody of example 5 are possible or that two different hearings are equally plausible, but rather that *both* the axial and the descending linear structures are heard *simultaneously* (unlike the rabbit-duck picture, where one view precludes the other). In contrast, on any given level in an analysis of Beethoven's melody, the doctrinaire Schenkerian would have to choose one version over the other, the reason being that his analytical reduction cannot accommodate the simultaneous multiplicity inherent in the structure of the music. That is, the higher-level symbology and the reductive apparatus of Schenkerian theory on the whole do not allow for simultaneously "incompatible" or "contradictory" reductions on lower levels.

Concerning measures 1–4, the Schenkerian would probably argue (in retrospect on this level) that the continuation (measures 6–15) favors the linear pattern rather than the triadic one (see the analysis and compare version *b* with version *a*). To maintain the linear E♭–D♭ over the prolonged E♭ in measures 1–4 in any given analysis is, however, to miss the point: the simultaneously dichotomous structure of these measures in Beethoven's Trio. The rabbit-duck figure above exemplifies not one thing or the other, but both. The same holds true for measures 1–4 of example 5.

To the extent that Schenkerian theory recognizes only one structural possibility in the first five bars of Beethoven's Trio (probably the E♭–D♭–C), it may be said to commit the a priori error. This point merits a little discussion. Although Schenkerians have argued that the *Urlinie* was not fabricated ad hoc, that it came into being over a long period of time, that it was fashioned carefully from empirical facts,[20] and that the Schenkerian system as a method is therefore analytic, not synthetic,[21] such apologists confuse genetic order with logical order. Like all theories, it is true that Schenker's system evolved gradually and that it underwent considerable change. But, regardless of its empirical origin, the logical formulation of the theory is idealistic, and more important—as we shall see—its use in analysis is heavily rationalistic. There is no reason either pattern in measures 1–4 of example 5 should take precedence.

And this is a good place to lay aside the usual Schenkerian appeal to our perceptual experience. For the argument that Schenkerian analysis is based on perception—implying that if we take the *Ursatz* as an

---

20. Babbitt, review of *Structural Hearing*, pp. 260–65.

21. The argument made by Susanne K. Langer, *Feeling and Form* (New York: Charles Scribner's Sons, 1953), p. 124.

axiom, that is, on faith, the structural voice-leading secrets revealed to us will confirm the theory, while insinuating that if we do not have this experience there is something wrong with our ears, which Schenker proclaims throughout *Der Freie Satz*—is no argument at all. For we now know that theories organize facts, not vice versa.[22] Taking the first five bars in example 5 alone on successive hearings, we can readily hear either the linear pattern or the axial one or both simultaneously depending on our cognitive set *and* our theoretical beliefs. The *Urlinie* cannot be justified by aural experience alone, because "believing is hearing."

THE *URSATZ* AS "DEEP" OR HIGH-LEVEL STRUCTURE

I have discussed various reasons why the *Ursatz* must be rejected both as a formal and an informal axiom. As a formal system, a belief in the inherent validity of I and V as axiomatic terms is illogical. In addition, I argued that such terms could not be accepted as undefined because they are so heavily endowed with prior semantic meanings, unlike the uninterpreted signs of mathematics and symbolic logic. Thus, we concluded that the acceptance of terms like I and V without predication simply represented too great an intellectual commitment. Major structural features of works would in effect become predetermined. As far as predication is concerned, it was shown that the predication on which the principal relations of the *Ursatz* depend (e.g., I–V–I in the bass and $\hat{3}$–$\hat{2}$–$\hat{1}$ in the soprano) could not be validly differentiated from similar relationships in the system. This, as we shall see, will prevent us from finding logical constants (whether based on synonymy, conjunction, or implication) or from formulating propositional functions (empirical constants) with any rigor—the sine qua non of the axiomatic approach.

As an *in*formal system, Schenkerian theory fails because it is based on the assumption that within the system the *Ursatz* stands for (and is therefore reducible to) a single chord (the tonic). This is problematic

---

22. Karl R. Popper, *Conjectures and Refutations: The Growth of Scientific Knowledge* (London: Routledge and Kegan Paul, 1963).

because, as we saw, if the tonic chord is taken as the axiom, we are led to the untenable position of having a relational stimulus pattern generate the syntactic patterns. Further, the *Urlinie* and *Grundbrechung* do not operate independently within the system but are derived from one another, which strips them of any independent axiomatic status. Finally, the use of the *Ursatz* has led to numerous contradictions in normal analytical work. All these things militate against the neo-Schenkerian view that Schenker's theory can be treated as an axiom system.[23] (Indeed, there is reason to be suspicious of any axiomatic approach in music.) And if Schenkerian theory does not satisfy the standards of the axiomatic approach, then Schenker is unquestionably guilty of the a priori error because in that case the *Ursatz* has to be treated as a high-level *structure*.[24]

That the *Ursatz* is a "high-level," "deep," or "background" structure—call it what you will—is in fact the view promulgated by several of Schenker's direct disciples (Salzer, Jonas, Weisse, et al.). Although the distinction between structures (*Ursätzen*) and prolongations (*Auskomponierungen*) is not a particularly happy dualism, because it is clear that prolongations must also be treated as structures on some level, the search for high-level structures in a work is nevertheless certainly a more desirable activity in music theory than the search for axioms. For, as we have seen, there is good reason to be chary of invoking the axiomatic approach in the analysis of music, since axioms

23. The possibility that Schenkerian theory can be classified as a "natural deduction system" where the *Ursatz* functions as an element of formation operating within a specified deductive apparatus will be considered in chapter 9.

24. Briefly stated, the a priori error consists in attempting to establish knowledge of fundamental synthetic truths on something other than empirical evidence. A priori facts are usually extracted from the language of which they are a part in order to give them an authority they do not deserve. Schenker puts forth the *Ursatz* as a basic musical "truth" without giving us acceptable a priori facts. Acoustical "facts," strictly speaking, are not part of the "language" of music. Though acoustical phenomena form part of the continuity from syntax to perception to cognition, they cannot be endowed with the sort of necessity in music theory that Schenker proposes. On a priori errors, see John Stuart Mill, *A System of Logic Ratiocinative and Inductive* (Toronto: University of Toronto Press, 1973), pp. 746–72.

are always prefabricated ad hoc, in contrast to high-level structures, which are presumed to be a "natural" part of the piece. In any case, no structuralist would ever be content with axioms alone, since he would always want to know what was "behind" the operations codified by the axioms. Thus the *Ursatz*-as-structure point of view, which takes the position that every good tonal piece has some form of the *Ursatz* as its highest level, is of considerable interest.

Before discussing the merits of this point of view, let us rid ourselves of the notion that in music a background configuration can be *both* structure and axiom. That this is nonsense has rarely been appreciated by either the neo-Schenkerians, who accept the *Ursatz* as an axiom, or by Schenker's followers, who believe the *Ursatz* is a structure. In mathematics, where symbols have no conventional meanings and the axiom system is uninterpreted and abstract, it *may* be that, since the structure of the theorems is derived and systematized from axioms and since axioms are also theorems,[25] axioms and the high-level structure are the same—the derivations and their axiomatic point of "origin" expressing a general type of structure. But this is not true in other fields. In biology, for instance, we may attempt to express the relationship of a high-level structure of a cell in mathematical terms, but the interpreted symbols used in such a logistic system are many steps removed from an accurate representation of the structure of the cell.[26] (The structural representations of a cell could best be shown, perhaps, through radiographs of some sort.)

Music lies somewhere between mathematics and biology. Like mathematicians, most music theorists, I believe, would like to represent structure in the subject-matter symbols at hand—that is, in some modified form of musical notation, since these symbols offer a precision and economy of communication that is lost when notes are translated to, say, roman numerals, or arabic numerals, or letters, or conventional

---

25. Some readers may not be familiar with this position. For a convenient explanation (and proof) of it, see Charles Parsons, "Foundations of Mathematics," *Encyclopedia of Philosophy*, reprint ed., 5:191.

26. For some examples of symbolic logic and their application to biology, see Woodger, *Axiomatic Method in Biology*.

words. But like biology, the high-level structure and the axioms from which the lower-level structures might be derived in music are necessarily separate and different things, even though in music (unlike biology) both axioms and high-level structures might be expressed through some modified form of musical notation (assuming we knew such axioms and such structures).

Schenkerians might thus take a single chord as the axiom of a piece—though I have already argued that this is a doubtful position—and by some sort of syntactic productions derive other structures from it. But such a chord cannot also be thought of as the high-level structure unless, of course, we wish to commit the a priori error. Or we might take something like the *Ursatz* and hypothesize that it is the high-level structure of such-and-such a piece and then go on to see whether this is the case. But if we treat the *Ursatz*-as-structure hypothesis as the axiom from which structures are derived, then (as we shall see) we make the mistake of affirming the consequent.

(I have dealt with this issue here because Schenker himself seems to have been unclear about whether the *Ursatz* was to operate as a generative axiom or to function as a high-level structure—though my guess is that ultimately Schenker believed the *Ursatz* to be *the* high-level structure in all good works, since he says in the third volume of *Das Meisterwerk in der Musik* [p. 22] that his analytical theory is an art and can never be a science. In any case, the structural logic of the analytical theory and the structure of the effects produced are often confused. The fact that the neo-Schenkerians treat the *Ursatz* as an axiom, whereas Schenker's disciples treat it as a background structure, is the direct result of this confusion.)

There are, of course, rigid criteria which a hypothesis-theory of structure must meet, and rather precise epistemological rules govern its formulation. For only by distinguishing and separating the rules of entailment in the analytical methodology—the "if" conditionals (i.e., the working hypothesis) from the "then" conclusions (i.e., the structural results)—can the analytical interpretations drawn from analyses be firmly grounded. Unfortunately, Schenker does not help us in this regard because in formulating the theory of the *Ursatz* he commits the error of affirming the consequent in its most blatant form.[27] What starts out as a working hypothesis (the *Ursatz*) ends up being the evidence of the structure itself. Even where Schenker instructs us to reverse our method and proceed from the lowest level to the highest, reaching the *Ursatz* is obligatory. The framework is known in advance:

> Yet I recommend that everyone take the small trouble to feel downward from the foreground to the middleground to the background; indeed one needs only to have learned in books and schools how to apply to detailed diminutions known methods of reduction, and he will always arrive at shorter settings, ultimately to the shortest: to the *Ursatz*![28]

The logical fallacy may be stated as follows: If the *Ursatz* is a structural hypothesis, then it will be successful in analysis. If it is successful, then

---

27. For a discussion of this in regard to hierarchies, see Mario Bunge, "The Metaphysics, Epistemology and Methodology of Levels," in *Hierachical Structures*, ed. L. L. Whyte, Albert G. Wilson, and Donna Wilson (New York: American Elsevier, 1969), p. 27. The syllogism for the fallacy of affirming the consequent: If p then q, and q, therefore p. Or: S implies T and T is true; therefore S is true. From Schenker's ontology to his epistomology: the *Ursatz* is the fundamental structure which implies the *Klang*; the *Klang* is an a priori fact of nature; thus the *Ursatz* is a true fundamental structure. See C. L. Hamblin, *Fallacies* (London: Methuen, 1970).

28. *Der Freie Satz*, p. 58. A word about the terminology of analytical models. Most discussions of hierarchies use the biological model of a tree as reference for terminology—thus the use of the words "high" and "low" to describe levels. In some ways, however, the tree is not such a good model for musical analysis because although in biology the visible tree itself is the high-level structure (so to speak), in music the highest level is not "visible" in the notes; it is "hidden" beneath the low-level, foreground surface. While, as we shall see, Schenker is fond of biological models, in reference to levels he and his followers perhaps have architecture rather than biology in mind when they speak of working "down" to the (high-level) *Ursatz*, that is, down to the "foundation" (though Schenker says in one place in *Der Freie Satz*, p. 30, that music should never be compared to architecture). The mixing of models has produced some interesting non sequiturs. For instance, Salzer, a disciple of Schenker, says that having arrived at the *Ursatz*, one must always work back to the foreground levels if one is "not to remain on the *surface* of the composition" (*Structural Hearing*, p. 208, italics mine).

it must *be* the structure. Simply put, there is no separation between Schenker's epistemology and his methodology. The circular reasoning can be illustrated in the following way:

ONTOLOGY

    1. *Klang in der Natur*

EPISTEMOLOGY

    1. Concept of *Brechung* (horizontalization of the *Klang*)

    2. Formulation of the *Ursatz*

fallacious   3. Hypothesis: Structure determined by the *Ursatz*

reasoning METHODOLOGY

    1. Conclusion: Always work to the *Ursatz*

Derivation and result are confused. Source and goal—cause and effect—are the same.

Three
SCHENKERISM AS INTELLECTUAL HISTORY

THAT THE URSATZ IS AN "EXTERNALIZATION" OF THE IDEA IN Nature (the *Klang*) and is therefore to be treated as an absolute is, of course, very close to the philosophy of Hegel. And like all idealism Schenker's philosophy is accompanied by the usual embarrassing metaphysics. Schenker claims, for instance, that the *Urlinie* was given to him in a "vision" (*erschauen*).[1] His view of history is also notoriously Hegelian, and it would be interesting to know to what extent his analytical concepts are indebted to Hegel's trichotomies. Does it stretch the imagination too far, for instance, to make an analogy between Schenker's concept that the *Ursatz* plus the *Auskomponierung* leads to a *Schicht* and Hegel's concept of thesis (= structure), antithesis (= prolongation), and synthesis (= level)? Several places in Schenker's writings seem to show Hegel's influence. On page 25 of *Der Freie Satz*, Schenker begins his discussion of the background by attributing to Hegel the quote that fate is "the appearance of that which is, for the determined individuality, like an internal and original determination."[2] Schenker then refers to the background, middleground, and foreground as origin, development, and presence, which perhaps resembles Hegel's division of logic into concept, essence, and being.

Other cultural historians would no doubt find a similarity between Goethe and Schenker. Goethe's *Urphänomen* (primal phenomenon) and his notion of the *Urpflanze* (primal plant) as a basic model from which all plants come, for instance, sound suspiciously parallel to the *Klang*

1. *Das Meisterwerk in der Musik*, p. 218 (Schenker, 2:41)

2. Schenker gives no source, and I have been unable to locate where in Hegel's work this quote comes from.

31

and the *Ursatz*.[3] We know, moreover, that Schenker was acquainted with Goethe's work.[4] Yet from such meager clues we can only conjecture about Schenker's intellectual sources.

But a strong case can be made for the affinity between Schenker's method and other intellectual trends of his times. The similarity between Schenkerism and Gestalt philosophy has been pointed out on several occasions[5]—quite rightly so, since the *Ursatz* is conceived as an immutable form—and I have noted Schenker's evolutionary view of music history. The parallel between Schenkerism and Gestalt philosophy will be considered first.

SCHENKERISM AND GESTALTISM

The central idea of Gestaltist structuralism is the idea of wholeness, particularly the notion that *Gestaltqualitäten* impose themselves on our perception from the start, giving us "immediate insight" into the nature of the structure at hand. Similarly, Schenker argues that we conceive the wholeness of a composition—its innate unity—from the appearance of the first chord of the *Ursatz*. To Schenker, a work ends, and achieves good form, when the last chord of the *Ursatz* appears—regardless of how much music continues afterward.[6] In like manner, on lower levels, a voice-leading progression (*Zug*) closes when the prescribed goal is reached.[7] Thus for Schenker closure of the parts is predetermined by the shape the *Ursatz* takes at the beginning.

3. Thomas Clifton also observes this in his article, "An Application of Goethe's Concept of *Steigerung* to the Morphology of Diminution," *Journal of Music Theory* 14 (Winter 1970):165–89.

4. There is a long quote in *Der Freie Satz*, p. 25, from Goethe's *Theory of Color*, for instance. And in *Das Meisterwerk in der Musik* (2:92) there is an interesting discussion (and quotation) of Goethe's attitude toward the artist's awareness of general principles versus his realization of the specific. Schenker relates this to the *Ursatz* and foreground diminution.

5. For example, Helmut Federhofer, *Beiträge zur musikalischen Gestaltanalyse* (Vienna: Akademische Druck- und Verlagsanstalt, 1950).

6. *Der Freie Satz*, p. 199. Such views that unity originates from the "womb of the *Urlinie*" or that unity emanates from the *Urlinie* and the *Bassbrechung* are common in Schenker's writings. See *Das Meisterwerk in der Musik*, p. 50 and p. 220 (Schenker, 2:235, 241).

7. Ibid., p. 124.

The superiority of the Gestalt view over associationism—over identifying a string of motivic relationships or ascribing roman numerals to a series of chords—has long been recognized. Our experience of a work—its concrete-object character, its perceptual constancy, its dimension in time and space, its self-induced frame of reference, its configurational aspects, not to mention its appearance of having "meaning"—argues strongly for the assumption of a unified whole. None of these things, for instance, can be accounted for by cementing the piecemeal elements of our sensations together like some mosaic. Since the parts of a whole appear different when observed separately than when observed together, the Gestaltists conclude that the whole must transcend the characteristics of the parts. Thus, in a Gestaltist fashion, Schenker argues that the part cannot exist without the whole[8] and that it owes its origin and continuing organic existence to the *Ursatz*, the immutable Gestalt.

Despite the spectacular advances of Gestalt psychology, putting Schenkerian theory in the same company is not necessarily complimentary. For in assuming a deterministic, unified whole at the start, the Gestaltists stumbled into a morass of methodological difficulty. The first problem with the notion that the whole is independent, causal, and dynamic—that it originates, selects, and organizes the parts—is simply that no evidence exists to suggest that a given whole is anything more than its parts working together. That a whole has a "character" significantly different from the sum of its parts remains, of course, an empirical truth, but the argument that the whole acts to control the parts, or that the "whole-character" comes from something other than (or more than) the set of conditions resulting from the combination of the parts is simply not tenable.[9] For the Gestaltists, the only way out of this problem was to fall back on the idea of a deterministic, supersummative agency. In Schenkerism this retreat is, of course, embodied in the *Ursatz*. And since the *Ursatz* is metaphysically based (on the *Klang in der Natur*), it is not by accident that as an im-

8. Ibid., p. 153.

9. For a good introduction to and discussion of the problems of Gestalt psychology, see Floyd H. Allport, *Theories of Perception and the Concept of Structure* (New York: John Wiley, 1955), pp. 112–47.

mutable, static form the *Ursatz* remains unpolluted by history from without or genesis from within.[10] In the Schenkerian scheme, voice-leading processes must preserve the *Ursatz*, contributing to the larger whole.

This notion of a deterministic, unified whole, assumed in both Gestaltism and Schenkerism, leads us directly to a second difficulty, the degraded status of the parts. If the whole determines the meanings of the parts, then the idea that the whole is prior to the parts must follow; this, as we have seen, is a major premise of Schenkerian philosophy. Since new parts are born from the background—Schenker says diminution, for instance, is present from "birth"[11]—the original whole (the *Ursatz*) can be arrived at by tracing part-meanings backward. From this Schenker concludes that the part has no independent status. In *Der Freie Satz* he asserts:

> Through authentically organic and precisely traceable voice-leading constraints, all diminution must be located firmly in a fixed membership in the whole. Every diminution, even that of the lowest order, lives and moves with the whole—not the least particle [exists] without the whole.[12]

Thus, as in Gestalt psychology, in Schenkerian theory only the whole gives meaning to the parts. This leads to a subtle form of the "genetic fallacy": that we must look to the antecedents of things in order to understand their meaning in the present.[13] Since the *Ursatz* is the origin of all art and since it was always present in the *Klang*, all parts are thus foreordained as agents of the *Ursatz*. The *Züge* have no real independence.

10. This is a criticism of Gestalt psychology made by Jean Piaget, *Structuralism*, trans. Chaninah Maschler (New York: Harper and Row, 1971), p. 55, which I have borrowed here.

11. *Der Freie Satz*, p. 31.

12. Ibid., p. 153.

13. The genetic fallacy confuses temporal or historical order with logical order. In Schenkerian theory, not only must we believe the dubious assertion that the historical origin of tonal music is attributable to the *Klang*; we must also assent to the fallacious conclusion that the structural "logic" of all tonal pieces is based on it as well. On the genetic fallacy, see Morris R. Cohen and Ernest Nagel, *An Introduction to Logic and Scientific Method* (New York: Harcourt, Brace and Co., 1934), pp. 388–90.

To the historian, of course, the Schenkerian (and the Gestaltist) blunder is obvious: for to achieve a unified whole, we must have organization, and in order to organize, we must have entities that already have relationships—relationships acquired in other times and other places, and *in other wholes*. This prior existence of *the part* utterly destroys the notion that any single whole (any single piece) or any original whole (like the *Ursatz*) can completely account for the meaning of the parts. For instance, representational paintings rely on a common stockpile of figures; poems have words; every musical piece contains motives and progressions found in other pieces and other styles; and so forth. As I shall argue with the implication-realization model, the way out of this problem is to frame part-meanings within one theory (a theory of implications) and whole-meanings within another (a theory of realizations). Neither part nor whole can be assigned conceptual priority in formulating explanations. But before considering where the Schenkerian assumption of a unified whole leads in analytical practice, let us briefly lay aside the parallel between Gestaltism and Schenkerism and consider the concept of the *Ursatz* in light of another analogy Schenker is fond of invoking—that between music and biology.

THE BIOLOGICAL METAPHOR

Schenker continually admonishes us to see tones as creatures. "We should learn to assume in them biological urges as they characterize living beings."[14] Each tone, he argues, has its own "egotism"[15] and, as the bearer of its generations,[16] strives to exert its will[17] as the tonic, as the strongest scale step,[18] by struggling "to gain the upper hand" [*Lebenskräfte reichen*] in its relationships with others.[19]

Yet in its "desire to dominate its fellow-tones,"[20] to "procreate" a

14. *Harmony*, p. 6.

15. Ibid., p. 30.

16. Ibid., p. 29.

17. Thus, Schenker's title *Der Tonwille* for his collection of essays published between 1921 and 1924.

18. *Harmony*, p. 256.

19. Ibid., p. 84.

20. Ibid.

tonally stable order for itself, a tone does not have absolute freedom. First of all, nature establishes a boundary line in the *Klang*; and, second, within a piece the freedom of a tone is always regulated by the background *Ursatz*. Thus new transformations in the system must preserve the unifying principles of the background. Growth, continuation, and improvement are always under the control of the *Ursatz*.[21] The diatonic system must prevail.[22] Hence, some tones must sacrifice their egos for "the common interest of the community,"[23] community being defined by the overriding tonality at hand. Despite the appealing suggestiveness of Schenker's analogies between biology and music, we can see in the biological conception the makings of a classic case of the free will–determinism problem.[24]

If a tone is a creature with a will, then what is the analogical function of the *Ursatz* in the biological model? As one might imagine, the *Ursatz* is to music what God is to nature. Although this statement sounds hyperbolic, Schenker actually proclaims in the foreword to *Der Freie Satz* that because a work "confesses but one background cause, it is arranged monotheistically."[25] And he believes that since all coherence is designed by God, including the *Ursatz*, and since this cause is unchanging, an art-monotheism theory is obligatory.

Thus, an exaltation of the spirit to the *Ursatz* is an exaltation to God.[26] The sympathetic relation between the *Ursatz* and the foreground is like the relationship between God and creature,[27] God being the creative will in life,[28] the *Ursatz*, the creative will in music. Through this creative will, nature shows us the way in the overtone series,[29] thereby insuring the diatonic system as the "only natural medium" for

21. *Der Freie Satz*, p. 49.

22. *Harmony*, p. 290.

23. Ibid., p. 30.

24. See Schenker's discussion on the "*Urlinie* and Freedom" in *Das Meisterwerk in der Musik*, pp. 150–51 (Schenker, 1:197–98).

25. *Der Freie Satz*, p. 18.

26. Ibid., p. 29.

27. Ibid.

28. Ibid., p. 22.

29. *Harmony*, p. 20.

expressing the artist's idea.[30] As Schenker says, the *Ursatz* "signifies an awakening of the life of the *Klang* by a living, natural force" so that "the original power of this once-induced motion wills to increase and continue on its own."[31]

As I have pointed out, however, this "induced motion" is always under the control of the *Ursatz*. Since no tone can exist in the foreground unless the background breathes life into it,[32] it is impossible for anything new to grow in the foreground unless it has already been born in the background. Transformations, it is true, carry forward the evolutionary process,[33] enriching the content of music and contributing to the differentiation of the foreground members, but in the process the background tones remain the same.[34] As Salzer has said, structural goals are "predestined" by the *Ursatz*.[35] In the Schenkerian scheme, the origin of life—musical or otherwise—is simultaneously the fate of life. Outcomes are, as it were, preordained.

A doctrine of predestination, of course, leads directly to a belief in final causes. And nowhere is Schenker's teleology more reprehensible than in his attitude toward other styles and other cultures in music history. That Schenker conceives tonality as the ultimate evolutionary goal of music history is obviously a logical outcome of his belief that art is an imitation of nature. From the beginning, according to Schenker, there has been a steady advance of the horizontal, but beneath it lay always the vertical *Klang*, whose mission was to induce the horizontal to comply with the basic arpeggiation up to the fifth overtone.[36]

> In past centuries ... music grew through the constant splitting off of spans [*Zügen*]: Content expansion grew

30. Ibid., p. 290.

31. *Der Freie Satz*, p. 57. From *Das Meisterwerk in der Musik*, 1:12: "Music is the living movement of tones in nature-given space, the compositional unfolding ... of the *Klang* given in Nature" (translation mine).

32. *Der Freie Satz*, p. 31. Schenker equates the high-level *Ursatz* with *Ursprung* (origin); ibid., p. 25.

33. *Der Freie Satz*, p. 50.

34. *Das Meisterwerk in der Musik*, p. 134 (Schenker, 1:188).

35. Salzer, *Structural Hearing*, p. 101.

36. *Der Freie Satz*, p. 173.

temporally to such an extent, that in accordance with its true origin, it became a play in space, in background, middleground, and foreground. The greater the progress of the art characterized by the continuous branching off of spans, resulting from the practice of the masters, the more the foreground resulted in a succession of time, in which the relationship of the foreground to the background was *all the more determining*.[37]

Thus, once tonality and the determining *Ursatz* were achieved through the German masters, Schenker argues, there could be no new style.[38] The major mode had been "indicated and ordered by Nature."[39] In contrast, the church modes, for instance, constituted an experimental stage of development,[40] and their demise was inevitable, since plainchant was "thrown together in a haphazard and irrational fashion" without a guiding harmonic principle.[41] The tonal system, once achieved, could "hardly be expected" to undergo any substantive change, since it alone stood in "complete conformity to Nature [*Naturhaftigkeit*]."[42] And every "good" piece necessarily had the *Ursatz* as the high-level structure behind it.[43]

The parallel between Schenker's biological view of music history and pre-Darwinian evolutionary theory is exceptionally striking. The following quotation from the history of science will illustrate my point:

All the well-known pre-Darwinian evolutionary theories— those of Lamarck, Chambers, Spencer, and the German *Naturphilosophen*—had taken evolution to be a goal-directed process. The "idea" of man and of the contemporary flora and fauna was thought to have been present from the first

37. *Das Meisterwerk in der Musik*, p. 196. Italics mine (Schenker, 2:28).

38. *Der Freie Satz*, p. 173.

39. Heinrich Schenker, *Harmonielehre* (Berlin: J. G. Cotta'sche Buchhandlung Nachfolgen, 1906), p. 68 (translation mine).

40. *Harmony*, pp. 58–59.

41. Ibid., p. 134.

42. Ibid., p. 279. See also *Der Freie Satz*, p. 41.

43. It may also be noted here that Schenker's notion of equating aesthetic value with organic unity comes directly from Hegel. I am grateful to my friend Professor Ruth Solie of Smith College for pointing this out to me.

creation of life, perhaps in the mind of God. That idea or plan had provided the direction and the guiding force to the entire evolutionary process. Each new stage of evolutionary development was a more perfect realization of a plan that had been present from the start.[44]

Like the pre-Darwinians, Schenker treats music history as a goal-directed process where an idea (the *Klang*), extrapolated from and present in nature from the beginning, evolves into the ideal, namely tonality. If we extend Schenker's historical view to include the *Ursatz* as the "idea or plan" providing direction and guiding force in the evolution of a piece, we then arrive at the Schenkerian biological philosophy of music in a nutshell. As in Lamarckian evolution, in Schenkerian theory "variations" (diminutions) in the habits of "organisms" (tones) are explained as adaptations to the influence of the "environment." Or, as Schenker would say—to use our earlier comparison with Gestaltism—"the whole is the atmosphere of diminution."[45]

It can be concluded, then, that Schenkerian theory in the field of musical anlysis is "pre-Darwinian" in concept and thus indefensibly teleological. As a first corrective, therefore, music theorists must recognize, as biological evolutionists have learned, that "evolution" in music history or in a specific composition is as dependent on moving *from* something—from a specific implication—as it is on moving *toward* a goal. Our notion of "evolution" in a work should depend on describing events not only as a succession of steps *toward* a solution, but also as a succession of steps *away* from one or more solutions to an original "problem." And we must recognize further that the meanings of specific implications are never wholly contained in the goals that are realized. In music we may experience a sense of "moving toward"—of "progress"—without necessarily being able to define precisely what goal will occur. And our retrospective knowledge of what actually does come to pass can never account completely for what was implied.

44. Thomas S. Kuhn, *The Structure of Scientific Revolutions* (Chicago: University of Chicago Press, 1962), pp. 171–72.

45. *Der Freie Satz*, p. 153.

In other words, part-meanings (implications) must always be kept conceptually distinct from whole-meanings (realizations).

Although related "species" in music (schemata) clearly evolve from common "ancestors" (archetypal patterns), it appears that the true "genetic" basis in musical process is to be found by discovering what patterns imply in prospect (their probabilistic nature) in relation to what they realize in retrospect. There is no reason to assume a priori that there is such a thing as a preexisting whole or a preordained goal. This is true in connection with both our understanding of music history and our explanation of musical works. In short, the "genetic unit" for both historian and music theorist resides in the relationship between that which is implied and that which is realized. But enough of the biological model: Nature's work and man's, after all, are not directly comparable.

Four

THE ASSIMILATION-ACCOMMODATION
PROBLEM: HISTORY VERSUS ANALYSIS

S CHENKER'S INSISTENCE ON TREATING THE *URSATZ* AS BOTH ORIGIN
and goal, original whole and ultimate determiner of part-meaning,
initiating plan and overall guiding force—in short, as both high-level
structure and axiom—becomes methodologically feasible and leads to
useful results only if the analysis favors one musical parameter over all
the others. In Schenkerian analysis the optimized parameter is harmony,
as is conceded by Schenker's most ardent disciples. As one writer says
about Schenker's theory of goal-directed musical energy, "The source
of this energy is neither melodic nor rhythmic, but harmonic, for it is
harmonic impulse, according to the concept of the *Zug*, that is the
activating, dynamical force in composition."[1]

Schenkerian theory's assertion that harmony and its voice-leading
rules govern every tonal piece leads to what may be called a one-way
"assimilation-accommodation" approach.[2] "Assimilation" refers to
the process by which we reproduce an analytical operation in order to
incorporate objects into a given system. Recall the discussion of
example 2, for instance. Melodic pitch patterns were first reduced to
harmonic patterns. These in turn became prolongations of structural
chords. Finally, the *Ursatz* was attained. Such analytical schemes of
assimilation are possible only if the theory underlying the analysis is
constructed in such a way that it can "accommodate" whatever is
new. In Schenkerian analysis the elements of every piece are assimilated

---

1. Slatin, "The Theories of Heinrich Schenker in Perspective," p. 186.
2. I have borrowed this dualism from Piaget, *Structuralism*, p. 63—though I put it
to a very different use.

analytically by the voice-leading rules of tonal harmony and, ultimately, by the rules of the *Ursatz*. In turn, the accommodating theory is structured in such a way that throughout the history of tonal music, disunity is not possible in the foreground or the middleground.

Thus, although elements may recombine in various ways, there is no room for any concept of virtual change.[3] All content is determined and eventually assimilated by the *Ursatz*.[4] Historical growth is theoretically accommodated in advance. No work establishes a sufficient degree of originality to absorb and thereby alter the preformed, high-level structure. "Prolongations" never become "fundamental structures." The *Ursatz* remains immune to transformation. The feedback exchange between the accommodating theory and the assimilating analysis works in one direction only.

Consequently, whatever genuine potential a piece has for transforming tonality cannot be accommodated in Schenkerian theory. Assimilating functionalism—the means-ends approach of the analysis—precludes the possibility of examining the transforming potential of the parts. Tones create "motion," to be sure, but they do not "act" to change their environment, which is predestined by the *Ursatz*. In the Schenkerian scheme tonality—fixed in eternity by nature—is not an expanding universe but a Copernican solar system. Tonal style exists as a completely synchronic system uncontaminated by history. Intrasystem potential is not possible.[5]

3. Certain rules always remain immune to change. See *Der Freie Satz*, p. 119.

4. According to Schenker, "all content of music" can be explained by considering only the connection of the *Urlinie* to the bass arpeggiation (*Der Freie Satz*, p. 45).

5. A minor, but interesting, dispute has arisen over whether Schenker's method is "static" or "dynamic." John Daniskas, *Grondslagen voor de analytische Vormleer der Musiek* (Rotterdam: W. L. and J. Brusse, 1948) argues that Schenkerian theory maintains a static notion of tonality, as does Leonard B. Meyer, *Emotion and Meaning in Music* (Chicago: University of Chicago Press, 1956), pp. 52–54. In contrast, Babbitt, review of *Structural Hearing*, Beach, "Schenker Bibliography," p. 17, and Allen Forte, "Schenker's Conception of Musical Structure," p. 16, all attempt to refute this view. I think the matter can be laid to rest here, because whether one views Schenker's system as dynamic or static depends on one's vantage point. Looking "from the inside out"—from the analysis of a specific piece—Schenkerian analysis definitely exemplifies a "dynamic systems theory." Looking "from the outside in"—from the point of view of Schenker's conception of tonality as a synchronic system—the theory

The modus operandi for the Schenkerian analyst, then, is nicely laid out. Guided by the structure of the bass line, the analyst decides which tone is the first note (*Kopfton*) of the *Urlinie*. From then on he need not be concerned with intraopus prospective meanings in any virtual sense.[6] Nor need he be interested in independent, interopus part-meanings, since the goal of every piece is already known. He has only to follow the proper assimilation schemes in making the analytical reductions. Even if a piece is new to him, once it has been classified as tonal the Schenkerian can predict the content of every level. For, as one theorist put it, the accommodating theory enables us to "know in advance the underlying organizational principles and the function of detail."[7] Inasmuch as we can understand how a theory works only by seeing what values are assigned to the parameters (melody, harmony, rhythm, etc.), let us examine the assimilation schemes.

Since in Schenkerism the foreground and middleground are theoretically based on the background—"organicism" being guaranteed by the background[8]—the background must assimilate these levels analytically. As to foreground harmony in Schenkerian theory, since only consonances can create new tonal spaces, it follows that foreground dissonance cannot be prolonged[9] and can never be a goal.[10]

---

is definitely static. In a more general sense, a static outlook is typified by a belief in "motions," whereas a dynamic view typifies a belief in "processes." But again, which view is relevant depends upon one's vantage point from within or without the hierarchy.

6. In this book I use the word "virtual" to refer to those inherent, essential, and substantive qualities in music whose potential power must be taken into account regardless of whether they are formally (materially) admitted in the theory. Prospective meaning is one such virtual characteristic. Diachronic meaning is another, and temporality and formation (implication), still others. The best theories, in my view, not only do not discount virtual meanings but make a special effort to include them in the formulation.

7. A claim made by Forte in "Schenker's Conception of Musical Structure," p. 27, the consequences of which I shall examine later.

8. *Der Freie Satz*, p. 28.

9. *Das Meisterwerk in der Musik*, p. 158 (Schenker, 1:203), and *Der Freie Satz*, p. 51.

10. *Das Meisterwerk in der Musik*, p. 187 (Schenker, 2:24). Mentioned by Oswald Jonas in the preface to Schenker's *Harmony*, p. xix.

Theoretically, only certain intervals are afforded a "real" status.[11] The ninth, for instance, can never be regarded as a "true interval";[12] further, sevenths and ninths as chord constituents have to be assimilated as passing tones (*Durchgänge*), neighboring tones (*Nebennoten*), or suspensions (*Vorhalten*).[13] As to foreground rhythm, since "all rhythm comes from counterpoint—and only from counterpoint,"[14] rhythm can automatically be reduced to contrapuntal structures where (presumably) durational differentiation disappears. Melody is accommodated in the same way: like rhythm, it is also reducible "to some simple principle of counterpoint,"[15] since all diminution originates from strict counterpoint.[16] Melody is essentially the horizontal expression of harmonic voice leading,[17] because "the urlinie is . . . the pre-stabilized harmony of the composition."[18] It follows then that the notion of the registral identification of melodic pitches as existing independently of the *Urlinie* is simply an illusion.[19] Obligatory register (*obligate Lage*), according to Schenker, is defined by the *Ursatz*, not by the actual melody at hand.

Thus, all the elements of the foreground are based on the strict counterpoint of the background.[20] Even free counterpoint has to be derived from strict,[21] because strict counterpoint is never "completely

---

11. *Harmony*, pp. 122–23 and throughout. "Harmonizability" is Schenker's key criterion for determining the status of intervals.

12. Ibid., p. 204.

13. *Das Meisterwerk in der Musik*, p. 207 (Schenker, 2:34).

14. *Der Freie Satz*, pp. 46, 65.

15. Jonas's observation in the preface of Schenker's *Harmony*, p. xvii.

16. *Das Meisterwerk in der Musik*, p. 511 (Schenker, 3:20–21).

17. Kalib, "Thirteen Essays," p. 453, in his commentary of *Das Meisterwerk*: Schenker "showed melody in diatonic polyphony to be essentially the horizontal expression of harmony."

18. *Das Meisterwerk in der Musik*, pp. 144–45 (Schenker, 1:195).

19. *Der Freie Satz*, p. 42. See also p. 166.

20. Ibid., p. 96.

21. *Harmony*, p. 156. (See particularly Jonas's footnote on this page.) Salzer, *Structural Hearing*, p. 131, says much the same thing: "So-called 'free' counterpoint is therefore possible and logical if it appears as a prolongation of a basic contrapuntal setting representing the techniques of pure counterpoint."

lost" in a composition.[22] And, furthermore, free composition can be understood only through the *Stufen*,[23] because, theoretically, *Stufen* are "responsible for the rise of free composition."[24] The "final unalterable nucleus," that is, the *Urlinie*, must be preserved.[25] Thus the simplicity of the method: criteria are formulated to differentiate free counterpoint from strict counterpoint, melody from *Urlinie*, harmony from the *Stufen*, and so forth. Once this is done, differences between the manifest object (the piece itself) and the desired object (the transformational structures dictated by the theory) can be reduced. Assimilation therefore becomes complete.

Perhaps the clearest way to understand the Schenkerian conception of assimilation is by a diagram. Essentially the whole theory can be seen as a grand "tree" design as illustrated in figure 1. On the left side of the tree are the voice-leading prolongations; on the right, the harmonic ones. All defining elements of the system are accommodated by the theory, so that on any given level any one of them can be assimilated completely in the analysis on the next higher level. Relationships and terms are bound together to form one self-contained, synchronously functioning system.

Thus, Schenkerian analysis is only partly useful to the historian, since obviously he must be concerned not only with synchronic aspects of musical systems but also with diachronic aspects. That is, the historian demands that analytical methods be historically operational, which Schenkerian theory is not.[26] To the historian, any analytical theory worth its salt must take into account how *systems* are

22. Heinrich Schenker, *Kontrapunkt* (Vienna: Universal Edition, 1910), 1:315.
23. *Harmony*, p. 158.
24. Ibid.
25. *Das Meisterwerk in der Musik*, p. 144 (Schenker, 1:194).
26. The attempts by Felix Salzer, Saul Novack, Roy Travis, and others to apply Schenkerian theory to earlier music have on the one hand been severely criticized as apostasies by the true believers (e.g., Oswald Jonas and Ernst Oster), while historians on the other hand have rarely accepted their results. It should be noted here that an attempt has also been made to extend Schenkerian theory to include contemporary music. See, for example, Salzer's *Structural Hearing*, any volume of *The Music Forum*, or Allen Forte's *Contemporary Tone-Structures* (New York: Bureau of Publications, Teachers College, Columbia University, 1955).

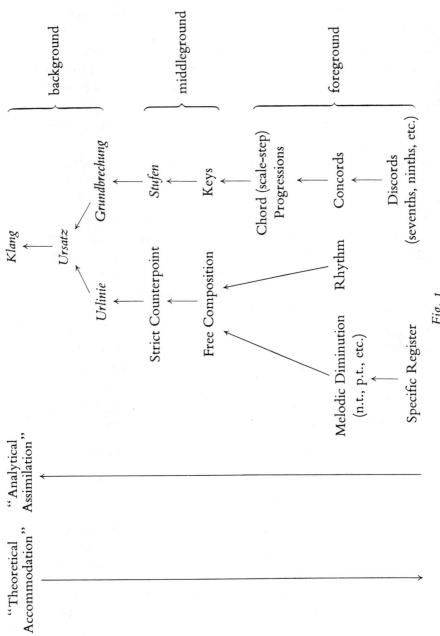

Fig. 1

assimilated into historical style. Consequently, he wants a *two-way* assimilation-accommodation scheme which deals with both synchronic and diachronic aspects. Quite aside from the fact that few sophisticated historians maintain that style systems are goals of historical processes, diachrony requires that the inherent *nontonal* tendencies in tonal music be recognized.

It is obvious, for instance, that from a harmonic point of view the historian wants to know when and how dissonances became goals, when and how sevenths and ninths began to become "real" structural intervals, when and how nonharmonic tones began to cease to function as such, and so forth. Or, from a voice-leading point of view, the historian wants to know how and in what way rhythm transforms the style. Schenker's absurd statement that the time factor "does not have ... the power to transform a musical phenomenon"[27] flies directly in the face of the historical *fact* of style change.

In short, because in Schenkerian theory the assimilation-accommodation scheme works only to the advantage of the synchronic aspect, and because nontonal potential—that which, when realized, eventually assimilates the tonal system—never appears in a Schenkerian analysis, many "Schenkergrams" (the analytical graphs) do not denote musical events accurately enough for the purpose of studying history, since the function of any foreground or middleground part is considered only from the standpoint of its contribution to the main or total purpose—the unity as exemplified in the preformed *Ursatz*.

27. *Harmonielehre*, p. 411 (translation mine).

Five
ANALYTICAL PROBLEMS: HARMONY

I T IS UNFAIR TO CRITICIZE A THEORETICAL SYSTEM EXCLUSIVELY IN terms of its formulation, because in the end what counts are the analytical explanations it generates. But if the foundations of a theory are weak and delimiting, as are those of Schenkerian theory, we can expect to encounter serious problems and unexplainable anomalies in the analytical results. Since, however, Schenkerian theory is based primarily on the premise that harmony is always the dominant parameter—where optimized voice-leading rules assimilate all the other parameters into a hypothetical unified whole—we might expect nevertheless to find Schenkerian analysis characterized by internally consistent rules of transformation, enabling the analyst to derive one level from another in a consistent way.

But this is not the case. To demonstrate, let us consider some trivial examples and try to construct some consistent rules of inference on which to base the theory. We are looking for logical or empirical constants. And the reason they are necessary is that before we can accept any propositions of analytic reduction in Schenkerian theory— those concerning strict counterpoint, free counterpoint, *Stufen*, prolongations, and so forth—we must know how certain are the deductions from the *Ursatz*.[1]

In order to understand the analytic problems inherent in the theory, suppose we assent to its central hypothesis and assume the "well-formed" status of both the *Urlinie* and the *Grundbrechung*. By his separate and lengthy discussions of each type of structure in *Der Freie*

1. On axioms of reducibility, see Whitehead and Russell, *Principia Mathematica*, pp. 59 ff.

Satz, Schenker seems to imply that the occurrence of either of these in a musical context signifies a closed shape. On the highest (background) level, the "achievement" of both structures congruently in the form of the *Ursatz* is asserted to indicate the closure of a composition. Since the *Ursatz*-shape can be the content of the foreground as well (*Der Freie Satz*, p. 47), we might thus infer from the occurrence of either the *Urlinie-* or the *Grundbrechung*-shape that a process of transformation (*Verwandlung*) signifying closure on the next level is to take place. In such a case we might reinterpret, say, an initial I–V–I bass—a foreground "*Grundbrechung*"—at the next higher level as simply a I (see example 6). In so doing, we might formulate a context-

Example 6

free "rule of synonymy." That is, we might infer an operation of transformation based upon a logical constant: the I–V–I "likeness" from one place (or one piece) to the next. Similarly, we might try to extend the rule to *Urlinie*-like structures and assume that in a foreground 3̂–2̂–1̂ pattern, the 1̂, as the closural tone, is to be taken to the next level (see example 6 again).[2]

2. Though I am relying on the 3̂–2̂–1̂ pattern here for the sake of the argument, I remind the reader once again that there are other forms of the *Urlinie* (e.g., 8̂ to 1̂, and 5̂ to 1̂).

For the *Urlinie*, however, such a rule of synonymy will not hold in Schenkerian theory. In a $\hat{3}$–$\hat{2}$–$\hat{1}$ pattern in the foreground, the $\hat{1}$ rarely, if ever, becomes the transformed tone beginning the next level. Instead, in Schenkerian analyses on the foreground level, the $\hat{3}$ subsumes the $\hat{3}$–$\hat{2}$–$\hat{1}$ pattern on the next level. The reason for this is that foreground melody can never close on its own. To allow it to do so would make the later (middleground and background) levels superfluous, since in Schenkerian theory higher levels bestow meaning on the content of lower levels, not vice versa. A $\hat{3}$–$\hat{2}$–$\hat{1}$ pattern becomes transformed to a $\hat{1}$ on the next level when and only when the *Ursatz* stands for the *Klang*, the unifying tonality.

Even if, in looking at Schenkerian analyses, we abandon our rule of synonymy for foreground *Urlinien*, we might still assume such a rule to be possible in reinterpreting a complete foreground *Grundbrechung*, since we can conceive of a bass as being independent of a soprano. Actually, however, such a rule cannot obtain here either. For instance, despite the I–V–I motion to measure 2 in example 7, the bass (bracketed in the example) does not constitute a *Grundbrechung*-form according to Schenkerian theory because a $\hat{2}$ in an *Urlinie*-form can never function as a lower neighboring tone. That is, a $\hat{3}$–$\hat{4}$–$\hat{3}$ neighboring-tone motion

Example 7

(prolonging the $\hat{3}$) has no descending counterpart in a $\hat{3}$–$\hat{2}$–$\hat{3}$ motion, because descending lines have a privileged status. In example 7, a return to $\hat{3}$ after the $\hat{2}$ is thus seen to interrupt the $\hat{3}$–$\hat{2}$ motion which, as Schenker says, points like a finger to the $\hat{1}$. Thus Schenker elaborates his theory to include a notion of interruption (*Unterbrechung*),[3] symbolized by the mark // between measures 1 and 2, and the interrupted *Urlinie* prevents the initial I–V–I in example 7 from being the *Grundbrechung*. In example 7, therefore, the V-chord of measure 1 points not to the I on the downbeat of measure 2 but, like the *Urlinie*, to the tonic in measure 3 (symbolized by the arrows in the example).

With respect to example 7, we must now abandon the earlier suggestion about separating the *Urlinie* and the *Grundbrechung*. On the basis of the theory of interruption, we must assume that both structures create an indivisible unit as formulated in the *Ursatz*. Consequently, our search for precisely specifiable rules continues. On the basis of examples 6 and 7, we might suppose that the synonymous relationship upon which to construct a rule of transformation should be not the completed $\frac{\hat{3}-\hat{2}-\hat{1}}{\text{I–V–I}}$ but rather the incomplete $\frac{\hat{3}-\hat{2}}{\text{I–V}}$ in the antecedent bar in example 7 (measure 1), which implies and eventually leads to the $\frac{\hat{1}}{\text{I}}$ at the end of the consequent (measure 3). And we would assume that everything between the initial motion and the terminal $\frac{\hat{1}}{\text{I}}$ would be somehow subsumed on a higher level as a prolongation of the overall $\frac{\hat{3}-\hat{2}-\hat{1}}{\text{I–V–I}}$.

Now, however, consider example 8. According to our newly formed rule of synonymy where the *Urlinie* and the *Grundbrechung* work in concert instead of separately, we might evaluate measure 1 in example 8 like measure 1 in example 7—that is, as a case which exemplifies "interruption" and in which the $\frac{\hat{2}}{\text{V}}$ points to and implies the tonic on measure 4. Though this seems consistent, it nevertheless will not hold in Schenkerian theory. In this instance, because the V in measure 1 is followed by a II, the V in Schenkerian theory is analyzed as having *no* implicative *harmonic* relationship to the tonic in measure 4. That is, harmonically the V in measure 1 of example 8 is said to have only a retrospective relationship to the initial I (symbolized by a connecting

---

3. *Der Freie Satz*, pp. 72–3, 78–9, 116 ff.

Example 8

slur; see the analysis underneath). The prospective relationship of the
bass to the D in measure 2 is said to be contrapuntal,[4] whereas the
Urlinie, contrary to what we have been led to believe from Schenker's
interruption theory about the indivisibility of the bass and the soprano,
is in this example separated from the bass and viewed as becoming part
of a neighboring-tone pattern prolonging the 3̂ (E). That is, the second
degree in the soprano in measure 1 (D) becomes a "composing out" of
the third degree (E) so that, overall, the first two bars become a contrapuntal motion to VI (again see example 8). Moreover, the rationalization of the second degree as a lower neighboring tone in this example,
despite the proscription of it pointed out earlier, is based upon circular
reasoning: the Schenkerian would argue that the soprano D is not part
of the *Urlinie* because it is not part of the *Grundbrechung*, though the
interrupted I–V bass (bracketed in measure 1 in example 8) occurs in
example 8 as surely as it did in example 7.

Curiously, Schenker admits the possibility of an implication even in
such neighboring-tone situations as example 8. He says, for instance,

4. For an example of the continuing ascending fifth patterns analyzed by Schenker,
see *Der Freie Satz*, appendix, example 68.

that a "lower neighboring note simulates an interruption of the *Urlinie*-progression."[5] Why then should an interrupted I–V bass with such a $\hat{3}$–$\hat{2}$ soprano be denied the same implicative status? Earlier, I stated that a concept of virtual implication is impossibile in Schenkerian theory because the goals are predetermined. Here, however, the contradictions between example 8 and example 7 demonstrate that even *within* the system a concept of implication cannot be consistently applied.

Finding consistent theoretical rules of inference is obviously no trivial matter in any analytical method. But it is particularly crucial in a system which concerns itself with levels, because without such logical or empirical constants, getting from one level to the next becomes merely a matter of conjecture and opinion, with the usual contradictory and disputed results. And it goes without saying that the whole notion of transformation has to depend to some extent on context-free rules of synonymy or on implication; that is, on inferring likeness in meaning from one place to the next.[6] Without this, there can be no adequate theory-building.

The dogmatic Schenkerian, however, may have some objections to the foregoing criticisms. He might say that the rule of interruption—of recognizing an initial $\frac{\hat{3}\ \hat{2}}{\text{I–V}}$ form as implicatively synonymous in every context—is not to be invoked where an "irregular" harmonic pattern occurs (i.e., a pattern specified as ill-formed by the syntax of the theory), such as the I–V–II progression between measures 1 and 2 of example 8. He might argue that in these cases context-sensitive rules are necessary. But this rationalization also leads to contradictory results. Take example 9. The "irregular" progression of I–V–IV–II–V–I occurs, but here we have no reason to tie the first V back to the first I, because, by following Schenker's voice-leading rules, the intermediate IV–II motion can easily be construed as a "composing out" of the

5. *Der Freie Satz*, p. 78.

6. This is an argument made by Roy Harris, *Synonymy and Linguistic Analysis* (Oxford: Blackwell, 1973). Throughout this essay I shall use the term "synonymy" not to refer to exact sameness of meaning—there is good reason to doubt that such a thing exists, particularly in music—but rather to "likeness in meaning" in accordance with the argument given by Nelson Goodman in his article, "On Likeness of Meaning," reprinted in *Semantics and the Philosophy of Language*, ed. Leonard Linsky (Urbana: University of Illinois Press, 1952), chap. 4.

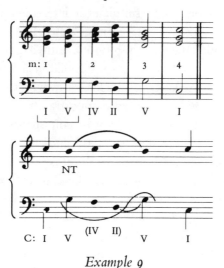

Example 9

initial V (see the analysis underneath). Thus, a synonymy rule of implication seems applicable here. That is, the initial I–V progression in measure 1 of example 9 could be envisioned as implying the I in measure 4, a conclusion supported by the voice-leading connections between the two dominants of measures 1 and 3. Indeed, if we look at example 8 again, we will see that if we choose a different voice-leading configuration in the soprano (in place of the neighboring-tone structure), the $\frac{3}{I}\frac{2}{V}$ form there can also be analyzed as implying the final tonic—that is, as leading directly to the tonic in a way similar to example 9 (see example 10; the dotted line signifies a "retained tone").

Example 10. An alternative analysis of example 8

A doctrinaire Schenkerian might have one ad hoc argument left. He might insist that the theory of interruption applies only where specific formal shapes occur, like ternary or binary forms or antecedent-consequent phrases. Though Schenker explicitly states that all forms are derived from the background and the middleground, and not vice versa,[7] in practice he does use the interruption precept mostly in conjunction with clear formal constructions. But in any case, this formal stipulation does not solve our problem of finding some logical constants in the theory. Example 11, for instance, taken from Felix Salzer's *Structural Hearing*—a study derived from the teachings of Schenker (but deviating in numerous and significant ways)—is in all important

Example 11. After Salzer (Mozart's Sonata, K. 576, measures 1–8)

7. *Der Freie Satz*, p. 200.

respects an antecedent-consequent phrase.[8] Yet Salzer invokes no interruption technique here for the precise reason mentioned in the discussion of example 8: The "irregular" harmonic progression from the V at the end of the antecedent (measure 4) to the II at the beginning of the consequent (measure 5) leads Salzer to conclude that such "incomplete" harmonic progressions (symbolized by the backward-pointing arrow in his analysis) have a harmonic relation only in backward reference to the structural I[9] and, because of this, that incomplete harmonic progressions make somewhat greater demands on the listener's capacity for structural hearing than complete harmonic progressions.[10]

Salzer notwithstanding, I seriously doubt that listeners find the I–II⁶–V–//II–V–I of example 11 any more "complicated" because of the "incomplete" harmonic motion than the "complete" I–V//I–V–I harmonic motion of any other antecedent-consequent phrase. And, further, I think we hear the I–II⁶–V progression in the antecedent phrase of example 11 as having not only a "backward" harmonic reference to the opening tonic but also a forward reference to the I at the end of the consequent phrase (measure 8). That is, the prospective relationship ending on the V in the antecedent phrase in example 11 (measure 4) not only is contiguously contrapuntal to the next adjacent chord (the II opening the consequent phrase in measure 5) but also has a discontiguous, implicative relationship to the tonic at the end of the consequent. The V-chord in measure 4 is *both* interrupted and connected. The V at the end of the antecedent "participates" in both an "irregular" progression (to the II) *and* a "regular" progression (to the I at the end of the phrase).

Like the "rabbit-duck" problem referred to earlier (example 4), the Schenkerian predilection to see musical events in only one way in any given analysis (e.g., Salzer's insistence that the V in measure 4 of example 11 has only a backward harmonic connection) is of course just another instance of the kind of misleading conclusions that result when

8. Salzer, *Structural Hearing*, 2:95.

9. Ibid., vol. 1; see the general discussion on p. 152 and the specific discussion of this example on p. 155.

10. Ibid., p. 155.

one accepts the a priori fallacy. The *Ursatz* is put forth as a prior "truth" without the empirical evidence. But I have dealt here with the application of the *Ursatz* in the most trivial harmonic examples imaginable—excluding, of course, example 11, Mozart's powerful "Trumpet" Sonata, which is anything but trivial—in order to show that the use of the *Ursatz* as an analytical hypothesis leads to one problematic conclusion after another. (If the *Ursatz* were a real axiom, of course, this would not happen.) But given the fallacious formulation of the *Ursatz*, this is perhaps not surprising.

What is surprising is that in a system so idealistically conceived and so heavily rationalistic in analytical methodology it seems impossible to formulate any firm rules about what is presumably its most distinct element. A true hierarchical transformation theory, of course, is supposed to reduce the number of rules needed. Each example here, however, seems to call for special rules, with little promise of future generalization. It is little wonder then that the analytical contradictions strain empirical credulity: We simply do not hear, for instance, the "incomplete" V in example 11 as having only a retrospective harmonic reference. As far as harmony is concerned, therefore, we are justified in questioning both the theoretical and the empirical foundations of the Schenkerian system.

Six
ANALYTICAL PROBLEMS: MELODY AND RHYTHM

Impoverished Explanations

Despite the preceding criticisms, Schenkerian analysis is often enlightening in passages that exhibit strong harmonic "control," particularly where such parametric dominance exemplifies the "heart of the style"—for example, in pieces where the voice-leading structures associated with the most common practice occur with great frequency. On the other hand, in idiosyncratic harmonic passages of unique and highly individualized works, Schenkerian analysis can identify deviations from the norm but can rarely explain them, since, according to the Schenkerian scheme, these passages must eventually give way to and support the assimilating structural organization dictated by the *Ursatz*.

To many theorists, however, Schenkerian analysis fails most markedly in dealing with the parameters of melody and rhythm.[1] As we have seen, the essential reason for this lies in its inability to come to grips with the "assimilation-accommodation" problem. In Schenkerian theory, the functional factors of harmonic voice leading always assimilate the functions of melody and rhythm; melody and rhythm can never irrevocably modify their harmonic-contrapuntal "origins." Let us first examine some of the analytical consequences of Schenkerian theory with respect to melody.

As is shown in example 12, Schenker analyzes the theme from the second key area in Beethoven's Fifth Symphony mostly as a series of

1. See Walter Riezler-Stettin, "Die Urlinie," *Die Musik* 22, 7 (April 1930): 502–10.

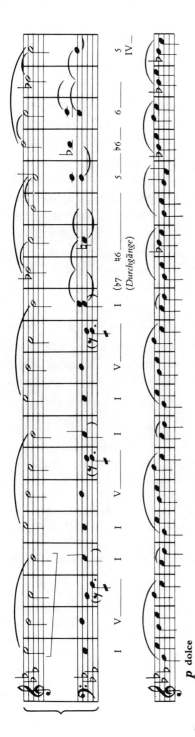
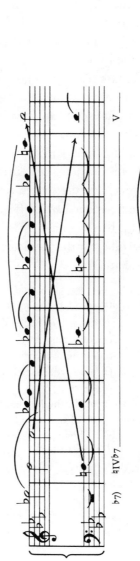

Example 12. After Schenker (Beethoven's Symphony no. 5, I, measures 63–94)

descending *Urlinie*-like patterns.[2] Underlying harmonic-contrapuntal structures are, of course, the rationale behind the linear reduction of the melody, and their existence is undeniable. Schenker's reduction, however, does violence to the melody. For if we listen to and analyze the melody prospectively from the viewpoint of its implicative patterns and its rhythmic phrasing, we will see that its power resides precisely in its refusal to conform to the descending voice leading that such harmonic patterns ordinarily generate. Indeed, understood from the point of view of implications, Beethoven's melody points more *upward* than downward (see example 13, → means "implies"). And the restless quality of that upward mobility—linear on the quarter-note level (D–E♭–F in measures 2–3) and triadic on the half-note level (B♭–D–F in measures 1–3)—contrasts with and complements the more patent descending line which follows the harmonic voice leading (E♭–D–C–B♭, measures 1–4).[3] Like the multiplicity of patterns inherent in the rabbit-duck picture shown earlier, *all* these melodic patterns are present in the first four bars of Beethoven's melody. To subsume the melody of these bars within the harmonic pattern not only is inaccurate but fails to account for the character of the first four bars—their lyrical and pregnant nature.

2. Heinrich Schenker, *Beethoven Fünfte Sinfonie*, ed. Karl Heinz Füssl and H. C. Robbins Landon (Vienna: Universal Edition, 1969). The analysis is from the foldout between pp. 6 and 7. The analysis originally appeared in *Der Tonwille*, vol. 1 (1921). A translation of Schenker's remarks about the first movement of this symphony (together with a reproduction of the analysis) may be found in *Ludwig van Beethoven: Symphony No. 5 in C Minor*, ed. Elliot Forbes (New York: W. W. Norton, 1971), pp. 164–82.

3. In a syntactic system like music, a level is defined by a span of time. Thus higher levels occupy longer spans of time than lower levels. In my view, it is unlikely that a tone will occur on a level lower than its actual duration, but a tone short in duration will often occur on a higher level because the parameter of duration can be transformed by, say, the parameters of melodic and harmonic pitch and meter. In such cases, a short note could "stand for" a higher level—a longer duration—even though it would still retain its identity as a short note. In example 13, for instance, pitch patterns establish melodic structures whose structural tones occur regularly every two beats in time (the B♭–D–F). Thus we may say that this structure occurs at the half-note level though the notes on which this pattern occurs are still quarter notes. I will say more about this later.

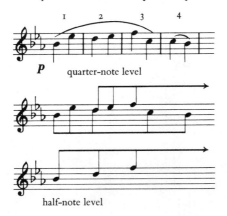

Example 13

Further, a failure to capture the importance of the triadic structure in measures 1–4, which is brought about by the regularity of the metric accents,[4] leads, as we can see in example 14, to a misunderstanding of what happens in the rest of the melody. There we see the realization of three different triadic implications: not only the initial B♭–D–F triad, repeated three times (measures 1–3, 5–7, 9–11, graph a), but also a B♭–D♭–F triad (measures 13–18, graph b), an E♭–G♭–B♭ triad (measures 21–32, graph c), and a higher-level B♭–E♭–G♭–B♭ structure as well (measures 1–32, graph d), which integrates the parts of the melody into a cohesive unit (see example 14, where ⤙ means "realized"— catching the "arrow" of implication).

Owing to a conformant relationship to the four-bar transition introducing the melody (example 15)[5] and the 3 + 1 phrasing, the implication of the first triadic pattern (B♭–D–F, measures 1–4, example 14) is at first not as strong as it would ordinarily be. But the direction the melody is to take becomes increasingly clear with the B♭–D♭ pattern in measures 13–17 (see graph b, example 14 again). In measures

4. Meter is a particularly important clue to melodic structure in additive rhythms such as Beethoven's melody, where the entire theme (except the last note) is written in quarter notes.

5. Charles Rosen, *The Classical Style* (New York: W. W. Norton, 1972), p. 406, also notices this conformant relationship.

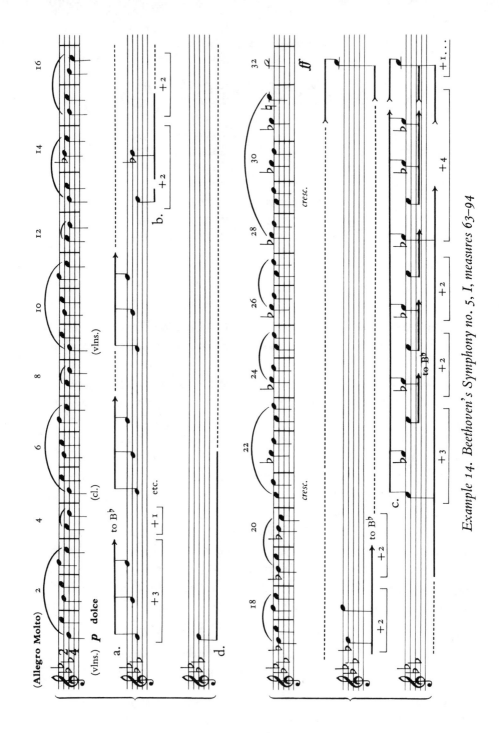

Example 14. Beethoven's Symphony no. 5, I, measures 63–94

Example 15

21–31, Beethoven carefully articulates the phrasing to make certain the E♭ and G♭ (graph c, example 14) gain in prominence: a three-measure grouping in measures 21–23 is followed by two two-measure groupings in measures 24–27; only then do we get the expected four-measure grouping (measures 28–31). Indeed, the manuscript is unambiguous about Beethoven's "intention" in this matter (example 16*b*): the more patent 2 + 2 grouping is scratched out and superseded by the slur encompassing three bars so that G♭ becomes the initiating tone from measure 24 instead of the preceding E♭ in measure 23. The reader may compare "what might have been" in example 16*a*

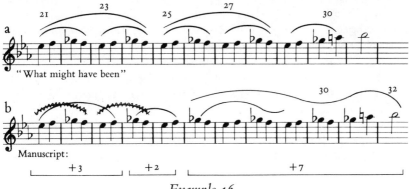

Example 16

with Beethoven's changes in example 16*b*.[6] Coming at this point in the melody—formally near the end and processively where the transformation from E♭ to G♭ takes place—the asymmetry of Beethoven's phrasing (3 + 2 + 7 in example 16*b*; 3 + 2 + 2 + 4 in the printed score, example 14) is all the more effective as the culminating B♮ in measure 32 realizes all the triadic implications.

Since in Schenkerian theory all rhythm is reduced to counterpoint,[7] details of phrasing and rhythm in Beethoven's melody are completely lost in Schenker's reduction on the next level—though rhythm is obviously crucial to any explanation of the melody.[8] Let us consider further how rhythm affects the triadic ascent in example 14.

One important feature of the melody, for instance, is that the reversal of direction following the ascent of the first two triads becomes progressively longer. For example, the reversal (C–B♭) following the B♭–D–F triad lasts one bar each time (example 14, measures 4, 8, and 12)—hence Beethoven's 3 + 1 phrasing (which Schenker reduces to a four-bar group)—whereas the delay from B♭–D♭ (measures 13–14) to D♭–F (measures 17–18, graph b) lasts two bars (measures 15–16, 19–20). Thus, beginning with measures 13–16 (primarily a prolongation of B♭) and continuing to measures 17–20 (primarily a prolongation of D♭), we would expect measures 21–31 to function formally as a higher-level delay to measures 13–20, except that the shift to E♭ (measure 21) and

6. Georg Schünemann, ed., *Beethoven: Fünfte Symphonie nach der Handschrift im Besitz der Preussischen Staatsbibliothek* (Berlin: Maximilian-Verlag Max Staercke, 1942). The 3 + 1 phrasing of measures 1–4, 5–8, and 9–12, mentioned earlier, also appears clearly in the manuscript. The last seven bars of the melody are usually represented in score as being 2 + 4, then +1 (the B♮ in measure 32). However, the manuscript (example 16*b*) shows the last phrase as one seven-bar unit including the B♮. Several two-hand versions for piano (e.g., Schirmer's) simply phrase measures 21–32 as 2 + 2 + 2 + 2 + 3 + 1, in wretched disregard of Beethoven's purpose.

7. For attempts to extend Schenker's concepts of rhythm into a more unified theory, see Morgan, "Delayed Structural Downbeat"; Komar, *Theory of Suspensions*; Yeston, *Stratification of Musical Rhythm*; and Anne Alexandra Pierce, "The analysis of Rhythm in Tonal Music" (Ph.D. diss., Brandeis University, 1968).

8. The reader may wish to compare Schenker's far-fetched explanation of the asymmetry in Beethoven's phrasing with the one given here. See Schenker, *Beethoven, Fünfte Sinfonie*, p. 10; or Forbes's edition, p. 174.

the prolonged G♭ (transforming the triadic motion in measures 22–31) intensifies *both* the ascending implication *and*, through asymmetrically grouped repetitions (3 + 2 + 2 + 4), the delay. The varied triadic approaches to the high B♭ in measure 32—the B♭–D–F, B♭–D♭–F, B♭–E♭–G♭ (perhaps even B♭–D♭–G♭, not shown)—and the constant reversal of motion (which delays the final ascent) together with the overall form (12 + 8 + 12), then, give this melody a subtle yet strong rhythmic direction that accounts for the forceful, culminating release felt on the B♭ in measure 32. This high B♭, incidentally, is prolonged until the closing of the entire exposition, which underscores the importance of the triadic structures that imply it.

Contrary to what Schenker would have us believe, therefore, the overall structure of Beethoven's melody owes its coherence not to the future completion of the *Ursatz*[9] or some other preformed supersummative agency like the *Urlinie*, but to the way its numerous parts are bound together by the realizations of different ascending triadic structures.

I do not wish to denigrate the unifying function of the harmony in Beethoven's melody, of course. But overall unity results not only from congruence of parameters but from noncongruence as well. We cannot assume, as the Schenkerians do, that melody always serves structurally at the pleasure of the bass line. The achievement of closure is not uniform from parameter to parameter.

Consider Beethoven's theme again. I have argued that the opening phrase (measures 1–12) is kept ongoing and "open" by the B♭–D–F triadic implication in the melody, and we may observe that these triadic melodic structures (a^1, a^2, a^3 in example 17) are noncongruent with the harmonic closure that takes place with the V–I progressions cadencing on the tonic E♭s in measures 4, 8, and 12 (see example 17). The situation is similar in the next two phrases. The fourth and fifth four-bar phrases (b^1, b^2, measures 13–20) are also harmonically "self-contained," in contrast to the implicative B♭–D♭–F there in the melody, but in measure 14 now the bass line in conjunction with the earlier phrases ending on E♭ unobtrusively establishes its own slowly

9. In *Der Freie Satz*, p. 47, Schenker says that "all forms receive their coherence from the *Ursatz*."

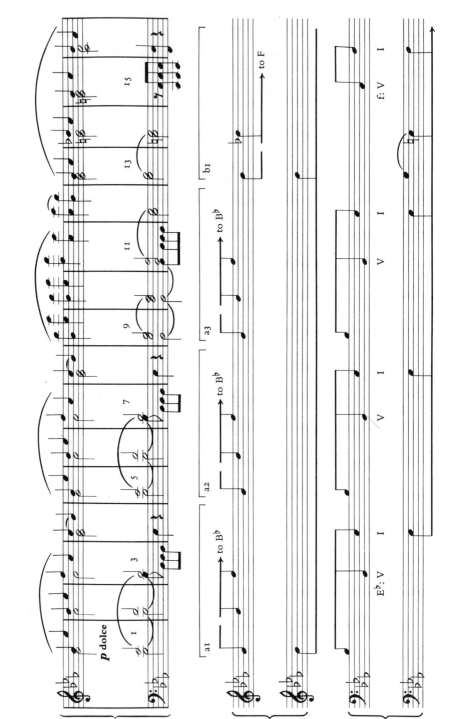

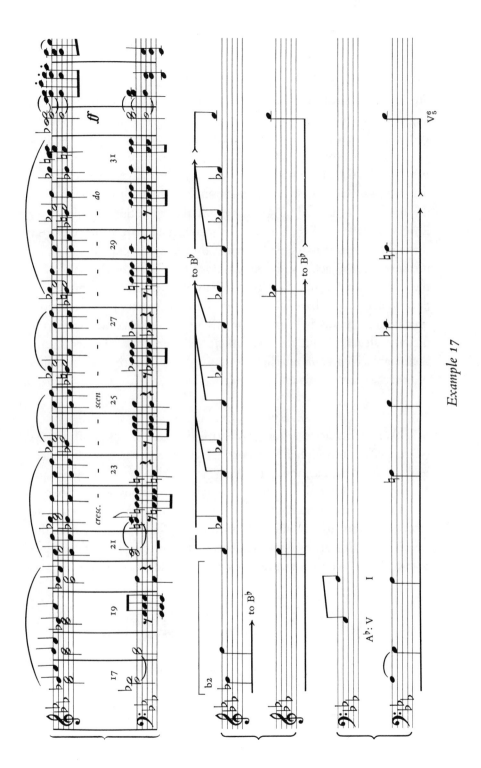

Example 17

ascending line (E♭–E♮–F–G–A♭), generating concomitant harmonic progressions through the related keys of F-minor and A♭-major. In prospect, the movement to the relative repose of the subdominant key in measures 17–20 (A♭) seems to be the end of the bass line's ascent. But with the ominous A♮ in measure 22 everything changes. The bass ascent gathers motion with increasing urgency in measures 22–29 (A♮–B♭–C♭–C♮), accompanied by equally portentous changes in the harmony—all acts of strong non-closure. Further, this nonclosure in the bass is coordinated to grind against the saturating repetitions of E♭–G♭ in the melody. Indeed, noncongruence remains the rule throughout this passage, and, even through the exploding V_5^6 in measure 32, the "actions" of one parameter are offset by the stability of the others. To be sure, Schenker's analysis (example 12) captures the importance of the bass line and the harmonies it supports, but how much more useful in explanation his reduction becomes when the melodic structure and the rhythmic/phrase structure of Beethoven's theme are given equal implicative status. I shall return to a discussion of other aspects of this melody later.

Erroneous Explanations

Schenker's insistence that foreground melody and rhythm must always be integrated into higher levels of the system according to the voice-leading rules of harmony, resulting eventually in the problematic *Ursatz*, leads not only to impoverished explanations where melody and rhythm are denied independent implicative status but also to erroneous conclusions that are completely at variance with our experience. We observed such an instance in our discussion of examples 8 and 11, and we may examine a similar melodic case in example 18,

Andante, ma non troppo

Example 18. After Salzer (Beethoven's Bagatelle op. 119, no. 11)

from Salzer's *Structural Hearing*.[10] The difference here is that the one-sided assimilating analysis prevents Salzer from structuring the foreground properly, resulting both in an untenable assertion about the relationships between the tones and in an incorrect evaluation of the implicative patterns in the melody.

The first problem in example 18 arises with the descending D–C–B♭ at the very beginning. The eighth-note C in measure 1 is treated as a passing tone, with the B♭ tied back to the D in accordance with the Schenkerian notion that all such patterns are *Terz-züge* (third-progressions). The problem is that in Beethoven's setting the C is the consonant tone (underneath lies a V without the third degree), whereas the B♭ eighth note is dissonant (see example 20 below). The assumption of the third-progression here, which exemplifies a Schenkerian rule of voice leading, leads Salzer to make the following claim:

> It would prove entirely misleading to follow the visible successions of tones, because they are often not indicative of the phrase's direction. For example, the eighth-note B♭ of the second beat is followed by a quarter-note E♭; one cannot for this reason assert that B♭ leads to E♭; nor does C lead to F, the downbeat of meas. 2. Instead the musical ear quite instinctively makes a larger connection and will register the upward motion of a third from D via E♭ to F as the actual melodic line—the melodic structure. The eighth-notes C and B♭ and the quarter-note C are embellishments and thus offshoots or prolongations of this melodic line.[11]

Although few would argue against the higher-level ascending D–E♭–F, the conclusions Salzer makes about the other foreground tones in measure 1 are mistaken. However "logical" his remarks seem in the context of Schenkerian dogma, it is simply absurd to assert that listeners do not make a direct melodic connection between the B♭ and the E♭ or the C and the F. The B♭ establishes a relationship with *both* the C preceding it and the E♭ following it. In fact, the way B♭ leads to E♭ followed by the conforming leap of C to F establishes an alternating pattern (brackets in example 19*a*) that brings out not only the

10. Salzer, *Structural Hearing*, 2:8.
11. Ibid., 1:41.

Example 19

D–E♭–F pattern on the beat but also a corresponding B♭–C pattern which implies a D. An acknowledgment of this latter pattern, of course, helps us explain the stable occurrence of this very tone in measure 3 (see example 19*b*). Such claims that the musical ear "instinctively" comprehends patterns only one way—either backward or forward according to Schenkerian principles of reduction—are, as we have seen, untenable, but they obtain necessarily in a theory which subsumes according to preordained wholes.

The biological metaphor in Schenkerism and the "slighting of the role of the part" in Gestaltism are pertinent here, for Schenkerians must always base their explanations on the next higher level—on what is to come, on what has been preformed by the *Ursatz*. In their view the part itself can be understood only by invoking the structure that assimilates it. Thus the very formulation of the theory leads them to incorporate the "genetic fallacy" in their explanations. This is clearly illustrated in Salzer's remarks. As he sees it, the B♭ eighth note and the C quarter note in measure 1 can be understood only by calling upon the "origin" of each tone, namely, the higher-level D and E♭. If, on the other hand, we take an implication view of these tones, we do not find ourselves in the "genetic" predicament. For the implicative meaning of, say, the D–E♭ pattern is "there" whether or not the goal-note F in measure 2 occurs. In an implication-realization theory, we thus need not cheat the independent status of the part, since its meaning need not be solely dependent on what eventually occurs. I shall elaborate on this later.

To return, however, to Salzer's analysis: a second problem arises in measure 2 (example 18). Here the descending tone E♮ is designated as the structural tone between the F on the first beat in measure 2 and the D in measure 3. But on what basis? Apparently the answer is that the eighth-note F on the third beat in measure 2 (and presumably the eighth-note D on the fourth) functions like an appoggiatura, clearing the way for us to hear the E♮ as a higher-level structural tone passing to the D in measure 3. Appoggiaturas are, of course, very common at semicadences in tonal music, and since Schenkerian theory attempts to reduce the melodic foreground to a contrapuntal-harmonic structure —preferably a descending line of some sort (like the F–E♮–D in Salzer's analysis)—Salzer's reduction appears to be within the rules. The trouble is that the chord on the third beat in measure 2 is a V⁶ (not a II⁶ or a IV), so that the dissonant tone is *not* the F, as we might expect in a real appoggiatura context, but rather Salzer's E♮ (a diminished fifth, over the A in the bass; see example 20). We should not, of course,

Example 20

automatically assume that dissonances are nonstructural, but there is no good argument in measure 2 for elevating the offbeat dissonant E♮ over the consonant F on the beat (a sixth), even though on the fourth beat we might argue structural primacy for the nonaccented C (a fifth) over the accented D (a sixth) on the basis of harmony. In all cases we must take into account the *actual* harmonic pattern in order to make analytical judgments about melodic structural tones. A preformed concept about voice leading and the contextual function of consonance and dissonance simply will not do.

Where does this leave us, then, with respect to the melodic connections from the F in measure 2 to the D in measure 3 ? Again, the implication-realization concept provides the answer. For by hearing the ascending leap from the C in measure 1 to the F of measure 2 as a structural *gap* that implies a descending fill, we can see the eighth-note pattern in measure 2 (discounting the neighboring tone G for the time being) functioning clearly as a realization of that implication,[12] taking the F back to the C before the D in measure 3 begins the two-bar phrase again (example 21*a*).[13] Similarly, we can construe the D in measure 3 as a delayed realization of the B♭–C line created by the

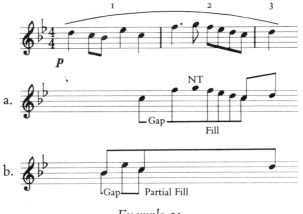

Example 21

12. On structural gaps, see Meyer, *Emotion and Meaning in Music*, pp. 130–35 and idem, *Explaining Music* (Berkeley: University of California Press, 1973), pp. 145–57. I myself have dealt extensively with a theory of gap implications in "The Melodic Structure of Tonal Music: A Theoretical Study," (Ph.D. diss., University of Chicago, 1974), chap. 4.

13. The F in measure 2 is not closed. On one level—that of the half note—the D–E♭–F pattern implies a G which is realized in measure 8 of the melody, while on the whole-note level the D–F implies a B♭ which is also realized in measure 8. The G–B♭ in measure 8 creates a gap which is filled in measures 9 ff.

partial filling in of the B♭–E♭ leap in measure 1 (example 21*b*).[14] So much for Salzer's contention that B♭ does not lead to E♭ in measure 1 and C does not lead to F in measure 2.

THE POLYPHONIC PROBLEM

As I have emphasized, the analytical reductions Schenkerians perform are possible only by presuming congruence of parameters dominated and controlled by harmony. Since they accept the premise that tonal music is an extrapolated horizontalization of the *Klang*, it seems natural to them that the quickest way to structure a piece is to reverse the process: conceptually verticalize all motion into chordal harmony, then reduce all stepwise relationships to voice-leading connections between these chords (passing tones, neighboring tones, appoggiaturas, suspensions, etc.).

Schenker's reduction of Mozart's Sonata, K. 545, shows the process clearly enough (example 22).[15] The harmonic progression in measures 1–4—in roman-numeral analysis, I–V$_3^4$–I–IV$_4^6$–I–V^6–I—is seen as a prolongation of the tonic because the V$_3^4$, IV$_4^6$, and V^6 chords function in terms of voice leading as neighboring-tone chords and appoggiaturas.[16] Thus the melody must follow. The C–E–G pattern in measure 1 is reduced as a rolled chord of the tonic; the motive in measure 2 is an appoggiatura, since the V$_3^4$ underneath is a neighboring-tone chord

---

14. The pitch fill to a gap need not be complete, nor need it always be linear. For instance, a leap upward of an octave could be partially filled by a leap downward of a fifth; a leap upward of a fifth, by a leap downward of a third. Thus in example 21*b*, the C functions as a partial fill to the B♭–E♭ gap. The degree of incompleteness in a fill has an important bearing on how the gap structure is transformed to the next level. The more incomplete the fill, the more likely it is that the leaped-to note will belong to a latent pattern on the next level. Thus in example 21*b*, the leaped-to E♭ functions both as part of a higher-level ascending linear structure (the D–E♭–F) and as part of a lower-level gap.

15. The example is from Schenker's *Der Tonwille*, vol. 2 (1923), appendix, p. 2. Another somewhat less distorted, later version of an analysis of this same sonata may be found in the appendix of *Der Freie Satz*, p. 82.

16. Though I think that roman-numeral symbology is theoretically and analytically problematic, throughout this essay I shall continue to employ it because it is the least clumsy nomenclature to use in writing prose about musical events.

Example 22. After Schenker (Mozart's Sonata K. 545, measures 1–5)

(not shown in Schenker's analysis); the A in measure 3 functions as an appoggiatura over the I, and so forth. Since the melody in measures 1–2 must be connected structurally in some way, Schenker asserts an *Urlinie*-like relationship, the 3–2–1, which, as a span of a third, prolongs the tonic chord (shown by the slur). The "middle voice" in measure 1 (the E) is made the structural tone on the foreground level; and since it is the "3," the sixteenth-note D in measure 2 is also elevated to the status of a foreground "2," despite its exceptionally weak rhythmic position. Similarly for the reduction of the melody in measures 3–4: the A in measure 3, as an appoggiatura over the I, sets up another descending line which follows down to the E in measure 4, a span of a fourth (again shown by the slur).

Once all this is done, some further analytical guide is necessary. Before we can begin the analysis in measure 5, measures 1–4 must be further reduced. Harmonically, they prolong the tonic, and so melodically, the structural tone must be $\hat{5}$ or $\hat{3}$ ($\hat{8}$ does not figure in the analysis). The $\hat{5}$ is chosen because measures 5–6 move to the sixth ($\hat{6}$) and fifth ($\hat{5}$) degrees of the scale.

Thus, at any given stage of his reduction Schenker must bear in mind where the analysis is to be taken, because on higher levels one chord is posited to be *the* chord (the tonic), one stepwise motion, *the* melody (the *Urlinie*), one bass-line structure, the support of *the* harmony (the I–V–I of the *Grundbrechung*), and one contrapuntal motion, *the* voice-leading structure (the *Ursatz*). There is no question that each of these things by itself is "chordal" or "melodic" or "harmonic" or "contrapuntal." The problem is that throughout the levels of the analysis Schenker promotes adjectives into substantives without convincing arguments, results, or explanations.[17]

Since all middleground and foreground phenomena are absorbed into a "structure of structures"—a structure that, horizontalized, is a voice-leading motion and, verticalized, is a melodically prolonged chord—Schenker concludes that *all* melodies are polyphonic in the sense that they exhibit many voices of chords. In example 22, for

17. I have borrowed this argument from Paul A. Weiss's article, "The Living System: Determinism Stratified," in *Beyond Reductionism*, ed. Arthur Koestler and J. R. Smythies (Boston: Beacon Press, 1969), pp. 34–35.

instance, Schenker would argue that the melody of measure 1 contains *three* voices—C, E, and G. On higher levels, once the *Urlinie*-tone is decided upon, all the rest of the tones of the melody function as either "inside" (*untergreifen*) parts or "outside" (*übergreifen*) parts prolonging the structural chord which supports the *Urlinie* tone.[18] Even the scalar *Urlinie*—when understood in terms of its origin (the *Klang*)—is conceived as having two voices, the $\hat{3}$ and the $\hat{1}$, the $\hat{2}$ being a passing tone made consonant by the structural V underneath.

The polyphonic nature of tonal melodies has been observed by many theorists and musicologists, of course, and there are many instances where a polyphonic analysis of a melodic line seems justified. But this certainly is not true in all cases. The melody of Mozart's Rondo, K. 511, for instance, is singled out by Salzer as one instance of a polyphonic melody (example 23):

Example 23. After Salzer (Mozart's Rondo K. 511, measures 1–4)

18. Throughout the essay I will use Salzer's translation of these terms to "inside" and "outside" voice, though the German might be better rendered as "underlapping" or "overlapping."

Although motion into and out of the inner voice and the effect of the retained tone [shown by the dotted slur in the example] are actually created by one voice alone, it appears as if this single voice has split into two parts, one retaining the structural value of E, the other performing the motion into and out of the inner voice of the governing chord.[19]

In fact, the melody can be more simply and elegantly analyzed as a single motion: an ascending filling in of a descending structural gap from E down to A. It is misleading (and confusing) in this example to assert that the stretched-out version of the E–A chordal interval is polyphonic. The leap from E down to A does not so much signify a motion to the middle voice of the tonic chord as it implies a melodic (linear) return to the E by means of an ascending filling in of the gap. As in geometry, where two points may define a line, so here too: E and A in example 23 create two points between which is *one* implied line, not the appearance of several polyphonic ones. If the melody of example 23 is a chord of several voices—or rather if A is a line in a polyphonic texture—then it must have its own two diverging points of reference, which clearly it does not. That is, it is obvious that genuinely polyphonic melodies must have two or more *separate* melodic motions implied *and* realized.

My disagreement with the Schenkerians about polyphonic melody is more than a different point of view. One cannot deny that harmony influences tonal melody in important ways. But it does not follow from this that tonal melody can be pulverized into voices of chords and reduced according to the parameter of harmony. About example 23 Salzer says, "This polyphonic manifestation proves that tonal melody is not based on a purely horizontal conception in spite of all the 'linear' tendencies it may demonstrate."[20] What proof? One does not have to be a "purist" about horizontal relationships to reject the notion that melody is merely a prismatic refraction of harmony. It is, after all, possible that many tonal melodies Schenkerians regard as polyphonic can be better explained in terms of what they in fact are

---

19. Salzer, *Structural Hearing*, 1:121. The example is from 2:58.
20. Ibid.

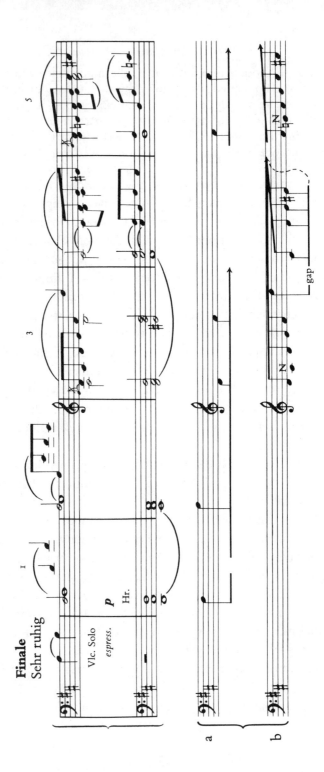

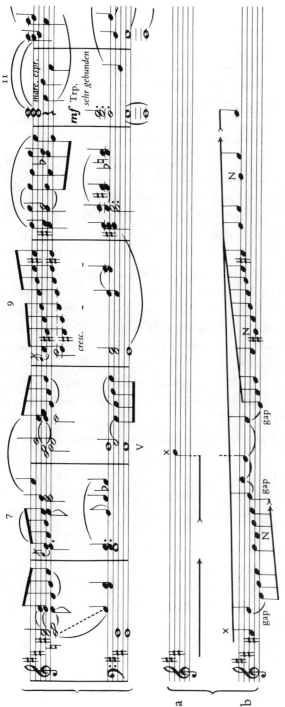

Example 24. R. Strauss, Don Quixote (Finale)

—namely, structures composed of one horizontal motion—before being viewed through the distorting voice-leading prism of the *Klang*.

Though their functions often overlap, this is a good place to emphasize that *voice leading and melody are not the same*. Voice-leading connections are understood primarily in terms of figured-bass symbolizations which represent the horizontal motion necessary to harmonic process. Melody, on the other hand, though influenced by harmony, nevertheless remains independent of it. It is possible for a piece to display regularity in voice leading and at the same time have a melody whose structure is quite at variance with—and therefore not capable of being absorbed by—the harmony. Observe the melody of example 24, for instance. The F♯ in measure 3, as the seventh of the chord, skips up to D (instead of resolving to E as a voice of the chord), and then that D skips back down to the C♯ in measure 4, creating a gap. Thus, in important ways, neither the F♯ nor the D can be assimilated into the voice leading, though the harmonic voice leading of the passage is, in all other respects, stylistically very regular. (The F♯ in the orchestral cellos, for example, does resolve to an E in measure 4.) Rather, the F♯ in the solo cello presages the overall triadic ascent (example 24*a*), which is renewed on the F♯–A in measure 5 and taken linearly up to the dissonant D in measure 8 (over the V) and eventually to the climactic A in measure 11 (example 24*b*). Much the same can be said about the melodic D of measure 3. It also cannot be subsumed as a simple harmonic motion to the C♯ in measure 4 through the specious Schenkerian technique of octave transfer (about which more in a moment). Rather, as the initiating tone of a descending gap (example 24*b*), it, too, reinforces the implication (begun in measure 3) that the melody will rise linearly and return to a D in that register, as indeed the melody does in measures 8–9. Thus, the melodic deviation from the voice leading in the solo cello in measure 3 is central to an understanding of the affect of the passage. Fractionating the melody of the solo cello into "polyphonic" voices of the harmony would obscure the importance of the F♯ and the D in measure 3. Moreover, by reducing the music to harmonic process, a "Schenkerization" would have distorted the cohesion and the reason for the intensity of the rising lines in the passage.

Example 25. After Schenker (Mozart's Symphony no. 40, I, measures 2–9)

On the other hand, example 25, an analysis of the opening bars of Mozart's Symphony No. 40 given by Schenker in the second yearbook of *Das Meisterwerk in Der Musik*,[21] clearly operates as a "two-story," polyphonic melody. In this case we might be tempted to go along with the verticalization of the intervals (shown in the analysis by slurs denoting the "outer" voice of the structural tones). However, because Schenker wants to absorb lower levels into higher, he misses, I believe, the real polyphonic structure in Mozart's melody. That is, Schenker wants to find what he considers the main chords, which then enable him to reduce the melody to the 5̂–4̂–3̂–2̂ structure by the legerdemain of an ascending octave transfer (*Höherlegung*) on the A in measure 9. Although the notion of octave equivalence belongs squarely to harmonic theory (and has no place in a genuine melodic theory)—which brings us to a major problem in the Schenkerian analysis of melody that I will discuss in a moment—there is nothing in the Fuxian fourth-species, contrapuntal model (example 26) to suggest the kind of melodic

21. To see how the 5̂–4̂–3̂–2̂ pattern presents a horizontalization of a chord, see *Der Freie Satz*, appendix, p. 44, example 89,3. For the sake of clarity I have omitted some of Schenker's detail from the analysis. Also I have added the numbers with carets.

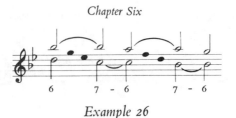

Example 26

convergence Schenker wants us to accept in example 25. That is, in a strict Fuxian pattern, two polyphonic lines like those found in Mozart's melody form a melodic sequence of 7–6 suspensions, and the parts never merge (see example 26). In Schenker's analysis, on the other hand, the lower line (D–C–B♭, the 5̂–4̂–3̂) is made to converge with the upper line in order to extrapolate the 2̂, thus making the *Urlinie*. Much credit has been given to Schenker for formulating his theory on thoroughbass models, but here we can see that the *theory* tends to distort such models because supersummative agencies like the *Urlinie* are invoked.

In an implication-realization model, however, both the polyphonic pattern behind Mozart's melody and the Fuxian model it exemplifies are preserved (see example 27). Moreover, this view enables us to understand the melody better: the "upper story" B♭–A goes on to the G, whereas the lower line (D–C) ends on the lower B♭. Specificity of

Example 27

register can be maintained, and the Fuxian model need not be misrepresented. In example 27 we thus see how an analysis based on a concept of implication and realization is much more consonant with our aural experience and how the implication-realization concept avoids a distortion of the "facts," namely, the specific registral identity of melodic pitches.[22]

THE POVERTY OF OCTAVE TRANSFER

Like many Schenkerian concepts, the idea of octave transfer often misrepresents the structure of melody. I have already pointed out that according to Schenker independence of register from the obligatory register (*obligate Lage*) of the *Ursatz* is an illusion.[23] This is nonsense, of course, but because Schenkerian theory essentially views patterns retrospectively in terms of predetermined harmonic goals, the concept of independent registral potential is all but ignored. And this leads to erroneous theories of melodic structure and a weakened sense of aural comprehension—in short, to a greatly impoverished theory of melody.

22. It should be pointed out in this example that the D–B♭ skip in measure 2 and the C–A skip in measure 6 also function as gaps that are filled in by measures 3 and 7, respectively. These gaps are not shown in example 27 because their fills do not completely close the high register. As I will argue later, tones are always *both* open and closed on any given level. There are several reasons for this with respect to example 27. First, the larger a direct leap is, the more its registers tend to separate. This is particularly true where rhythm itself adds no differentiation to bind the pitches of the leap together, as in example 27, where the leaps D–B♭ (measure 2) and C–A (measure 6) occur as quarter notes. Second, the rests which follow directly upon each leap in example 27 tend to emphasize the independence and potential of the high notes. Third, the fills themselves to these two leaps (G–E♭ in measure 3 and F♯–D in measure 7) are incomplete triads (incomplete relative to linear fills)—set up on the half-note level by the *differentiated* ♪♪ ♩ rhythm—with the result that the leaped-to notes (B♭ in measure 2 and A in measure 6) connect and create the implication to the G in measure 10. If the gap filling had been shown, of course, the reader would have noticed some overlap between my analysis in example 27 and Schenker's in example 25. The point I wish to stress here is that, because in the implication-realization model tones are viewed as being simultaneously open and closed on the same level, the notion of gap filling is radically different in concept from Schenker's idea of filling in the tonal space (the *Tonraum*). Recall examples 21 and 23.

23. *Der Freie Satz*, p. 42.

One would think, for instance, that a cardinal feature of Beethoven's rondo theme in example 28 is the lack of a G♯ in the "right" register. The repeated A's in measures 2–3, the accompanying crescendo in measure 3, the forcefully unfolding, descending bass line from the start,

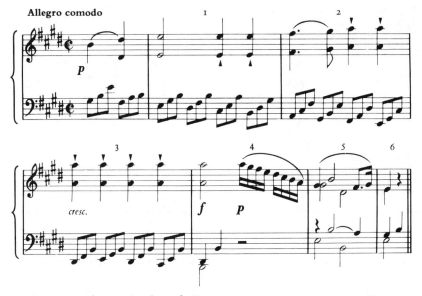

Example 28. Beethoven's Sonata op. 14, no. 1, measures 1–6

the harmonic seventh over the V in measure 4—all these point to a G♯ of substance and character in the upper register. But the melodic power of Beethoven's melody is completely flattened out in a Salzerian analysis (example 29).[24] By the specious technique of octave transfer (symbolized by the arrow between measures 4 and 5 in the example), the repeated A's merely become the 4̂ in a typical 5̂–1̂ *Zug*, leading to a structural G♯ (the 3̂) in measure 5.

In fact we do get a "good" G♯ in the "right" register on the fourth hearing of the theme (example 30, arrow). The overpowering effect of the third recurrence of the rondo theme, however, is not due just to the realization of the registral potential at the beginning. The first and second recurrences set up a peculiarly rondoesque "norm of omission" in the work, so that by the third recurrence we have all but forgotten

24. Salzer, *Structural Hearing*, 2:72.

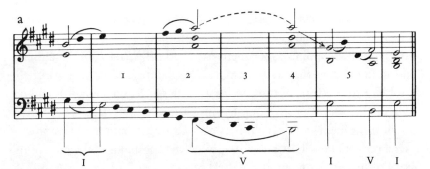

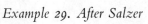

Example 29. After Salzer

Example 30. Beethoven's Sonata op. 14, no. 1, measures 108–16

the registral implication. The high G♯ thus functions as both a witty surprise and a brusque jog to our memories.

Obviously my point is not to deny a function of partial *harmonic* closure on the low G♯ in the first hearing of the theme (the V7 in measure 4 resolving to the I in measure 5), as it occurs in Salzer's analysis and in each of the other hearings, but to emphasize that by virtue of registral implication Beethoven's melody is not congruent with the harmony— that a potential implication is "there" at the beginning, which helps us explain the development in the third recurrence of the theme, and that the eventual realization of the high G♯ contributes to the overall closure of the rondo theme. More generally, registral potential is an important part of the *structure* of Beethoven's piece, and that potential should find a place in an analytical representation if the melodic structure is to be accurately explained.

Seven

ANALYTICAL PROBLEMS: FORM
AND METER

Form and meter function like other nonprivileged elements in Schenkerian theory.[1] That is to say, they are assimilated into the harmonic-contrapuntal analysis. Because all forms, on every level, are derived from the *Ursatz*,[2] according to Schenker they "receive their coherence only from the *Ursatz*."[3] "Repetitions reach explanation and confirmation only from the background and the middleground,"[4] and since "repetition is . . . the prerequisite of meter and rhythm,"[5] meter, like rhythm, must obey the rules of counterpoint and harmony. The element of time cannot alter the meaning of a musical phenomenon.[6] Prolongations are independent of temporal "size."[7] And so on. That form and meter are not explicit factors in the formulation of Schenkerian theory has been noticed by many writers.[8]

We observed earlier the assimilation of form and meter in connection with Schenker's analysis of Brahms's Waltz op. 39, no. 1 (example 2), and we saw in Schenker's analysis of the theme in the second key area of Beethoven's Fifth Symphony (example 12) that the factor of meter with respect to melodic structure was in many instances disregarded. It

---

1. See *Der Freie Satz*, pp. 197 ff., for Schenker's main ideas of form, and pp. 183 ff. for his ideas of meter and rhythm.

2. Ibid., p. 200.

3. Ibid., p. 47.

4. Ibid., p. 184.

5. Ibid., p. 183.

6. *Harmonielehre*, p. 411.

7. *Der Freie Satz*, p. 202.

8. Regener, "Layered Music-Theoretic Systems," p. 55.

will be recalled that Schenker analyzed the first twelve bars of the melody as descending voice-leading patterns of E♭–D–C–B♭ (example 31*a*), even though meter emphasized an *ascending* B♭–D–F (see example 31*b*).

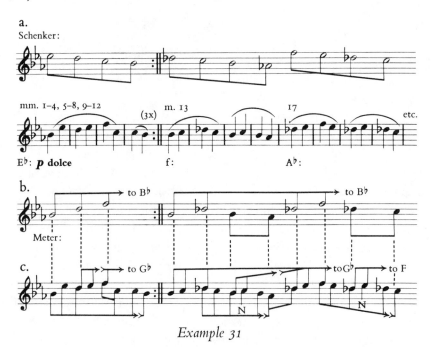

Example 31

Schenker's treatment of form presents two general problems. First, the predilection for lines structured according to voice-leading rules often elicits false comparisons. In the same Beethoven example, for instance, one might think from Schenker's analytical reductions that measures 13–16 and 17–20 conformed not only to each other but also to measures 1–4, 5–8, and 9–12, since all the phrases show the same descending pattern of fourths (again see example 31*a*).[9] In fact, as one

9. I have borrowed the word "conformant" from Meyer's *Explaining Music*, chap. 3. The word is used to denote formal events that are related by similarity, regardless of level. Thus, in example 31 each measure is conformant in terms of meter; measures 1–4, 5–8, and 9–12 are conformant in every parameter (except instrumentation—see the score of the symphony); measures 13–16 are partially conformant to measures 17–20 in terms of melody and harmony but not in terms of mode, and so on.

can see from Beethoven's melody, measures 13–16 and 17–20 are significantly different from measures 1–4, 5–8, and 9–12. Indeed, the analysis of measures 1–12 and 13–20 in example 31c shows that foreground differences are great enough to affect higher-level structures: measures 1–12 encompass three notes of a triad (B♭–D–F), whereas measures 13–16 and 17–20 are each structured on two notes of a triad (B♭–D♭ and D♭–F, see example 31b). Thus, in a Schenkerian reduction similarities between prolongations may or may not be meaningful in terms of the actual music. In contrast, in an implication-realization model, differences and similarities are detailed much more rigorously.

This leads us to the second problem with form. Because Schenker's theory absorbs form under the dominant parameter of harmony, a Schenkerian analysis often obscures manifest parallelisms in the actual music. Consequently, formal relationships which are important to an understanding of the structure can be overlooked. Let us consider such an example. In his book *Structural Hearing*, Salzer gives the following structural reduction of a passage from the D-minor Fantasy of Mozart (example 32; half notes represent those tones of greatest importance; quarter and unstemmed notes are ornamental; *a* and *b* designate levels).[10] The dominating parameter thought to be most important in determining structure is again obviously harmony, and it establishes a voice-leading motion of $I-V_3^4-V_5^6-I$. Both the melodic line and the bass are subsumed into a neighboring-tone figure (symbolized "*N*" in the example).

Harmonically, the analysis can hardly be faulted. The part for the left hand (example 33) shows clear evidence of the prolongation of the I by means of the $V_3^4-V_5^6$ motion: the bass voice leads unambiguously from D to the E-C♯ neighbors and back to D. Furthermore, in the left hand the four-bar phrase with its $1 + 1 + 1 + 1$ divisions (each bar being halved as well) seems to articulate the neighboring-tone structure.

Melodically, the analysis is much less convincing. The melody by

---

The term is useful, for it lets us talk about purely analytic relationships—in other words, about formal synonymity—without reference to function. Schenker was fully aware of such relationships (see examples 118 and 119 in the appendix of *Der Freie Satz*).

10. Salzer, *Structural Hearing*, 2:60.

Example 32. After Salzer (Mozart's Fantasy K. 397, measures 12–15)

itself suggests no 4 × 1 division; it is clearly cast into two-bar phrases (again see example 32). The second conforms closely to the first; that is, each two-bar phrase is made up of two distinctly structured motives: the ♩ ⋯ ♬ ♪♪♪♪ | ♩ and the ♪ ♫. The obvious question then is, Why in Salzer's analysis (example 32) does the double-dotted F in measure I receive more structural weight than the double-dotted G

Example 33

90

in measure 3? Both, after all, function as the initiating tone in each two-bar motive which marks them for "consciousness"—the 2 + 2 relationship clearly underlining a connection between the long notes: the double-dotted F in measure 1 and the double-dotted G in measure 3 and the quarter-note C♯ in measure 2 and the quarter-note D in measure 4. Further, the parallel between the latter two notes is structurally emphasized by the anacrustic eighth-note motion which leads to them (measure 1: G–F–E–D; measure 3: A–G–F–E). Why then in Salzer's analysis should the E in measure 2 be regarded as on a par with the G in measure 3 (both N's symbolized as quarter notes) while the F in measure 4 (on the weak beat) is given a greater structural role even though it is formally parallel to the E in measure 2?

From a melodic, formal, rhythmic, and metric point of view, Salzer's analysis is replete with such questions. Although within the biases of the theory we can find answers, they are not satisfactory. Melodically, it is true, the ear hears four discrete events (the two motives, repeated once, referred to earlier). But the tones transformed from these motives to the next level are the result of other processes besides harmony. Rhythmically, the thirty-seconds point up the third beats of measures 1 and 3 (♬) ending on the pitches G and A respectively; see example 34*a*), which in turn initiate the anacrustic eighth-note continuations that culminate on the quarter-note C♯ in measure 2 and the quarter-note D in measure 4 (♩♩♩♩ ♩ ; again see example 34*a*). Moreover, from the end of measures 1 and 3 to the beginning of measures 2 and 4, meter stresses descending triadic patterns—however noncongruent thay may be with the harmony (dissonances are marked with "x")—which underscores the anacrustic nature of the eighth-note rhythm and implies the self-same long notes in measures 2 and 4 (G–E–C♯ and A–F–D; see example 34*c*). Further, the notes G and A on the third beats in measures 1 and 3, together with the preceding ascending linear thirty-seconds (E–F–G and F♯–G–A, respectively), easily offset the descent of the eighth notes in those bars so that the whole melody in the upper register remains open and ongoing to measure 5 (see example 34*d*). In short, Salzer's summation

Example 34

is too glib. There are other important forces in Mozart's melody besides the harmonically generated neighboring-tone pattern.

We have a right to demand that our analytic representations agree as closely as possible with our aural experience and with the empirical "facts"—the notes on the printed page. There should be a direct relationship between the form, the rhythm, and the meter of Mozart's melody and our note reduction. The failure of Salzer's analysis to come to grips satisfactorily with the relationship between analytical representation and the manifest patterns printed in the music is indicative of a fundamental problem in Schenkerian theory: its inability to deal with a given part on closural terms other than the predetermined whole (in the case of example 32, the $\frac{3}{1}$). Often this cannot help but make the Schenkerian concept of levels suspect: transformational derivations often appear mechanistic and irrational.

What sort of higher-level melodic pattern would emerge if we took into account length of note, formal relationships, and motivic similarity? The answer, as we have seen, is that instead of a neighboring-tone structure in the melody, dominated by the parameter of harmony and the voice-leading rules of the I–V$_3^4$–V$_5^6$–I pattern so clearly evident in the left hand, we would have a two-story pattern of discontiguous seconds: F–G and C♯–D (example 35). In this analysis the factors of

Example 35

duration (the double-dotted quarters in measures 1 and 3 and the quarter notes in measures 2 and 4), form (2 + 2), conformance (A + A'), and meter would be taken to militate against the fact that the G in measure 3 is a dissonant diminished fifth over the C♯ in the left hand (though with respect to some of the other tones, some of the metrically strong notes are clearly ornamental—e.g., the dissonant, nondiatonic D♯ in measure 2). This, however, should not disturb the Schenkerian greatly, since Salzer also takes the G in this measure as the structural, upper neighboring tone instead of, say, the more consonant A on the third beat. Thus, although there seems to be evidence of a polyphonic pattern in this example by Mozart, such a bilinear melodic structure shown in the alternative analysis is completely overlooked in Salzer's reduction, where the parameter of harmony is allowed to dominate.

By allowing that the two-story linear pattern of the melody may be noncongruent with the neighboring structure of the harmony, we can assess *both* the closure and the nonclosure of the four-bar phrase. That is, in contrast to the neighboring-tone closure of the harmony, the nonclosural F–G linear pattern in the melody implies a continuation beyond the four bars—to an A (example 36, note the noncongruence

Example 36

of F–G and C♯–D with the neighboring-tone structure in the left hand). And this latter tone does indeed occur in the very next measure (example 37). But the F–G–A relationship, so crucial to understanding

Example 37

Mozart's melody, does not figure in Salzer's analysis, not only because form and rhythm and meter are ignored, but also because implicative relationships are not really accounted for.[11]

I shall continue to discuss the matter of form in the next chapter.

11. I discussed earlier the argument that if Schenkerian theory were a true axiomatic system there would not be so many discrepancies between different theorists' analyses of the same piece. Jonas's analysis of Mozart's Fantasy is a case in point. In contrast to Salzer, Jonas does see the higher-level F–G–A melodic relationship—though he omits in his discussion an analysis of how he derives the pattern in terms of the harmonic structure and the bass line (Jonas, *Einführung*, p. 6). Moreover, Jonas's representation and derivation of the ascending melodic pattern is significantly different from the one I have presented here in that Jonas shows the high-level F–G to be more important than the culminating A in measure 5. That is, the F and G are represented by Jonas as whole notes and the A is shown as a half note—distortions of Mozart's rhythm brought about by Jonas's adherence to Schenker's rules that harmony and voice leading must perforce assimilate all the other parameters.

Eight
OF TREES AND NETWORKS, SYSTEMS
AND HIERARCHIES

O NE CONSEQUENCE OF THE WAY SCHENKERIAN THEORY WORKS IS
that every analysis results in a treelike structure like that of
example 38 (cf. with example 32). Given the one-way assimilation-
accommodation scheme, it could hardly be otherwise (see again fig. 1).
Since the I–V$_3^4$–V$_5^6$–I harmony above the neighboring-tone structure
in the bass in example 38 seems clear, a treelike generation might
seem reasonable were it not that such a parsing distorts melodic,
formal, rhythmic, and metric facts. A second consequence of Salzer's
analysis—where in example 32 the melodic structural tones are made
congruent with the neighboring-tone structure of the bass—is that it
neglects implicative, nonclosural elements. In example 32 this led to a
misinterpretation of the high-level, implicative F–G in the melody in
measures 1–4 and would if carried further result in a misconstruction
of the function of the A in measure 5 that clearly realizes the F–G
implication.

In Schenkerian theory, only the preparatory *Anstieg* and the various
forms of the *Ursatz*—because of their privileged status in the theory—
stretch across from one "branch" of the tree to another on successive
levels. If, however, as has been implied, the normal state of affairs in
tonal music is *non*congruence of parameters between levels instead of
congruence,[1] it follows that analytical reductions should be concep-

1. To those unfamiliar with hierarchies, this generalization may seem a bit puzzling.
It is true that a level can arise only if it is closed; but it must also be remembered that
the same level cannot connect to other levels—become part of the system—unless it is
also open and incomplete. Thus every level is Janus-faced, both open and closed
simultaneously. Hierarchies are possible only if parameters are noncongruent on
lower and middle levels. It is this Janus-faced quality that gives hierarchies their
discontinuous character. I shall speak about this in more detail later.

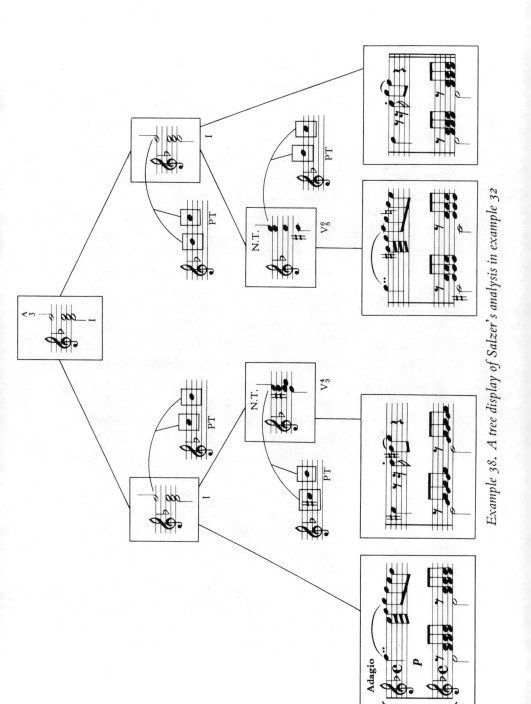

Example 38. A tree display of Salzer's analysis in example 32

tualized not as trees—except perhaps in the most simplistic kinds of music where each unit (form, prolongation, whatever) is highly closed—but as *networks*. That is, musical structures should not be analyzed as consisting of levels systematically stacked like blocks, as in example 38, but rather as intertwined, reticulated complexes—as integrated, nonuniform hierarchies.

Unity would then be a result of the interlocking connections that occur when implications are realized between parts rather than as a result of relationships determined by the assumption of a preexisting whole. The coherence of the little melody in example 39, for instance, would be explained not in terms of a treelike parsing subsumed under a prolonged 3̂ (cf. with example 18) but in terms of the complex way the melodic tones are welded together in varying, yet collaborating, structural realizations of implications—linear, gap filling, and so forth (cf. example 40 with example 39). And, although levels are clearly present in example 40, no treelike analysis could do justice to such complex structural interlacing.

In a hierarchical network-analysis based on an implication-realization model, all levels would be only *partly* closed or, as Herbert A. Simon says, partially "decomposable."[2] Thus, in order to describe a partially decomposed level in a true hierarchical system, we would have to attend to *both* closural and nonclosural aspects *on the same level at the same time*. That is, it would be necessary to account for why and in what specific ways a given part is closed *and* unclosed *without* invoking reasons from a higher-level structural realization. Our evaluation of either the closural or the nonclosural aspect would therefore have to be made on the basis of the *internal* evidence in the part, not from "outside"—that is, not on the basis of the realized whole which the part eventually joins.

That hierarchies are defined by partially decomposable levels indicates that Schenkerian theory is not concerned with hierarchies at all but rather with *systems*—although this may come as a surprise to the Schenkerians who have thought *Ursatz*-analysis is synonymous with

2. Herbert A. Simon, *The Sciences of the Artificial* (Cambridge: M.I.T. Press, 1969), pp. 99–107.

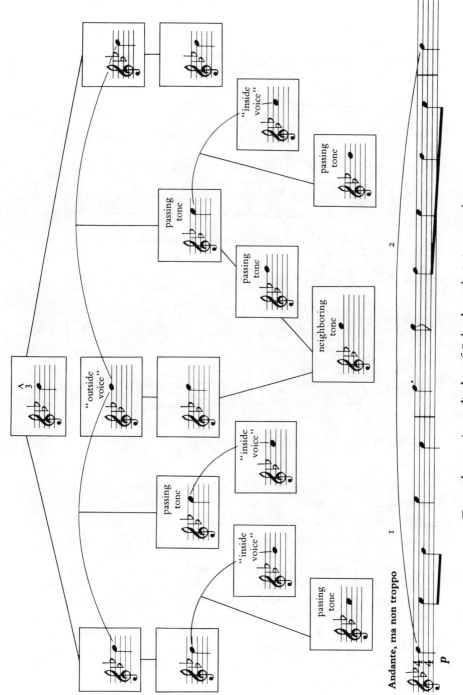

Example 39. A tree display of Salzer's analysis in example 18

Example 40

hierarchical analysis.[3] For levels in Schenkerian theory are not partially decomposed but are in principle disconnected according to the rule of the optimized parameter, harmony. Pattee's remarks describe the situation in Schenkerian analysis perfectly (re. examples 38 and 39).

3. There is a common misconception among Schenkerians that Schenker "discovered" the notion of levels in music theory. For instance, Forte, in "Schenker's Conception of Musical Structure," p. 4, refers to "Schenker's achievement—which might be termed the deepening of musical understanding through the discovery of the principle of structural levels." Actually, the conception of hierarchical levels may be found very clearly stated in Gottfried Weber, *Versuch einer geordneten Theorie der Tonsetzkunst*, 3d German ed. (Mainz, 1830–32), which antedates Schenker's work by some seventy to one hundred years.

One central aim of control in dynamical systems is to avoid instabilities at all costs, since instability generally leads to a new dynamical regime. A second common goal in control theory is to optimize certain parameters under a given set of fixed constraints. . . .

. . . dynamical systems theory emphasizes holistic, single-level descriptions, avoidance of instabilities, optimization under fixed constraints and artificial isolation of adjacent levels.

. . . the essential behavior of real hierarchical systems [however] depends on the *partial* decomposition of levels.[4]

The parallel is striking: Schenkerian theory avoids most instabilities by regarding parts as wholly closed and by reducing pieces to the *Ursatz*. The instabilities in tonal pieces which historically lead to nontonal dynamical "regimes" (atonality, pantonality, modality, etc.) are controlled under the voice-leading constraints of the optimized parameter, harmony. The description of the whole is what counts in Schenkerian analysis . . . and so forth.

In the analysis of Beethoven's Bagatelle shown in the tree design of example 39, for instance, the B♮ in measure 1 is viewed as the end of a passing-tone pattern. The tone displays no instability (despite the fact that in the music it is dissonant against a V chord); it does not imply a continuation down to A; it does not connect directly to the E♭ that follows it; it functions only as an "inside voice" to the initial D. All that matters in the analysis is the assimilation of the tones into the next-level whole. The downbeat F in measure 2, despite its function as the apex of the phrase, is just another "outside voice" serving to prolong the $\hat{3}$.[5] Segmentation of parts is complete. The designation of the function of each tone in Schenkerian terms (neighboring tone,

4. Howard H. Pattee, "Unsolved Problems and Potential Applications of Hierarchy Theory," in *Hierarchy Theory*, ed. Howard H. Pattee (New York: George Braziller, 1973), p. 149.

5. Salzer's analysis in example 18 does not actually take the melody to the level of the *Urlinie*, as I have done in example 39, but there is no question that under the rules of the theory the D is the structural tone (the $\hat{3}$) and the F an outside part. See the harmony and the bass line—Schenker's criteria for discovering the *Urlinie* tones—in example 20.

passing tone, inside voice, outside voice, etc.) leads to a wholly artificial isolation of the parts.

The argument that the name V_3^4 designates an unclosed prolongation in a case like example 38 and that the form at that point is only partially severed, therefore rationalizing the Schenkerian system as hierarchical, will not do because the very assessment of such a V_3^4 as an unclosed part and the evaluation of its degree of nonclosure are made exclusively of and defined in terms of a whole at a *higher* level—in example 38 the $\frac{3}{1}$. In a true hierarchical system, the nonclosure of a level or a part has to be decided *internally* without recourse to higher levels which have not occurred. Schenker always evaluates the closure of a level or a part from *above* the level of its occurrence, where the actual notes of the level under consideration are not present. As Schenker says, "the progressions in an upper, middle or lower voice are at an end as soon as they . . . have arrived at the destination required by coherence."[6]

In contrast, a hierarchical approach would have to explain why a pattern ("progression") "ends" (closes) without reference to a higher, "required" level. And it is the inability of Schenkerian theory to do this which renders it more a "dynamic systems approach" than a hierarchical one. For the cardinal rule of the hierarchical approach and the characteristic which distinguishes it from systems analysis is that, in order to understand the near-decomposability of forms, a true hierarchy theory must describe and define a given level in two *internal* stages *simultaneously*: the closural aspect (that which enables us to comprehend the specificity of something *internally* as a form) and the nonclosural aspect (that which enables us to comprehend the specificity of something as *internally* incomplete). And since in music the relationship between closure and nonclosure is never uniformly balanced within any one level, complex network structures rather than simplistic trees are bound to result.

What makes the theory and analysis of music exceptionally difficult, I believe, is that pieces display both systematic and hierarchical tendencies *simultaneously*. And, as we shall see, this suggests that both "tree" and "network" structures may be present in the same patterning. The possibility of such dualistic complexity should not really be

6. *Der Freie Satz*, p. 124.

surprising, however, since music "contains" both synchronic (systematic) and diachronic (historical and temporal) relationships and meanings. But it does serve to emphasize one of my main points: in music, noncongruence of parameters is the natural circumstance between levels.

The most common examples of tree structures in music theory, of course, are those found in formal analysis (see figs. 2 and 3). Such tree

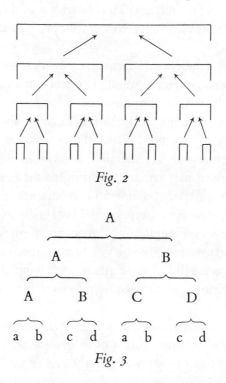

Fig. 2

Fig. 3

structures are established on the basis of optimizing closure over nonclosure, assuming a whole, disregarding implicative connections, and so forth, so that each level (a bracket or a letter) can be treated as an integral entity. Formal analysis is of limited value, however. As Pattee says about formal hierarchies,

> There is seldom any doubt that such structures are lifeless. What is missing is some recognizable "function." No matter how intricate a structure may be, permanence is not

compatible with the concept of function. Function is a *process* in time, and for living systems *the appearance of time-dependent function is the essential characteristic of hierarchical organization.*[7]

And as Schenker knew well, other than yielding descriptions of the molar-molecular variety, the analytical generalizations offered by formal analysis are weak and nonexplanatory because they cannot deal with time-dependent function. Thus Schenkerian theory was formulated as a vigorous alternative to the "empty" structures of formal hierarchies.

Yet it is ironic that because Schenkerian theory must posit completely decomposable components, resulting in treelike structures, it finds itself confronted with precisely the kinds of problems it sought to avoid. For, like formal analysis, Schenkerian theory also deals with and generates treelike structures. Thus the limitations of Schenkerian analysis and formal analysis are similar: neither can explain the closural function of a given part without referring to the next higher level—meaning that the part only becomes an agent of something else, allowing "growth." Or, seen conversely, both Schenkerian analysis and formal analysis suppress real implicative connections, particularly between *non*adjacent parts on any given level, because the realizations of such implications, necessarily discontiguous and nonuniform, upset the systematic ordering and the geometric progression of the analytical tree structure.[8]

Although Schenkerian analysis is a great improvement over purely formal analysis—because it forces us to grapple with the problem of time-dependent function without grossly oversimplifying it—it nevertheless remains deficient because it does not recognize, as Pattee points out, that time-dependent relationships are *processive* and therefore not completely decomposable. We may recall Schenker's ludicrous remark that the time factor "does not have . . . the power to transform a

7. Howard H. Pattee "Physical Conditions for Primitive Functional Hierarchies," in Whyte, Wilson, and Wilson, *Hierarchical Structures*, pp. 165–66 (italics mine).

8. For a further discussion of hierarchical structures and how they might pertain to music, see Leonard B. Meyer, *Music, the Arts, and Ideas* (Chicago: University of Chicago Press, 1967), p. 309 ff. Also see the same author's *Explaining Music*, chap. 4.

musical phenomenon."[9] But I need not reiterate here all the evidence discussed earlier that shows the erroneous results of Schenker's dismissal of the temporal factor. Is it not doubly ironic, however, that someone so avowedly enamored of the biological metaphor should create a theory that produces only tree structures with decomposable parts, structures so incompatible with present concepts of living systems?

FORM RECONSIDERED

This is a good place to reexamine the whole matter of form. For however lacking in time-dependent function formal analyses are, and however "untreelike" most musical processes may be, formal structures exist as indisputable musical facts which cannot be casually shunted aside in note-reductive theories. Whatever theory we choose as a model to study connections within and between events—whether we opt for an *Ursatz*-theory where structures are generated from the highest levels to the lowest or choose an implication-realization theory where structures of pitch are generated from the lowest level to the highest—the structures of pitch reductions and the structures of forms must be coordinated. One should reflect the other.

For the structural function of events on many levels and the formal descriptions of these many-leveled events take us straight to the heart of the epistemological relationship between material and symbol— between our abstraction of experiential relationships and their representation. And the persistent *disagreement* between the reality of forms in a piece and the note-reduction theory in Schenkerian analysis simply cannot be treated as a non-problem. Schenker was on the right track with his notion of interruption technique, although, as we saw in the antecedent-consequent phrase of example 11, the *Ursatz*-theory cannot be consistently applied even in these cases. But the reason coordination between form and note reductions is necessary is this: any form (i.e., any recognizable part) *is* a form simply because a sufficient degree of closure is present. This is a psychological fact. The recognition of a form testifies to the presence of closure. The recognition of a form is possible only when a perceptual threshold is crossed. And such closure is not imposed "externally," from a higher level, though our evaluation

9. *Harmonielehre*, p. 411 (translation mine).

of it may depend on prior learning, but is the *internal* result of the specific way parameters interact in the creation of patterns.

Out of that internal interaction, some tones come to be more closed than others. These more closed tones function in two crucial ways. First, they contribute to the creation of form on that level in the sense that they become "events" of closure. And at the same time, by virtue of their more closed status, they emerge as the tones which create the beginning of the next level—that is to say, which emerge transformed, creating implicative patterns on the next level.

Reconsider the melody of example 34, for instance. The F on beat 1 in measure 1 and the G on beat 1 in measure 3 become closed because of their duration, their metric position, and their function as the initiating tones in the melodic and rhythmic process. The G on beat 3 in measure 1 and the A on beat 3 of measure 3 become closed because of their function in terminating one rhythmic pattern and one pitch pattern (the thirty-second notes, example 34a, and the E–F in measure 1 and F♯–G in measure 3, example 34d)—yet at the same time initiating still others (the eighth-note rhythm, example 34a, and the linear-triadic patterns shown in example 34c). Similarly, the C♯ in measure 2 and the D in measure 4 become closed because they terminate the pitch and rhythmic patterns begun in measures 1 and 3. Likewise the eighth-note E in measure 2 and the eighth-note F in measure 4, as terminal notes in rhythmic, melodic, and harmonic processes, become *transformed* linking measure 2 triadically to measure 3 and measure 4 triadically to measure 5 (see example 34c and d). Thus, F–G–C♯–E and G–A–D–F become the closed, transformed tones in those four bars (shown by the dotted vertical lines in example 34). And this transformation (together with the neighboring-tone structure in the bass) partly accounts for the emergence of these four bars as both a complete and an incomplete form: two of the transformed tones (F and G) create the *formation* of an implication—implying the A in measure 5 (example 34d). Hence, every form displays both transformative and formative aspects on the same level.

Forms therefore can be heuristically useful in theory-making, for they tell us where to look for levels and, to some extent, structural tones. In short, by narrowing the choice of possible transformations they offer helpful guides for formulating explanations, since the stipulation of a form depends on the *internal* definition (and recognition) of rules by which certain tones become more closed than others. To repeat: formal relationships and pitch-pattern relationships are two interdependent aspects of the same musical phenomenon. The relationships do not exist separately.

Thus, when a given Schenkerian pitch transformation shows no direct correspondence to what are manifestly clear formal events on the same level, we suspect that something is wrong. Put another way, when Schenker implies in his discussion of form in *Der Freie Satz* that foreground forms come to verification through the middleground and background,[10] he has put the cart before the horse. For exactly the opposite is the case: closural tones of the foreground forms become the basis for the verification of the middleground transformations, and those of the middleground in turn become the basis for the background.

The process is recursive. As closure occurs, a form emerges. As one branch of the formal tree begins to take shape, the closural tones simultaneously create implications and a cohesive nonclosural network begins to overlap the previously emerging tree. If these implications become realized, a new form emerges (with new implications). And so on, until the piece ends.[11] A form literally cannot be generated from a level above, nor can its occurrence on lower levels ever be completely absorbed by a higher-level pattern.

10. *Der Freie Satz*, pp. 197–200. Schenker tells us that we have to ignore what is manifestly "visual" in the music in order to perceive the laws of the *Urlinie* (ibid., p. 74); yet elsewhere (ibid., p. 152) in contradiction he points out that composers often wrote ornamental notes (appoggiaturas, graces, etc.) as small notes.

11. In one sense, of course, pieces do not end. They continue to reverberate in our subconscious and go on to become part of our experience about our universe, culture, epoch, geographical locale, and so forth.

Nine

THE LINGUISTIC ANALOGY

M ANY NEO-SCHENKERIANS AS WELL AS SCHENKERIANS HAVE NOTICED
an apparent similarity between Schenkerian theory in music and
transformational grammar in linguistics.[1] In this light, Schenkerian
theory is viewed as a kind of natural deduction system (rather than as
an axiom system), and the *Ursatz* is seen to function as a high-level
structure of formation, a "kernel" from which other middle- and
lower-level structures are to be derived. Like the various forms of the
Schenkerian *Ursatz* in diatonic tonality, transformational grammar relies
on innate "kernel" sentences to generate the syntactic structures of a
given language; and, as in Schenkerian analysis, the linguistic structures
generated by transformational grammar turn out to be treelike, the
levels being completely decomposed (see fig. 4).[2] Surface-structure

1. E.g., Milton Babbitt, "The Structure and Function of Musical Theory: I,"
College Music Symposium 5 (Fall 1965):59–60; Regener, "Layed Music-Theoretic
Systems," p. 61; Howard Serwer, "New Linguistic Theory and Old Music Theory,"
Report of the Eleventh Congress 1972, International Musicological Society, vol. II
(Copenhagen: Wilhelm Hansen, 1974), pp. 652–57. In the same congress report
(1:43–45), I. D. Bent, "Current Methods in Stylistic Analysis, Summary of Remarks,"
argues against making an analogy between Schenkerian theory and Chomskyan
linguistics. The reader is also referred to essays by Harold Powers and Leo Treitler in
volume I of this report (pp. 58–61 and 61–70, respectively) that deal with this subject as
well as to the discussion at the end of the session on style analysis (pp. 121–30).

2. The example is taken from Noam Chomsky, *Syntactic Structures* (The Hague:
Mouton, 1957), p. 27. The symbol "S" for "sentence" could be replaced with the
symbol "I" for "idea," which has the advantage of paralleling more closely the
Schenkerian outlook in which the "idea" of a piece is the prolongation of one chord,
the tonic. As absurd as this sounds, it is in fact the Schenkerian position—that pieces
are "about" tonality, the *Klang*, the original Idea.

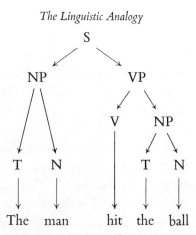

Fig. 4. S = sentence; NP = noun phrase; VP = verb phrase; T = article; V = verb; N = noun.

differences between sentences with the same deep structure (e.g., the same sentence content cast in the active form or the passive form) are explained through rules of transformation. We need not discuss in great detail either the triumphs or the failures of transformational grammar except to say that in postulating innate kernel structures as the bases of all sentences in a given language, Chomsky, the godfather of transformational grammar, has, like Schenker, been accused of the error of affirming the consequent.[3] (Unlike the Schenkerians, however, Chomsky openly admits and defends the rationalistic basis of transformational grammar.) Nor need we discuss at the moment the degree to which linguistic theory is analogous to music theory, or whether it is at all, for that has been dealt with elsewhere—though to a limited extent.[4]

3. See Rulon Wells, "Innate Knowledge," in *Language and Philosophy*, ed. Sidney Hook (New York: New York University Press, 1969), pp. 99–119. Roughly speaking, Wells accuses Chomsky of arguing the following fallacy in his later works: The transformation rules governing syntactic structures are so consistent from language to language that they suggest language is an innate ability in man. The transformation rules appear to be true, and so language must be innate. The most recent criticism of Chomskyan linguistics may be found in Ian Robinson, *The New Grammarians' Funeral* (Cambridge: Cambridge University Press, 1975).

4. See, for instance, Benjamin Boretz, "Meta-Variations: Studies in the Foundations of Musical Thought (I)," *Perspectives of New Music* 8 (Fall–Winter 1969), p. 51 ff; Terry Winograd, "Linguistics and the Computer Analysis of Tonal Harmony,"

Suffice it to say that Schenker himself gives ample reason for drawing upon the linguistic analogy. He asserts, for instance, that his theory establishes a note grammar for the first time,[5] whose growth is controlled and derived from an indestructible, innate Idea, the *Ursatz*.[6] According to Schenker the *Urlinie*, as one representation of the diatonic system—the "language"[7]—exercises "constraints" (regulations) with respect to all the counterpoint in a given diatonic composition[8] and, indirectly, also on all bass arpeggiation, since, originating from the innate *Klang* in nature, soprano and bass are mutually derived and indivisibly linked. The *Urlinie* selects all the melodic intervals in a work, and since it itself obeys the laws of strict composition, even melodic prolongations in free composition operate under these same laws.[9] Schenker then concludes that the laws of diminution are innate and that "the laws of voice-leading, organically anchored, remain always the same in the background, middleground and foreground, even though they undergo transformation."[10] This last statement, of course, is nearly identical to the rationalist position held by some linguists that all the "deep-structure" rules of the language system are innate and invariant. A neo-Schenkerian would maintain, for instance, that because all structures are governed by invariant rules, neighboring-tone prolongations with properties like those of example 32 can be reduced to tree structure generations of a single chord (with the root in the bass and the $\hat{3}$ in the soprano; see example 38), regardless of the level on which such a prolongation might occur.

Journal of Music Theory 12 (Spring 1968):2–49; Steven Feld, "Linguistic Models in Ethnomusicology," *Ethnomusicology* 18 (May 1974):197–217; and Otto Laske, "In Search of a Generative Grammar for Music," *Perspectives of New Music* 12 (Fall–Winter 1973):351–78.

5. *Der Freie Satz*, p. 37.

6. On the other hand, Salzer, in *Structural Hearing*, says Schenkerian analysis avoids all the problems of chord grammar; but he is obviously using the word "grammar" differently than we use it in linguistics.

7. *Der Freie Satz*, p. 40.

8. Ibid.

9. *Der Tonwille* 1, no. 2 (1922):4.

10. *Das Meisterwerk in der Musik*, p. 5 (Schenker, 1:12). The quote comes from *Der Freie Satz*, p. 29.

SOME ELEMENTARY DISTINCTIONS CONCERNING LINGUISTICS

Since linguistic models, past and present, are so popular in current music theory, it might be well to review briefly some features of different types of grammar. Several are possible. Indeed, we have already encountered one type in the neighboring-tone structure of example 32, a case exemplifying "immediate constituent" grammar. As we have seen, this type of generated structure is displayed in a tree diagram (example 38). The rules which generate such trees are of the form $X \rightarrow Y$, where X is a single element (part) and Y is a sequence of symbols (a "string"). The formula $X \rightarrow Y$ may be interpreted as an instruction to "rewrite" X as Y. The derivation begins with an initial symbol (the highest level) and ends with terminal symbols (the foreground level). At least one initial symbol (or string of symbols) is taken as given by the theory (the "primitive" base), which in the case of Schenkerism would be the *Ursatz*. Terminal symbols (the foreground events as defined by the rules) obviously never appear to the left of the arrow.

Thus the neighboring-tone structure which we saw in Salzer's analysis of Mozart's D-minor Fantasy (example 32) and which was represented in the "tree parsing" of example 38 could be "generated" as in example 41. Reading the example from the top down, we can see that the D-minor chord in the position of the third—the "primitive base"—is rewritten as a string with posterior and anterior inside parts (the slurred Ds). Each of these prolongations serves as an initial symbol and is in turn rewritten—and so on through the parts of each string until the "terminal symbols" (the actual notes) are reached. (To help the reader trace the derivation, dotted lines have been put in the example.)

Some of the rules governing structural generation can be said to be "context free" in the sense that no context need be referred to in which the symbols to the left of the arrow (X) are to be rewritten on the right (as Y). We might say generally, for instance, that any tone interpolated between any two others is a passing tone regardless of context. Or we might say specifically about example 41 that the symbol E is always a passing tone in the element F–E–D.

The analytical importance of discovering the rules of generation is

Example 41

obvious: by reversing our operations, we can deduce in a formalized sense structures on foreground and middleground levels without having to move from the transformations back to the initial point of generation, even though the "primitive base" would remain implicit in our derivation. If we had a sequential neighboring-tone melodic structure in the foreground, for instance, in which all the internal relationships from model to copy were maintained, as in example 42, we could invoke the same set of rules each time, ending up in the case of example 42 with a linear structure on the next level. In short,

Example 42

through such context-free rules we could perhaps discover those elusive logical and empirical constants that we searched for earlier (recall examples 6–10). The ultimate goal of such linguistic formalization is, of course, to give the temporal a nontemporal mathematical or logical foundation.

Strict context-free rules, however, are limited because they can deal only with contiguous events, and, as is well known, many of the most important syntactic relationships in music (and language) are discontiguous (nonadjacent), like the delayed "resolution" of an "interrupted" half-cadence in the antecedent part of an antecedent-consequent phrase (as we saw in example 11). The possibility of augmenting context-free rules with context-sensitive rules thus presents itself. Whether something is a dominant or a tonic depends, of course, on context, as we saw in our discussion of the "core-context" fallacy (chap. 2). In the harmonic progression of the chord C–E–G moving to the chord F–A–C, the F–A–C may be a I or a IV, depending on how the chord interacts contiguously *and* discontiguously with its "environment."

Although context-sensitive rules can be drawn up to deal with such situations, the improvement comes at the cost of obscuring the relationship between immediate constituents that was established by using the context-free grammar in the first place. Furthermore, given the manifold permutations and combinations of structures operating in context-sensitive grammars, analytical rules proliferate and become unmanageable. Indeed, we witnessed exactly this kind of problem earlier in trying to put the *Grundbrechung* on a firmer basis (examples 6–10).

One solution to the problems of both context-free and context-sensitive grammars, therefore, is to develop a theory of transformations. A transformation theory reduces the number of rules necessary for analysis without losing the immediate constituent structure, while at the same time allowing for relationships between parts not temporally adjacent.

Transformation theory operates on the assumption that the number of transformations is finite. That is, although the concatenation of *events* is indefinite and therefore theoretically unbounded, the *rules* governing events are by no means so. They are presumably systematic and can, to some extent, be studied without reference to their historical development. For example, general functional relationships of pitch in tonal style—our hypothetical "language" in this discussion—appear to be relatively (but only relatively) constant from one context to another. One does not have to know the history behind each kind of tonal structure to recognize regularity of pitch function between such disparate pieces as, say, a nursery-rhyme tune and a Verdi aria. The syntactic "rules" by which "London Bridge Is Falling Down" and "La donna è mobile" are understood overlap considerably (but obviously not completely). Thus, within the system it may be argued that syntactic rules exist independently of both the "speaker" (the composer or the performer) and the listener in the sense that, for an exchange of information to take place between speaker and listener, both must assent to the same rules.

Perhaps the favorite analogy in linguistics for this synchronic point of view is the game of chess. Just as one assumes that the value of a playing piece in a chess game does not exist independently from the entire set of rules of the game, so one also assumes in the language of tonal music—tonal music being defined as the entire corpus of pieces the grammar generates—that an element (i.e., a tone) takes its meaning from its place in the whole system. If we know the rules of the game, we can walk into a room where chess is being played and understand by deduction the positions of the pieces on the playing board without knowing the relevant historical data (how the pieces arrived at these particular positions) and without having witnessed the peculiar arrangement on the board in dozens of other games.[11] The relations hold a priori if we know the rules. Similarly, if we know the rules of tonality, we can switch on our FM radios and find ourselves in the middle of a piece we have never heard before and yet have no difficulty understanding where we are in terms of the form. To date, all theoretical deduction in music has to a large extent exemplified this synchronic orientation.

In the synchronic viewpoint so prevalent in linguistics and music, variations between pieces (or games) can be accounted for as differing "strategies." Since the rules determine what counts as a "move," not vice versa, acceptance in or exclusion from a given system is also determined by the rules.[12] Thus changing the rules changes the system. Deviations from obligatory norms must be dealt with either as anomalies requiring an expansion of the system (since in such cases the rule cannot account for the facts) or else as ill-formed utterances not exemplifying the system and therefore not part of it. We can now see why the choice of "initial primitive base" is so crucial in generating the grammar: rules act to identify *and* to explain anomalies.[13]

Given the similarity between transformational grammar and Schenkerian theory, music theorists thus have been attracted to the possibility of putting Schenkerian analysis on a less ad hoc basis. If the number of transformations that "map" the deep structure (the *Ursatz*) onto the surface structures, whose terminal symbols (the actual notes

11. Z. Vendler, "Summary: Linguistics and the *A Priori*," in *Philosophy and Linguistics*, ed. Colin Lyas (New York: Macmillan, 1971), pp. 253–58.

12. Piaget, *Structuralism*, p. 11.

13. On this, see Willard C. Humphreys, *Anomalies and Scientific Theories* (San Francisco: Freeman, Cooper and Company, 1968), particularly chap. 2.

of the composition) represent the "output" form of the music, are finite in diatonic tonality, then the rules must be finite, since rules are inextricably tied to the transformations. And if, as Schenker says, the laws of voice leading remain fixed and the specific operational conditions of these rules could be made explicit, then it should be possible to formalize the properties of tonal syntax. And inasmuch as such rules, by virtue of their fixed connections to the transformations, prescribe what is permissible in the system, excellent descriptions of structure might be attained.

THE PROBLEMS

However plausible the transformational outlook may seem as a theoretical modus operandi in music, and however convincing its epistemological rationale, it is nevertheless inherently defective in many ways. First, there is the problem that the *structure of the grammar* cannot be evaluated separately from the *structure of the transformations*.[14] In essence this is the criticism made earlier: Schenkerian analysis is unable to separate methodology from its assertion of structure. For example, a harmonic configuration like example 43*a* would, as we have seen, be reduced on the next higher level to a root-position chord with the third in the soprano, according to neighboring-tone rules. Example 43*b*, on the other hand, would reduce to a VI–V–I progression (in the key of F) according to passing-tone rules, even though the first three harmonies are identical to the first three in example 43*a*. Example 43*c* is also ruled according to the law of passing tones except that, in contrast to example 43*b*, it moves chromatically and goes farther afield in key. Now if we want to know in example 43*b* how the formulation of the *rule* governing the relationship between the V^6_5 (measure 1, beat 3) and the F-chord at the end of the phrase differs from the formulation of the rule governing the relationship of the V^6_5 and the B-chord at the end of the phrase in example 43*c*—a comparison of discontiguous, context-sensitive relationships for which transformational grammar was specifically designed—then we must look to the difference in the *structure* between the two examples. That

14. Winograd, "Linguistics and the Computer Analysis of Tonal Harmony," p. 9.

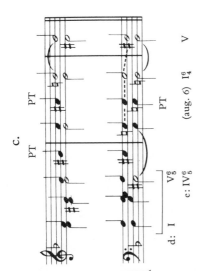

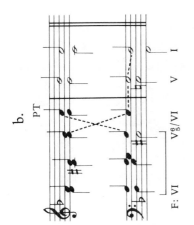

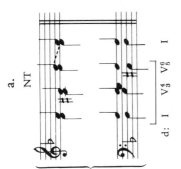

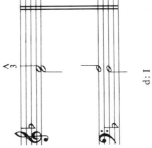

Example 43

is, transformational grammar does not produce a logical language of analytical rules separate from the effects created by those rules. We must always refer to specific contexts. With respect to examples 43*b* and *c*, a rule would take the following form: "Whenever the harmony of . . . (V_5^6/VI or $V_5^6 = IV_5^6$) in the key of . . . (F, D, E) is followed by a harmony of . . . (V, augmented sixth) over a period of . . . (two beats, three beats) and passes (diatonically, chromatically) to the cadence of . . . (V–I, I_4^6–V), a transformation of . . . will take place." And so forth. The rules of transformation are thus inextricably bound to what they produce. They form no logical language of their own.

If the rules were separate from the structure, however—an impossibility in strict transformational grammar—not only would we be able to observe that examples 43*a*, *b*, and *c* have identical beginnings (see the brackets in the examples), but we might also be able to decide what such synonymous *formation* might mean in the explanation of the various transformations. For regardless of the outcome of the phrases in examples 43*a*, *b*, and *c*, the implications of the opening patterns—identical in each example—are important. The opening harmonic processes in each example are *formative* events in their own right. Therefore they must figure in the explanation of the structure. That is, even though the harmonic implication of the I–V_3^4–V_5^6 pattern is realized only in example 43*a*, the *denial* of it in examples 43*b* and *c* is necessarily important to our understanding of the transformations. In example 43*b*, for instance, the denial of the harmonic implication pattern is less forceful than in example 43*c* because the dissonant diminished–fifth harmonic implication in the tenor (on the G, measure 1, beat 4) is eventually resolved on the F of the I in the V–I cadence (see the dotted lines). The voice leading is thus delayed but satisfied, whereas in example 43*c* the denial of that diminished fifth (measure 2, beat 1) is never satisfied in D minor, since the tenor stops on the F♯ of the V chord, the half-cadence in E minor. In a Schenkerian reduction these implicative features would all but go unrecognized, since the implications of the harmonic pattern in examples 43*b* and *c* would be subsumed as mere passing motion to the cadential goals.

Because in transformational grammar the rules of the transformations are tied to their effects (what they generate), the subject of formation to higher levels—of low-level implications generating higher levels—never arises in Schenkerian theory except as a gratuitous after-the-fact observation. The Schenkerian finds the structural tones in accordance with the rules, then looks back in time to see how the tones were implied. The transforming arrow of time becomes a finger pointing to a known goal.[15] And if one accepts the external evidence on which the rules of Schenkerism are founded—that such and such a motion (neighboring tone, passing tone, etc.) implies such and such a rule (and that such rules constitute the conceptual framework of diatonic tonality)—then, as in the game of chess, the correlations between events hold a priori, as necessary truths. Thus, as we saw in our discussion of examples 43*b* and *c*, the various passing-tone rules governing the transformation between the V_5^6 chords and their different goals could be applied without reference to the synonymous implication of the opening harmonic patterns. The notion of a *virtual* hypothesis of formation in such a synchronic system therefore ultimately becomes unimportant, since if all the finite rules are known all the transformational actualizations can be dealt with.[16] That is, though transformational combinations within the system are theoretically infinite in number, if we knew all the correct rules Schenkerian analysis would become simply a matter of retrospectively applying the finite rules in order to get the reductions.

It is this kind of rationale that enables Forte to say—erroneously, I believe—that "in tonal works ... we know in advance the underlying organizational principles and the function of detail."[17] However, this prevalent "a priori" attitude among Schenkerians belies our experience of music in which virtual prospective meanings are as important as retrospective ones. Moreover, it leads not only to doubtful analyses and impoverished explanations but to a distorted sense of history and a fundamentally mistaken concept of the time element in music. All things considered, the "advance knowledge" view of tonal works says in effect that what happens in a work is simply a product of

15. *Der Freie Satz*, p. 29.
16. For my use of the word "virtual," refer to chapter 4, note 6.
17. Forte, "Schenker's Conception of Musical Structure," p. 27.

delay.[18] But I doubt that any of us would listen to music if its main attraction were simply the postponement of "advance knowledge." For in that case music would be insufferably boring. The way an artwork shapes our temporal experience, after all, is infinitely more than a mere prolonging of something preordained.

But the main point, to repeat, is that Schenkerian analysis in no way addresses itself to the matter of virtual formation—to the matter of how transformations are obtained to begin with. For every pattern, every form, can be viewed on any given level as both a formation of something and a transformation of something else. Every form is both the basis *for* an implication and the result *of* a realization. To the historian, to proceed under the rationale that the *Ursatz* is an axiom or a "kernel" structure "cheats" the whole subject of formation. For by taking advantage of the labor of those who identified neighboring-tone and passing-tone transformations as part of an intuitive system in the first place, the whole issue of *con*struction is avoided.[19]

Moreover, let me emphasize again that transformations in Schenkerian theory are not only tied to the *Ursatz*. For the a priori kernel in some form is also allowed to generate the grammar on *every* level. Because of that, it therefore to some extent always interferes with the independence of the transformations on those levels. This is not true in transformational linguistics, where phonemic, morphonemic, and phrase-structure rules are kept separate. And it is the employment of

18. On p. 50 of *Der Freie Satz*, Schenker states quite clearly his view that transformations are simply delays in reaching the goal. This is implied throughout his writings.

19. Piaget, *Structuralism*, pp. 12–13: "If what is wanted is a *general* theory of structure, such as must meet the requirements of an interdisciplinary epistemology, then one can hardly avoid asking, when presented with such non-temporal systems as a mathematical group or a set of subsets, how these systems were *obtained*—unless, of course, one is willing to stay put in the heavens of transcendentalism. One could proceed by postulate, as in axiomatic systems, but from the epistemological point of view this is an elegant way of cheating which takes advantage of the prior labor of those who constructed the intuitive system without which there would be nothing to axiomatize."

the *Ursatz*-principle on every level that renders Schenkerian theory practically useless in identifying real elements of implication.

The neo-Schenkerians would doubtless argue, however, that circumventing the question of virtual formation is the very thing for which the transformational-grammar model was designed. It was meant to avoid all the problems inherent in diachrony—for example, the (Lamarckian) notion that all the characteristics of transformations are gradually acquired in the evolution of history (which simply cannot be proved or disproved). Since few are still foolish enough to adopt the belief that the Germanic version of tonality, as exemplified in the Masters (Bach, Beethoven, Brahms), is the final goal of history—predestined and sufficient for all time—the neo-Schenkerians argue that once the evolutionary scheme is admitted, once the idea of nonrecurring change taking place in nonrecurring time is allowed, once the history of an event becomes necessary to its explanation, once our perception of something becomes unique with respect to time and place, then an *infinite* number of rules exist. And the possibility of formulating an explicit theory under such time-contingent circumstances seems to the neo-Schenkerians (and the transformational grammarians) all but lost. Linguists since the time of Saussure, after all, have argued long and often successfully for the necessity of keeping the synchronic aspect separate from the diachronic one. And on the whole, art and music historians have in practice accepted the epistemological separation of the two. Like good Marxists, historians have believed that styles have terminal stages and that in the terminal stages of a style we can assume that the "rules" are operating in a pure state and can simply argue backward.[20]

But the fact is that we do not have to choose between a synchronic view, with all the inherent problems of a transformational grammar based on a kernel structure, and a diachronic view, with all the inherent problems of virtual formation, raising the question of how the characteristics of a style are transmitted. There is a third possibility.

20. For a discussion of Schenker and Marx, see Heinrich Hartmann, "Heinrich Schenker und Karl Marx," *Oesterreichische Musikzeitschrift* 7, no. 2 (1952):46–52.

Ten
AN ALTERNATIVE: TOWARD AN
IMPLICATION-REALIZATION MODEL

I NSTEAD OF SEEING A DESCENDING SERIES OF TRANSFORMATIONS
generated from a postulated organizing original whole (the *Ursatz*),
we might view a given system as generated from the bottom up. In
that case, *the characteristic implications of the individual parameters would
be taken as the postulates,* instead of the combining action of the realized
whole, *and we would look for rules of dynamic structuring rather than for
rules of dynamic wholes.* The whole would therefore be conceived as a
by-product of this structuring rather than structure being conceived
as a by-product of the organizing activity of the whole. Schenker's
"terminal symbols" (the foreground notes on the printed page of
the composition) would be conceived not as just another transformation mapped onto a lower level from middleground structures and
background kernel in the synchronic system, but rather as the *initiating
formation* of something that becomes transformed on the next higher
level. And since the rules governing such dynamic structuring would
be concerned with implications of parameters, implications would have
to be formulated separately from their effects. Whatever structures
actually occurred would always be related to what was implied. *But
what was implied would not necessarily be realized.* In other words,
implications (formations) would be evaluated separately from realizations (transformations), even though rules of transformation would
always seem to depend to some extent on rules of formation.

Since every structure is a system of transformations (and not just a
collection of elements together with their properties), we would never
be justified in assuming that either formation or transformation rules

are innate and immutable.[1] Structural transformation is the necessary *outcome* of what happens in a piece. But from this it does not follow that the rules of transformation can be conceptualized as the prior condition for those events. Though the structures of style are the basis for implication, the syntactic meaning of realizations on either the lowest or the highest level in an individual piece cannot be predetermined.

It is important to realize that such an implication-realization view treats the matter of formation very differently than does the Schenkerian transformational grammar approach. In Schenkerian theory, as one can see in figure 5, formation rules on middleground and foreground levels are assimilated by transformation rules as we *descend* the hierarchy, rules being fixed in their effect on the structure, since lower levels are generated from the *Ursatz*. In the Schenkerian model the act of generation is visited from above, as it were, from levels *where the actual notes that generate the structural derivations are not present.*[2]

Conceiving generation from the "internal" formation of the individual parameters in the foreground, on the other hand, is radically different from the Schenkerian concept, in the sense that no preformed, middle-level transformation or high-level structure need be stipulated. The multiple implications of each parameter—as derived from the actual notes on the printed page—would play a crucial role in creating the transformation as we *ascend* the hierarchy from any given level (see fig. 6).

Observe in this diagram that not all implications could be realized. In any given realization some would be left over. Thus, in contrast to the Schenkerian (transformational grammar) diagram, formations would *not* be completely assimilated by transformations. Potentiality would always remain. Pieces would stay unclosed. Further, these left-

1. Again, hear Piaget, *Structuralism*, p. 12: "One finds outstanding workers who . . . jump straight from the *stability* of transformation rules to their *innateness*.

2. Komar, *Theory of Suspensions*, p. 16: "A peculiarity of the language associated with tonal theory is that one speaks of generating a note *q* by virtue of some operation at level *x*, but note *q* is not *present* until the next lower level *y*. In other words, the act of generation is visited upon the notes of level *x*, but the result of that act first appears only in level *y*." The neo-Schenkerians regard this only as an odd way of speaking; the non-Schenkerians think it an analytical travesty.

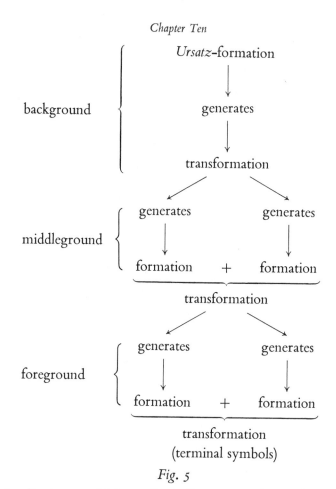

Fig. 5

over implications could be realized discontiguously, so that an over-lapping network would result instead of a tree. The closural characteristics governing the parts would face downward, so to speak (⌐⌐), while the nonclosural characteristics would face upward (∟∟).

Thus, each level is Janus-faced. The nonclosural aspect represents ongoing processes in time, and the closural aspect, events in time. An event in the hierarchy (implications plus realization) functions as it does because it is the point of contact between a closing process on one level and an ongoing process on another. Put another way, an event is the juncture, the link, between transformation on the lower level and formation on the higher. In the sense that an event operates as a time point in the hierarchy, separating what went on

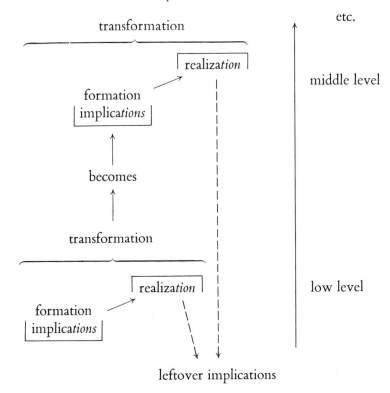

Fig. 6

before from what comes after, it helps to establish a form.[3] In the sense that it serves to connect successive levels, it becomes a process. But that immediate connection will never satisfy all the implications; potentiality will always remain. Thus, and this is absolutely essential, *the structure of an event lies in the dichotomy between process and form—a relationship of implications to both realization* AND *nonrealization.*

Structure is *never* mere realization. It cannot be formulated in the simplistic relationship between antecedents and consequents. Since all pitch patterns evidence simultaneous, multiple, parametric implications on any given level—often with mutually exclusive realizations (e.g., a gap fill in the opposite direction of the leap vs. the continuation of the

3. I have relied partly on Allport for this discussion (*Theories of Perception*, chap. 21).

interval in the same direction)—the realization of any one pitch implication will always exclude the immediate realization of another. Thus it follows that "indeterminism" in the sense of psychological probability has to be introduced, which altogether rules out *in principle* the notion of predictability. For if pitch implications are multiple on any given level, then every realization involves a *denial* of implication. Thus, in retrospect, every realization is in a crucial sense *not* a consequent. Therefore implications cannot be conceived in prospect as simple antecedents.[4]

The advantages the pluralistic implication-realization model offers over a transformational grammar approach are many, but two are paramount: (1) the structure of the formational *and* the transformational rules could be formulated independently of the structure of their effects; and (2) the model would parallel more accurately the actual act of listening to music, since a listener's understanding of a piece is "built up" temporally from low level to high level.

In an implication-realization model, then, we would look for the explicit rules that govern the internal interaction of parameters as they form and transform the part. Since we would want to formulate a genuine hierarchical theory where levels are partially decomposed, we would have to conşider two internal aspects: (1) that which creates closure (self-regulation, stability, equilibrium, and so on—all those things that enable us to call a whole a whole); and (2) that which creates nonclosure on the same level (the implicative, potential, "developmental," unstable aspect—all those things that enable us to identify a part as incomplete). Closural characteristics would determine connections *within* parts; nonclosural characteristics would determine connections *between* parts (contiguous *and* discontiguous).

The Janus-faced nature of a part, however, would not be uniformly balanced between closure and nonclosure. Within any one part, multiple implications would sometimes diverge, sometimes complement. A part would, moreover, display implications in varying

4. If, of course, music perception were a simple matter of expectation, prediction, and antecedent-consequent relationships, then music theory could become a tidy little branch of information theory, and the embodied meaning of antecedent and consequent events could be evaluated according to, say, Markoff chains.

strengths for *each* operative parameter—harmonic, melodic, metric, rhythmic, registral, dynamic, and so on; and those implications would often be noncongruent. Being multiple, the nonclosural implications would bear a relationship not to a single realization, but to many realizations—hence, the conception of a reticulated, intertwined network.

The recognition of implication in any parametric pattern would depend on the relative resemblance (degree of functional and conformant synonymity) of the pattern to its predecessors both within and without the piece. Style—intra- and extraopus norms—thus becomes both the source of specific implications and the framework by which they are evaluated. Strength of implication would be directly related to the number of times such and such a realization had followed such and such an implication. From without, a listener would recognize an implicative pattern and judge its strength by remembering various statistical recurrences of syntactic relationships in the style. From within, the realization of an implication already anticipated by the listener on the basis of prior knowledge and learning would contribute to the systematic aspect of the style. Further repetitions of these implied realizations would serve to reaffirm the systematic (synchronic) aspect, whereas a novel realization or a novel denial would weaken the system and emphasize the diachronic aspect of style—as a historical process undergoing change. A new style would be established once a novel realization or a novel denial recurred.

Thus within a piece a realization would always involve synchronic and diachronic feedback in the style. But again, because of the hierarchical nature of musical structure, the anticipation-feedback scheme between synchrony and diachrony would not occur in a continuous and uniform manner like a symmetrical spiderweb. Rather, a nonuniform network of discontinuous relationships would result. Levels would be generated by the collective interaction of elementary structures. These structures, however, would not be limited by their inherent properties. Instead, they would generate *emergent* properties (new implications) which, when realized, could result in *new contexts*—in new intra- or extraopus relationships or both.

Imagine, for instance, a historical style based on a "repertory" of only two pieces ("Piece 1" and "Piece 2," examples 44*a* and *b*) that utilized only three parameters: melody, rhythm, and meter. Ignoring levels, we could say (roughly speaking) that the melodic forms upon which the style is built are two: C–D–E–F–G and G–F–E–D–C. We could say the same about the rhythmic forms—also two: ♩ ♩ and (perhaps) ♩ ♩. Meter, the remaining parameter, would consist only of one form, the 3/4 measure (see example 44*c*). Even though our hypothetical "repertory" is exceptionally stable in style, there are nevertheless unrealized implications. Say an inventive composer comes along and recognizes two of them: E–F–G could imply A, and the rhythm of ♩ ♩ could continue in quarter notes (♩ ♩ ♩ ♩). He thus writes a piece realizing these implications ("Piece 3," example 44*d*). We now have the beginnings of a transformation in the style: New tonal material (A), a new melodic pitch structure (G–A–G), and a new rhythm (♩ ♩ ♩ ♩) have been created. Because "Piece 3" creates new emergent properties in the form of new implications (example 44*e*), we also have a new intraopus context. Say, however, that other contemporaneous composers do not recognize (or do not choose to realize) the potential inherent in these new structures. They are interested only in the new neighboring-tone structure (G–A–G); the new rhythm holds no attraction for them. Thus, their compositions ("Piece 4," example 44*f*) imitate only the neighboring tone of "Piece 3." The result is that the neighboring-tone structure becomes part of the style, and we have an instance of diachronic change in the form of style transformation—a new extraopus context. (At the same time, of course, "Piece 4" reinforces the older, synchronic aspect of the style, since it realizes basically the same style structures as "Piece 1" and "Piece 2.") The new rhythm in example 44*d* (♩ ♩ ♩ ♩), however, does not become part of the style even though it was written during this "period." Say that some time passes before anyone recognizes the implicative power of that structure. Finally "Piece 5" (example 44*g*) is written, and the last parameter in the old style—meter—is transformed. Again the result is a new context with a new, emerging potential (example 44*h*).

Example 44

To be sure, the stylistic history of musical structures is vastly more complicated than the simplistic schemes of example 44. Genetic development and logical growth rarely coordinate so clearly. Nevertheless, musical works do seem to have implicative ancestors. The high-level descending chromatic linear bass lines that generate such striking changes of harmony in the works of Beethoven (e.g., Symphony no. 7, first movement, introduction), Brahms (e.g., Piano Concerto no. 1, first movement, beginning), and Tchaikovsky (e.g., Symphony no. 5, second movement, second theme), for instance, find their progenitors in the more localized, diatonic chaconne and passacaglia basses of the Baroque. What I wish to argue here, however, is not just that familial relationships exist among certain structures in the history of music—which is well-known—but rather that structural changes in style result partly from realizations of latent implications.

We can see, for instance, in example 45 (the excerpts of which are offered for the purpose of discussion rather than to demonstrate any historical necessity between them) how logical growth and development might take place. All the excerpts—chosen from the early fifteenth century to the middle of the nineteenth century—exemplify to a greater or lesser degree rising melodic lines (between the outside voices) governed by the harmonic pattern of 5–6 (i.e., $\frac{5-6}{3\ 3}$ or $\frac{3\ 3}{5-6}$). (See the model in example 45*k*.) This very prevalent melodic-harmonic pattern, which interpolates a first inversion chord between two consecutive harmonic fifths—Schenker called it the 5–6 *Auswechslung*—is in common usage in the Renaissance and is discussed in practically all the treatises on figured bass in the eighteenth century.

What is interesting about the excerpts is that as we move chronologically through either the Renaissance examples (45*a–e*) or the seventeenth, eighteenth, and nineteenth century examples (45*f–j*), we see evidence of both diachronic change in the sense of growth and synchronic codification in the sense of replication. (Again I emphasize the didactic nature of the example; the samples from the various centuries cannot be taken literally; exceptions to the argument can be easily found.) In examples 45*b–d*, for instance, there is increasing extension and replication of the 5–6 structure. Thus, each elaboration can be thought of in some sense as a "realization" of the implications of example 45*a*. At the same time, there is stylistic codification. Even by the late sixteenth century, we can still find an excerpt by Lasso (example 45*e*) that is little different from that of the fifteenth century composer Dufay (example 45*b*). Both excerpts represent a typical treatment of the 5–6 melodic-harmonic figure in the Renaissance. Much the same can be said about the examples from the later centuries. Examples 45*h* and *j*, for instance, might be said to extend further the implications of example 45*f*, whereas example 45*g*, somewhat similar in the abstract to example 45*f* in that both excerpts function as 5–6 sequential preparations for a cadence, might be said to conserve or strengthen certain melodic-harmonic features of the style.

Interpreting the evolution of the nine excerpts as an increasing structural expansion brought about by the melodic-harmonic realization of the 5–6 pattern brings other things to our attention as well. All of the Renaissance examples, for instance, are *beginnings*, either of sections within pieces (examples 45*a*, *b*, and *d*) or of pieces themselves (examples 45*c* and *e*). In contrast, the seventeenth, eighteenth, and nineteenth century examples (examples 45*f*, *g*, *h*, and *j*) foreshadow *endings* (i.e., cadences). How do structures with histories of initiality become transformed to structures portending closure? The answer may again be found, I believe, in the implication–realization concept. For as a style structure grows, it also becomes codified. Extension and replication go hand in hand. Thus, as style structures increase in length, they tend to become more closed, with the result that the parts themselves undergo change. That is, a kind of entelechy takes place where a given part of a "full-grown" style structure points more toward closure than the same part did before its growth and replication in the style. And once that evolutionary step is reached, a given part can no longer function effectively as a real beginning, as a new point of prospective interest and generation—not without undergoing internal change of some sort, without some liberating mutation. But it can operate very effectively as a sign pointing to closure and arrival. And this is the case with the 5–6 structures in examples 45*f*, *g*, *h*, and *j*, where we feel sure upon the occurrence of the 5–6 pattern that a cadence will ensue.

By example 45 I mean only to suggest that one possible pattern of

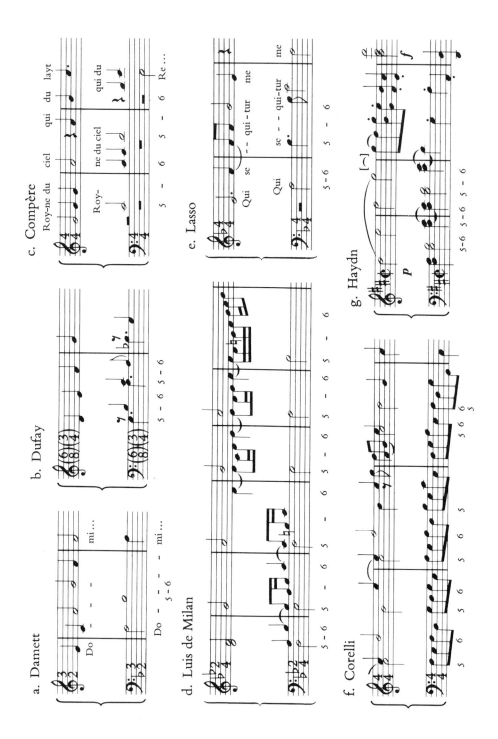

h. Beethoven

j. Schumann

k. Model

Example 45. (a) Damett, *Hymn, Beata Dei genetrix*; (b) *Dufay, Christe, Mass Sancti Jacobi*; (c) *Compère, Rondeau,* "Royne du ciel"; (d) *Luis de Milan, Fantasia*; (e) *Lasso, Motet,* "Qui sequitur me"; (f) *Corelli, Sonate da camera, op.* 4; (g) *Haydn, Symphony no. 104, I; (h) Beethoven's Sonata op. 26, I, variation III; (j) Schumann's Symphony no. 1, I;* (k) *a synthetic model.*

evolution in the history of musical structures is that beginnings gradually extended through realization become endings. The converse, endings becoming beginnings, is also possible—witness the number of pieces that start with V–I cadences (e.g., the trio of Mozart's Symphony no. 41 or the beginning of the first movement of Beethoven's Symphony no. 1)—though in the case of this kind of evolution, it seems to me that extension applies "backward": throughout the nineteenth century, dominant preparations at the beginning become increasingly larger, making pieces sound more and more like they start in the middle, as if what was already going on in one's subconscious had suddenly materialized.

THE HISTORICAL IMPERATIVE

The theory that pieces are generated by the formation of implications on the lowest level, transformed by realizations (or denials) on higher levels, is much more consonant with our actual perceptual experience of music. Equally important, however, the implication-realization model allows for the emergence of new contexts and potentially new contexts during this generating process and this corresponds more closely to our understanding of music history. Musical function is always formative as well as transformative, whereas in the Schenkerian synchronic view formation is based on an idealistic rationale that the number of transformations is finite, that the internal rules governing them are invariant, and that the boundary conditions of tonality (the language) are definable. But none of these premises, however attractive they may be to music theorists, will bear serious scrutiny.

Take the synchronic viewpoint by itself. One of the cardinal epistemological premises of the synchronic view is that it is logically impossible for the rules to "generate" structural results external to the system within which they operate. Yet there is an immediate difficulty in accepting this premise in music history because we know historically that tonality *did* yield "external" results. That is, it is an inescapable diachronic fact that the tonal system "led" to chromaticism, atonality, pantonality, and so forth. Hence, the earlier analogy of tonality as a chessboard where the value of the playing pieces (the referential elements) is always dependent on the entire set of rules of the game is *not* the real situation confronting either the music theorist or the historian. Rather, it is as if the rules of chess were transformed to those of backgammon *during the game*—as if the surface of the playing board were to change gradually from squares to triangles and the chance roll of dice were introduced while the player was plotting his move.

Even the assumption of internal invariant laws, which is necessary to the synchronic view, is problematic in music. For although the Schenkerians can give the *defining attributes* ("these laws apply to this repertory and, taken together, form the definition of tonal language")—which are arbitrary, and which one may or may not accept—they have never been and probably never will be able to formulate the *criterial attributes.*[5] To do this one needs a theory in which the logic of the rules of inference can be studied separately from the musical structures generated in the analysis. As we have seen, this is not possible in the transformational grammar approach. The Schenkerians, to be sure, are able to discriminate the features which distinguish exemplars from nonexemplars in their system. But they cannot formulate the *inferences of identity*—the necessary and sufficient conditions to posit a system operating with invariant laws. Although we have good reasons for thinking that invariant laws (real constraints and not just norms) exist—they are probably more psychological than exclusively musical— the fact is that in our present state of theoretical knowledge we are simply not able to establish the criterial attributes of tonality and thus cannot distinguish invariant laws from variable rules—which obviously creates an epistemological impasse for the use of transformational grammar as a model of music theory.

But in the implication-realization model, this impasse does not obtain. For the internal laws of tonality can be treated as statistical probabilities operating within the confines of generalized style schemes. And in contrast to the Schenkerian system, these internal laws can be treated as *implicative*, not causal or predictive. And their application in

5. I have borrowed the terminological distinction "criterial attributes versus defining attributes" from J. S. Bruner, J. J. Goodnow, and G. A. Austin, *A Study of Thinking* (New York: Science Editions, 1959).

the analysis of tonal structure would be subject to prospective interpretation, not retrospective formalization. Transformations would then be conceived not as a finite list of things but as realizations of implications in which the systematic aspect of the style itself could undergo transformation.

This is of course not to deny the existence of systematic features in the style, but music theory must always be formulated to allow for the possibility that elements of reference may in prospect have the potential to *transform* the rules, the boundary conditions, or both. The theorist cannot in good conscience examine the properties of these elements only within the realm of a hypostasized system. Structures may "contain" nontonal potential. New contexts may emerge. In short, the synchronic concept of tonality the neo-Schenkerians advocate cannot stand alone, because tonality is not just "system" but is also a historical style which itself is undergoing transformation. I shall explain more about how synchronic and diachronic aspects can be dealt with in the implication-realization model in chapter 11.

Meyer's Approach

The conceptual model I have just outlined obviously owes a great deal to the work of Leonard B. Meyer, particularly to his most recent book, *Explaining Music*, the second half of which is entitled "Implication in Tonal Melody." It is interesting to follow Meyer's development as a theorist. His notions about implication can be traced back to certain Gestaltist theories of expectation that are discussed in his *Emotion and Meaning in Music* (1956).[6] With the publication of *Music, the Arts, and Ideas* (1967), we note a shift in emphasis as he begins to replace the expectation idea with a concept of implication.[7] And in *Explaining Music* (1973) this change in emphasis is all but complete.[8] The reasons Meyer prefers implication over expectation are many, no doubt, but from my point of view it boils down to a belief that the concept of expectation is too subjective in content to enable the

6. Meyer, *Emotion and Meaning in Music.*

7. Meyer, *Music, the Arts, and Ideas.*

8. For Meyer's views on why he prefers implication over expectation, see *Explaining Music*, pp. 114–15.

establishment of a systematic theory of music. That is, what we know about expectations is based too heavily upon percepts, introspection, internalizations, and so on, with all the insoluble epistemological problems so well known to phenomenologists. Because of this, it is clear that the concept of expectation taken as an exclusive basis for building an analytical system has a fatal flaw in a theoretical sense because it cannot be formulated in falsifiable terms[9]—the sine qua non of a genuine theory. Implications, on the other hand, can be based on objectively specifiable evidence (the printed notes themselves), and their realizations can be precisely defined. As intellectual history, the shift we see in Meyer's work from the Gestaltist concept of expectation to a concept of implication roughly parallels the shift taking place in psychology from associationism, functionalism, Gestaltism, and so forth, to structuralism.

The main task in constructing a theory of implications and realizations is to formulate a unified set of analytical rules. By what principles can we safely determine patterns of implication and realization? What criteria can we invoke in the choice of structural tones? How do we avoid the pitfalls of expectation in the building of the theory? In *Explaining Music*, Meyer relies partially on a rhythmic theory of accents and nonaccents—which he and Grosvenor Cooper developed in *The Rhythmic Structure of Music*[10]—to discover the structural tones on which to base patterns of implication and realization. Consequently, the notion of "poetic feet"[11]—metric accents and nonaccents func-

9. On the importance of falsifiability in the constructing of theories, see Karl R. Popper, *The Logic of Scientific Discovery* (New York: Basic Books, 1959), chap. 4.

10. Grosvenor Cooper and Leonard B. Meyer, *The Rhythmic Structure of Music* (Chicago: University of Chicago Press, 1960).

11. The poetic feet tradition can perhaps be traced as far back as Saint Augustine (*De musica*). In tonal music, however, explicit treatments can be found in Johann Mattheson, *Der vollkommene Capellmeister* (1739); Johann Adolph Scheibe, *Der critische musicus* (1737–40); Joseph Riepel, *Anfangsgründe zur musikalischen Setzkunst* (1754); Heinrich Cristoph Koch, *Versuch einer Anleitung zur Composition* (1782–93); Antoine Reicha, *Traité de mélodie*, 2d ed. (Paris: A. Farrenc, 1832); Gottfried Weber, *Versuch einer geordneten Theorie der Tonsetzkunst*, 3d German ed. (Mainz, 1830–32); Rudolph Westphal, *Allgemeine Theorie der musikalischen Rhythmik* (Leipzig: Breitkopf and Härtel, 1903); Mathis Lussy, *Le rythme musical*, 3d ed. (Paris: Librarie Fischbacher,

tioning in various rhythmic groupings (iambs, trochees, etc.)—plays an important part in determining Meyer's structural patterns.[12]

There are several problems, however, in using metric accents and nonaccents to generate structural tones on which to build patterns of implication and realization. First, such rhythmic groupings are *summarizing*.[13] In any given situation, a poetic feet pattern attempts to "evaluate" a *number* of interacting parameters and represent them in *one* set of symbols.[14] Moreover, this representation is of the "either/or" variety. A tone belongs to either the closed, focal point of the grouping—the accent—or the unclosed part of the grouping—the nonaccent.[15]

1897); Hugo Riemann, *System der musikalischen Rhythmik und Metrik* (Leipzig: Breitkopf and Härtel, 1903); and Theodor Wichmayer, *Musikalische Rhythmik und Metrik* (Magdeburg: Heinrichshofen Verlag, 1917), to name but a few. For a brief history of this tradition in the nineteenth century, see Howard E. Smither, "Theories of Rhythm in the Nineteenth and Twentieth Centuries, with a Contribution to the Theory of Rhythm for the Study of Twentieth-Century Music," (Ph.D. diss., Cornell University, 1960), or Yeston, *Stratification of Musical Rhythm*, chap. 1. For a more detailed discussion, see Wilhelm Seidel, *Über Rhythmustheorien der Neuzeit* (Munich: Francke Verlag, 1975) or Gudrun Henneberg, *Theorien zur Rhythmik und Metrik* (Tutzing: Hans Schneider, 1974). The poetic feet tradition culminates in Cooper and Meyer, *Rhythmic Structure of Music*.

12. "Meter is regarded as the prime, though by no means the only guide to structural importance" (Meyer, *Explaining Music*, p. 121).

13. Cooper and Meyer, *Rhythmic Structure of Music*, pp. 117, 123, and 182.

14. Referring to *The Rhythmic Structure of Music*, Meyer says, in *Explaining Music*, pp. 27–28, "Rhythmic relationships were analyzed as *patterns* in which a stable accent and one or more weak beats were grouped together in different ways. Though the terminology of prosody was employed, our fundamental concern was with the nature and basis of temporal patternings seen as the result of the interaction of all parameters of music—melodic, harmonic, dynamic—as well as durational relationships."

15. In the Cooper-Meyer system, the placement of the accent determines the type of grouping. Only one accent can occur in any one grouping. Specific degree of closure is indicated by the type of grouping. End-accented patterns (iambs and anapests) are in general considered more closed than beginning-accented ones (trochees and dactyls). Middle-accented groupings (e.g., amphibrachs) are perhaps best viewed as a combination of an iamb pivoted to a trochee (‿ ⌐ ‿) (see Cooper and Meyer, *Rhythmic Structure of Music*, p. 64). If end-accented patterns are considered to be more closed than beginning-accented ones, then it follows that the accent in a grouping has to be considered the most closed part. For Meyer's views on the relative closure of groupings, see *Explaining Music*, p. 28, and *Rhythmic Structure of Music*, chap. 2.

This means that if a tone is *both* closed and unclosed on the level of its occurrence—as I insist it must be—then in a grouping by poetic feet only one aspect of that tone's function can be represented.[16] Thus an analysis relying on poetic feet to generate patterns of implications and realizations may omit important relationships. For example, a closed tone (say, one ending a process) might function simultaneously on the same level as an unclosed tone (as a medial tone in another process, for instance). If we only ascribed to that tone a closural function in the form of an accent, we might overlook its connection as an unclosed tone in the other process.

The second problem is that in our present state of knowledge the notion of metric accent as the closural tone in a rhythmic grouping necessarily has to be taken as an "axiomatic concept which is understandable as an experience but undefined in terms of causes."[17] Since I have already discussed in detail the problem of axioms in music analysis, it need only be mentioned in this connection that the use of metric accent (or nonaccent) as an hypothesis to identify patterns of implication and realization results in the generation of processes from the summarization *above*, as it were, instead of from the individual parameters themselves. That is, in an analysis relying on poetic feet to generate the patterns, a hypothetical rhythmic-metric outcome is "imposed" upon the music in order to derive the structure. The parallel to the Schenker method may be noted.[18]

16. The "double function" of a tone usually involves a two-level evaluation in the Meyerian system. That is, a tone can be closed on one level (an accent) and open on another (a nonaccent). There is one exception. Occasionally, on the same level Meyer will analyze a tone as both open and closed. Thus the symbols ⌣ and ⌣̇ (see the glossary in *Rhythmic Structure of Music*, p. 204). These two symbols, however, do not evaluate the *degree* of closure or nonclosure, which is what is needed. One simply offsets the other.

17. Cooper and Meyer, *Rhythmic Structure of Music*, p. 7.

18. Meyer does not give operational rules for "weighting" parameters in determining the rhythmic summarization, though he makes it clear that these summarizations come about as a result of such "weighting." Since an accent or a nonaccent can display only one aspect of a tone's function, one or more parameters must be chosen as the "dominating" factor in designating the rhythmic grouping. This is somewhat like Schenkerian theory, where one dominant parameter (harmony) is used to generate the structural tones on the levels below. Meyer's viewpoint, however, is more flexible in choice of parameter. Although the lowest level is often organized only by

Finally, the use of poetic feet to determine structural tones creates the risk of generating only tree structures, with all the inherent problems we saw in Schenkerian analysis—for example, the faulty explanation of discontiguous relationships, the ignoring of relationships between adjacent events, the disregarding of network connections between various parameters, and the problem of supersummation in a Gestaltist sense.

In many instances Meyer is able to avoid these problems because, as I have pointed out, he does not rely exclusively on the concept of poetic feet.[19] Moreover, the poetic feet theory is formulated in conjunction with a number of other rules—the presence of similarity and difference, the separation of events, the repetition of events, and so forth.[20] In putting all these to use, however, intuition plays an important part. That is, in each case the analyst has to decide whether, say, similarity is more important than difference in the analysis of events, or whether repetition takes precedence over separation. Thus the problems that arise in coordinating the use of these types of theoretical rules with the axiomatic ones of the poetic feet theory are dealt with on an ad hoc basis.[21] Consequently there is no attempt in Meyer's concept of implication and realization to formulate the rules into a unified body of knowledge organized under a parsimonious set of *operational* laws. Perhaps the reason for this lack of operational rules

---

meter, on higher levels other parameters (and combinations of parameters) can be invoked in order to generate the patterns of implication and realization. Thus Meyer is not bound by a commitment to any one parameter as Schenker is.

19. Only about half the examples in *Explaining Music* utilize rhythmic groupings. Moreover, one of Meyer's principal rules of thumb is that the metric rule can be nullified in harmonic patterns where a goal tone takes precedence over metric accent: "A general exception to this rule [of metric accent] is that goal tones—tones of resolution . . .—are considered to be structural on the hierarchic level on which they are goals, regardless of their metric position. It follows from this that appoggiaturas, though metrically emphasized, are *not* construed as structural tones. In an appoggiatura figure, the structural tone is the note of resolution" (*Explaining Music*, p. 122).

20. Ibid., p. 83.

21. "Tones which occur on a main metric accent are analyzed as being on a higher structural level than those which occur on secondary metric accents, with exceptions that are explained on an individual basis" (ibid., pp. 121–22).

is that Meyer has doubts about the inherent validity of such rules in the first place. In *Explaining Music*, he says, for instance, "It is doubtful whether hard and fast criteria can be devised for distinguishing ornamental from structural tones."[22] Indeed, throughout the book he argues strongly for the necessity of individual judgment (intuition) in the critical analysis of artworks:

> The reasons used to explain a particular musical event will
> ... be of two different sorts: rules reasons, derived from
> style analysis and music theory, which will tend to be
> constant, and strategy reasons which will be of the *ad hoc*,
> common-sense variety. Because they depend upon particular
> circumstances, strategy reasons are generally eclectic. Some-
> times they will be drawn from established disciplines such as
> acoustics or psychology; at other times they will be based
> upon common sense. Rule reasons, too, at least for the
> present, will from time to time be eclectic. This, because
> music theory is still rudimentary and style analysis only
> somewhat less so.[23]

Meyer is certainly right in that analytical criticisms of artworks can never be based completely on theoretical rules. There is no question that room must be left for critical insight. Nevertheless, if music theory is to become less "rudimentary," I do not see how we can avoid trying to find "hard and fast" rules for identifying structural tones, however elusive they may be. For theories become refined only when anomalies are recognized, defined, and explained. And the most economical way to recognize anomalies in music theory is to try rigorously to derive hard and fast rules for determining structural tones. Indeed, it is safe to say that the future of music theory depends on just such rigor.

22. Ibid., p. 121.

23. Ibid., p. 14. From p. 18: "Because its reasons are often *ad hoc* and its explanations eclectic, criticism may at times seem somewhat improvisatory. But this does not mean that it is arbitrary or illogical. Different sorts of arguments from a variety of sources may be employed, but they must be applied *objectively*: rules and techniques, arguments and evidence must be used in the same way in each analysis; and though not systematized, reasons must be consistent with one another."

PARAMETRIC GENERATION OF IMPLICATION

Although the development of a rigorous set of rules is beyond the scope of the present book, it is clear that in order to do so, we must look directly to an analysis of the individual parameters. The reason is that, although *tones* are both open and closed on any given level, *parameters* are by no means so. That is, a parameter at any given temporal point is either open or closed. Therefore, the "structuralness" of a tone—its degree of closure relative to its nonclosure—depends directly on the implication and realization displayed in each separate parameter. Bluntly put: If the implication-realization model is to live up to its promise in critical analysis, we are going to have to avoid generating structural tones from the level above their occurrence. And if the implication-realization model is going to be useful in style analysis, we are going to have to put our summarizations—harmonic ("ursatzean"), rhythmic, and otherwise—on a firmer basis.

Let us contrast the analysis of one piece in *Explaining Music* with an analysis based on the individual parameters. The point is not necessarily to criticize Meyer's analysis, since he intends it only as a didactic exemplar of certain features of implication he wishes to write about.[24] Rather, my point will be to demonstrate how a parametric analysis might work and how it might help us identify the kinds of problems that must be dealt with in the use of the implication-realization model.

In example 46—the "Soldier's March" from Schumann's *Album for the Young*—Meyer sees the B–D trochee in measure 1 as setting up three main implications: a gap, which is immediately filled (graph 1); a triadic continuation, the realization of which does not occur until the very end (measure 32, graph 3); and a descending motion from the third degree, B, to the tonic, G, in measure 4, the realization of which on a higher level implies a low D "around which the middle part of the piece centers" (graph 4).[25]

24. Moreover, whatever implicit criticisms there are apply to my own previous work as well.

25. Meyer, *Explaining Music*, p. 127. The example is taken from p. 126. The D in graph 4 symbolizes the Ds in the middle section (measures 17–24), not the D directly above it in the music of the example.

Example 46. From Meyer, Explaining Music (*Schumann's " Soldier's March," from* Album for the Young, *measures 1–8, 25–32*)

The first curious feature of Meyer's melodic analysis is that the E in measure 2 does not figure in the implication-realization patterns, even though it is clearly part of the melody. Meyer sees the E in measure 2 in harmonic terms, as a neighbor note: "The D [in measure 1] is understood to have been 'prolonged' by the neighbor-note, E, after which the melody descends by conjunct motion, filling the gap and moving on to the tonic."[26]

In a parametric analysis of the melody, however, E does not function only as a Schenkerian type of neighboring tone.[27] Rather, in looking at the melodic pitches alone—without reference to the meter or Meyer's rhythmic summarization—we can see that the E creates a linear pattern (B–C–D–E) which, in implying F♯, helps us explain the closure of the final cadence (example 47a).[28] The unclosed character of the line in measures 1–2 is assured by the parallel tenths created in conjunction with the bass (47c).[29]

The E in the soprano line, however, not only is open in the sense of implying a continuing ascent; it is also simultaneously closed because of the harmony. That is, the motion from the I⁶ in measure 1 to the root position IV in measure 2 transforms the E (47c). Thus, the E in measure 2 becomes the structural tone on the next level in the soprano instead of the D in measure 1. It follows, then, that the gap governing the descent in measures 2–3 is B–*E* (see example 47b), not the trochaic-ally defined B–D in measure 1 (as shown by Meyer in example 46).

26. Ibid., p. 126

27. Meyer acknowledges his debt to Schenker (*Explaining Music*, p. 109). Schenker, however, has no use for the poetic feet system. See *Der Freie Satz*, pp. 195–96.

28. The G in measure 7 realizes the B–D triadic pattern, though the pitch is weakened by the harmony (see Meyer's analysis in example 46). The F♯ in measure 7 (see the music in example 46), however, does not follow the B–C–D–E line shown in example 47a, because it is a medial part of a descending gap filling (again see example 46, measures 6–8, graph 1). Its place in this descending process prevents it from functioning also as part of the linear ascent. In contrast, the D in the bass in measure 7 does function to realize both the G–B triadic implication and the G–A–B–C linear implication (see examples 47d and e).

29. For a study of the relationship between bass-line structure and melodic structure, see Reed J. Hoyt, "The Bass-line in Tonal Music: Its Relationships to Melodic and Harmonic Structure" (Ph.D. diss., University of Pennsylvania, 1977).

Example 47

Finally, note that the bass-line melody is also both open and closed. Like the melody, a gap (G–C) is created by the rhythm and the harmony (47c), but the same C also implies a linear continuation to the D in measure 7 (example 47d). As the analysis shows, the realization of the lines between the bass (measure 7) and the soprano (measure 32) is not congruent (cf. example 47a with 47d).

If a parametric analysis makes suspect the B–D gap shown in measure 1 in example 46 in the soprano, there can be no question about the validity of the B–D triadic implication. Parametrically, D emerges as the closed tone connecting back to the initial B because of the cumulating ♪♪ ♪ rhythm and the harmony. The reason these two parameters transform the D is that their processes exemplify the Gestalt

145

principle of return.[30] The terminal eighth note in the rhythm is a partial return to the long note which initiated the pattern (the dotted eighth), while the sixteenth note functions as a kind of "digression" in the process (see example 48c). The same could be said about the

Example 48

harmony—symbolized in figured bass in example 48c (the $\begin{smallmatrix}3&3&3\\8&7&6\end{smallmatrix}$): the $\frac{3}{6}$ created by the closure of the cumulating rhythm is a partial return to stability, though, as we shall see, it is open on the next level, moving to the $\frac{3}{5}$ in measure 2. As before, these transformations affect the bass as well as the soprano. G–B in the bass implies a triadic continuation to the D in measure 7 (example 48d).[31] To repeat: in measures 1–2 tones are *both* open and closed on the same level. An either/or approach will

30. On the Gestalt principle of return, see Meyer, *Emotion and Meaning in Music*, pp. 151–56.

31. I will not discuss the middle part in the melodic analysis. It is processive mostly in terms of harmony. Melodically, the G–F♯–G–F♯–G in the middle voice in measures 1–4 exemplifies the Gestalt principle of return and is therefore closed.

not do because parametric processes create networks of relationships, often noncongruent with one another.[32]

I suggested earlier that parametric analysis could put summarizations on a more secure footing. If the analysis above is right (example 48), it follows that measure 1 could be more accurately summarized as the pivoted rhythm of, say, ⌞–⌞◡⌟–⌟ rather than as the trochee shown in example 46 (⌞–◡⌟). However, even if we could establish as a stylistic rule the proposition that durational patterns like ♪♩♪ create summarizations of the ⌞–⌞◡⌟–⌟ sort, such a rule would not enable us to use such summarizations with any great degree of confidence in generating structural tones. For, as I have emphasized, one aspect of the function of the tone—its simultaneous closed and unclosed quality on the level of its occurrence—is always omitted in the either/or symbolization.

32. The reason a tone is both open and closed on the same level has to do primarily with melodic and harmonic implication. In the pluralistic implication-realization concept, all intervallic motion implies both a continuation in the same direction and a gap with a fill in the opposite direction (the motion of a half-step being the sole exception). The interval G–B, for instance, implies a continuation to D (or E, depending on the harmony) and a fill to A. Multiple implications in melody are rarely equiprobable, however, because other parameters like durational rhythm and harmony usually give us "cues" to which implication is the stronger. For this reason harmony and rhythm are often involved in the creation of melodic transformation on higher levels, as we see in example 48. Melodic pitch is not solely dependent on other parameters for the establishment of closure, however; it is governed by its own rules of closure. For example, an immediate return to the initial pitch of a pattern—for example, G–A–G (a neighboring tone) or G–D–G—creates a sense of closure, as does a return to the initial note in a gap (e.g., G–B–A–G). In continuation patterns, the achievement of the octave (e.g., G–B–D–G in example 48*b*) also establishes a degree of closure. The closure inherent in returns and octave achievement, however, is not absolute. The line B–A–G in a gap fill of G–B, for instance, also implies a continuation to, say, F♯, which may or may not occur. Similarly, G–B–D–G in any octave implies a replication of the whole triadic pattern an octave higher. In the implication model, we have to have rules for knowing when to retain multiple contrasting implications in the analysis of the structure and when to omit them. The listener remembers only what is necessary to comprehend the music. Not every implicative relationship can be represented in an analysis—only the realizations that establish processes. But we should recognize that the richness of a structure depends as much on what is implied and *not* realized as on what is realized.

The same kind of omission, however, could occur in a note reduction that did not rely on poetic feet. In measure 4 in example 46, for instance, Meyer disregards his trochaic summarization and analyzes the cadential G on the nonaccent as the closed tone (graph 1). Thus, in this case, harmonic cadence is seen to take precedence over metric accent in closing the descending D–C–B–A–G line in measures 2–4 that follows the B–D gap (again see graph 1 in example 46). If, however, the melodic G in measure 4 is viewed *only* in terms of being closed on the lowest level, then measure 4 becomes cut off from measure 5 even though it is immediately adjacent. That is, in Meyer's analytical symbology in example 46, the G in measure 4 has *no* relationship to the B in measure 5—though the G–B–D melodic connection from measure 4 to 5 in Schumann's melody surely constitutes an important reason why the second phrase (measures 5–8) regenerates the triadic implication of the first phrase (compare example 48*b* with graphs 3–4 in example 46).[33]

Omitting the G–B connection between measures 4 and 5 is, of course, a direct consequence of conceptualizing a tone as being only closed or only open on its given level, instead of both. To be sure, example 46 shows the G in measure 4 as being open on the *next* level (graph 4): the G in measure 4 becomes part of a high-level, descending triadic pattern implying the D in the middle section. But if we analyze all the processes in measures 1–4, parameter by parameter, we will see that in certain respects the G in measure 4 is also unclosed on the lowest, note-to-note level, implying—and helping us to explain—the events that follow.

The rhythmic-durational pattern of which the G in measure 4 is a part, for instance, is implicative: We expect the continuing eighth notes in measures 1–4 to culminate on some longer note, as indeed they do on the dotted eighth notes on the downbeats in measures 5, 9, and 13 with the restart of each four-bar phrase (see example 49).

An explanation of this expectation and the way it affects the rhythmic nonclosure of the G in measure 4 is necessary. Example 49 shows a

33. Unlike the G of measure 7 over the C♯ (creating a diminished fifth), the G at the very end of this piece (measure 32) thus completes the octave on a harmonically stable sonority, which is another reason it is so important to the closure of the composition.

Example 49

processive analysis of the rhythm of the whole piece—rhythm being defined here as durational patterning instead of parametric summarizations (i.e., instead of poetic feet). On level one, the motion from each dotted eighth to the sixteenth note in measure 1 (and measures 5, 9, and 13) is implicative in that the durationally *countercumulative* pattern (♪♪) implies a return to a note of relatively the same duration as that that initiated the pattern. Since a level is defined by a span of time, nonclosure (and implication) in a durational process is always created when a note of longer duration moves to a note of shorter duration. And vice versa: a degree of rhythmic closure is always created when a short note moves to a long note.[34] Thus, closure is supplied by the *cumulative* eighth note to which the sixteenth moves.[35] Since the ♫♪ rhythm is closed, the dotted eighth (♪.) and the eighth note (♪), as the initial (♫) and terminal (♪) tones of the process, become transformed as the structural tones on level two, where a new rhythmic process begins: the motion from the dotted eighth to the eighth note— again countercumulative in duration—so that what is needed to close this pattern is a return to the dotted eighth note. This we get in measure 5 (see example 49). Thus, measures 1–4 are rhythmically processive on

34. Since higher levels occupy longer spans of time than lower levels, a tone rarely occupies a level lower than its actual duration. This does not mean, however, that a tone relatively short in duration cannot occur on a higher level. If the high level were four bars in length, for example, and the eighth note were the structural tone transformed to that level, then the note would "stand for" the level of four bars even though it would maintain its identity as an eighth note. I am grateful to my student Robert Frankel for bringing this to my attention.

35. I cannot go into the whole theory here. Essentially I believe that *countercumulative* patterns like ♫ are *durational gap patterns*. Thus the pattern in measure 1 of example 49 is the following rhythmic process: ♪. ♪ ♪ . The complete filling in of a gap, as I have pointed out, exemplifies the Gestalt principle of return. In this case, the fill (the ♪) is incomplete. There are basically three kinds of rhythms in music: cumulative (e.g., ♪♪), countercumulative (e.g., ♫), and additive (e.g., ♫).

level two, and the G in measure 4 (beat 2) which falls on one of those implicative eighth notes is rhythmically open.[36]

On level three, the transformed tones are the dotted eighth notes in measures 1 and 5.[37] Like the continuing eighth notes on level two, on a higher level these dotted eighths are *additive*. Additive patterns exemplify the Gestalt law of continuation—that once a pattern is initiated it tends to be continued in the mind of the listener.[38] Thus the continuing implication of these additive patterns can be closed only by a realization at a higher level—that is to say, by a note of longer duration. This cumulation in rhythm occurs on the long notes in measures 17–18, which, themselves becoming transformed to a new level, establish another additive pattern of continuation (see level four in the example). The fact that the cumulations on the dotted eighth notes in measures 5, 9, and 13 are interrupted each time with an abrupt return via the sixteenth note to the short eighths in measures 6–8, 10–12, and 14–16 partly accounts for our satisfaction in hearing the sustained quarter notes in the middle section (measures 17–18 and 21–22) and at the end (measures 29–30).

If the eighth notes at each cadence (measures 4, 8, 12, 16, and 28) are

36. Partly because our theory of harmony is so well developed, we have long been accustomed to thinking that a perfect authentic cadence like that in measure 4 (and measures 8, 12, and 16) is completely closed. Thus it may be difficult to imagine the cadential tones in those bars as having any implications. Yet I think both rhythmic and (as we shall see) melodic evidence suggests that a summarization according to harmony—in which the closural V–I dominates and subsumes the other parameters in those bars—is mistaken.

37. To repeat: although the dotted eighth represents a level of four bars, the note does not *become* four bars in length. That is, the dotted eighth retains its durational identity even though it becomes transformed.

38. The principle that once a pattern is initiated it tends to be continued in the mind of the listener comes from Gestalt psychology. For a discussion of the "law of good continuation," see Meyer, *Emotion and Meaning in Music*, chap. 3. In additive patterns, I believe, the listener relies heavily on meter to structure his perceptions. That is, when a pattern becomes rhythmically undifferentiated through unrelieved repetition—when the process of rhythmic continuation is realized over too long a time span—the listener invokes measured regularity to help him get the next-level transformations. The reader may wish to compare my notions of rhythmic process with Schenker's. See *Der Freie Satz*, appendix, example 140, p. 100.

rhythmically open in the sense of implying a cumulating long note, as I have argued, then the reader may well ask whether the piece ends rhythmically unfinished, since the last two notes of the piece are eighth notes. The answer is no if the last note of the composition, though written as an eighth note, is played on the piano with the damper pedal down (preferably only on the second time through), thus creating a long note despite the notion (as shown in example 49). (To insure rhythmic-durational closure, a performer would take care to hold the last eighth note longer than a quarter note, thereby cumulating the rhythmic implication of the quarter notes in the middle section as well; see example 49, level four. Moreover, the performer might also slightly—but only slightly—retard the tempo of the last two beats in order to underscore the cumulation.) The answer becomes perhaps, however, if the last note of the composition is played strictly as written—as an eighth note, unheld and unpedaled.[39] Aesthetically speaking, we could find delight in either the rhythmically closed or the rhythmically unclosed rendition. Pedaling the last note would give the "Soldier's March" a sense of satisfying finality, whereas playing the note "as is"—as a short eighth—would create a mildly jolting surprise.

As we have seen, some of the parameters—namely, melody and harmony—contribute to the closure of the last two eighth notes in the piece. Thus the implication of the final durational pattern to cumulate is not strong. Moreover, in order to evaluate closure, we have to take into account the rests—the amount of silence—following the cadence. Silence in music functions like pitch. It is both open and closed and is therefore subsumed into the musical hierarchy according to the way the parameters interact. When rests are *equivalent* in duration to pitch, they tend to reflect the summarization of the process in all the parameters. (I use the word "summarization" here not in Meyer's rhythmic

---

39. It is difficult to develop a good theory of music without considering what the performer does. If the reader doubts that the eighth-note rhythm keeps the melody open in measures 4, 8, 12, and 16, he should try playing all the eighth notes as quarter notes (with the pedal down). The hideousness will be readily apparent and the overall effect on the rhythmic process of the piece ruinous. We are in great need of a theory of performance, but that can come only after we have a more rigorous theory of music.

sense, but in the sense of a *pitch* summarization of the interaction of all the parameters. This will become clearer when we get to example 52.) In measures 2–4, for instance, the eighth-note rests function to close, by articulation, the eighth-note pitches, but because the pitches are on the whole implicative (both rhythmically and melodically), the rests also reflect the nonclosure. That is, the silences, as equivalent in duration to the pitches that precede them, do not impede the overall process. When rests are *longer* than the notes they reflect, then they tend to emphasize closure (separation, articulation, etc.). Conversely, when they are *shorter*, they tend to reinforce the aspect of nonclosure (bringing connection, conjunction, etc. to our attention). And if nonclosure is relatively strong, then rests shorter than the notes they reflect will serve to "dramatize" the degree of nonclosure. On the other hand, if closure is relatively strong, then longer rests will increase the degree of closure. In example 49, for instance, the ⁊⸲ in measure 32 emphasizes the closural aspect of the eighth notes in the cadence. Thus, silence itself enters into covariant relationships with the pitch processes of music.

So much for the rhythm. Let us return to the G in measure 4 and discuss its nonclosure in terms of pitch. For not only is the G rhythmically open in measure 4, it is also melodically open: The descending line begun in measure 2 and continued in measures 3 and 4 (E–D–C–B–A–G) implies an F♯ and beyond (see example 50a). But in comparison to the realizations of the rhythmic implication, where the cumulating long notes followed immediately after the cadential G in measure 4 and establish regular closural patterns on the cumulations in measures 5, 9, 13, and 17, here there is a difference. For the temporal distance between the E–D–C–B–A–G in measures 2–4 and an F♯–E–D pattern which could fulfill that implication is relatively long: the F♯ does not occur until measure 17 (again see example 50a). Does this argue for or against making the relationship? The question brings up one of the most difficult problems in using the implication-realization model. What are the rules for making (or ignoring) relationships between widely discontiguous events? Although I argued in example 47 that the ascending B–C–D–E pattern in measures 1–2 connects to the F♯–G in measures 31–32 and thus in effect that temporal separation is not sufficient reason to omit making a relationship, I do not believe that the F♯ in measure

153

17 in example 50 functions to continue the G in measure 4 downward.

For if we evaluate all the parameters on the G in measure 4, we will see that two parameters contribute to closure while two others contribute to nonclosure. Both the bass melody and the harmony are closed in measure 4, and these two parameters balance out the nonclosure of the soprano melody and the durational rhythm. That is, the G in the bass in measure 4 prolongs (via the D preceding) the G in measure 3, the G that closed the initial G–C gap in the bass (see example 50*b*).[40] In like manner, the harmonic process closes on the $\frac{8}{3}$ sonority in measure 4[41] (see example 50*d*). In contrast, the soprano is open, as is the dura-

---

40. I cannot discuss the whole theory of intervals here. The G–D pattern in measures 3–4 of the bass does imply a continuation to the low G, but when D moves back to the G in measure 4 (on the cadence), it exemplifies the Gestalt principle of return. Recall that in the implication-realization model tones are simultaneously both open and closed. I would argue that the melodic implication to the lower octave is "forgotten" by the listener and that, because of that, G–D–G on the I–V–I is construed as a closed pattern. (Of course, harmony contributes to the closure.) Such "intersticed" patterns are common—the melodic neighboring tones (G–F♯–G–F♯–G) in the middle voice of example 50, for instance. Although as yet we have no terms for relatively distant, intervallic "neighbors," Schenker's concepts of *Ausfaltung* (unfolding) and *springender Durchgang* (leaping passing tone) were on the right track.

41. Again I cannot discuss the whole theory here, but I believe there are basically two harmonic processes in tonal music: (1) patterns of continuation (e.g., those moving toward more consonance like $\begin{smallmatrix} 7 & 6 & 8 & 8 \\ 5 & 5 & 6 & 5 \\ 3 & 3 & 3 & 3 \end{smallmatrix}$ and those moving toward more dissonance $\begin{smallmatrix} 8 & 8 & 6 & 7 & 7 \\ 5 & 6 & 5 & 5 & 4 \\ 3 & 3 & 3 & 3 & 3 \end{smallmatrix}$, the latter patterns more evident in the nontonal music of our century than in tonal music); and (2) patterns of gap filling (e.g., $\llcorner$ gap $\begin{smallmatrix} 8 & & 7 & 6 & 8 & 8 \\ 5 & & 5 & 5 & 6 & 5 \\ 3 & & 3 & 3 & 3 & 3 \end{smallmatrix}$).
Fill

The harmony from measures 1–2 in example 50*d* is a gap-filling process ($\llcorner$ gap $\begin{smallmatrix} 3 & 3 & 3 \\ 8 & 6 & 5 \end{smallmatrix}$ Fill), though the fill is not only partial: measure 2 would have been more closed if the harmony on the downbeat were a return to the $\frac{3}{8}$ rather than the slightly more "dissonant" $\frac{3}{5}$. The implication-realization model I am outlining is thus able to make use of the tradition of figured bass which symbolizes harmonic process—one other example of its worth in the sense that it builds upon and synthesizes previous theories. Observe, however, that figured-bass symbols in themselves are summarizing in several ways. The *symbology* of $_{minor}\frac{3}{6}$ to $_{major}\frac{3}{6}$ in measures 2–3 of example 50*d*, for

tional rhythm (examples 50*a* and *c*, respectively). This balance among parameters may be expressed as a ratio of 2:2—the two closed parameters of bass melody and harmony versus the two implicative parameters of melody and rhythm. In other words, the evidence for closure on the lowest level on the G in the soprano in measure 4 is roughly equal to the evidence for nonclosure.[42]

In the face of such patterns—where closure and nonclosure are more or less equivalent—the listener, I believe, always favors closure over nonclosure because this is the most efficient way he can continue attending to the piece intelligently. That is, the listener must transform measure 4 into something he can immediately store in his memory and

---

instance, does not accurately portray how processive this progression is, because the diminished fifth (C–F♯) between the soprano and alto on the $_{M}6^{3}$ in measure 3 is not shown. That is, the internal character of the intervals is not symbolized in the figures. Thus, a more accurate, less summarizing symbology would have to show not only the relationship of the upper tones to the bass but also the inner voice relationships as well. The $_{M}6^{3}$ in measure 3, for instance, is really

> diminished 5 (soprano to alto)
> minor 3 (soprano to bass)
> major 6 (alto to bass).

Moreover, figured bass symbology is often not indicative of the actual ordering of the vertical events from the bass upward in the music even though soprano position is clearly an important factor in determining degree of chordal stability. If we accept the relationship between the outside voices as being a valid summarization in consonant sonorities, and if we accept the historical notion that harmonic intervals are divided into perfect and imperfect consonances and dissonances, and also accept the normal rank ordering of these intervals from most consonant to most dissonant (e.g., unisons, octaves, fifths, thirds, sixths, fourths, seconds, sevenths)—then clearly a $\frac{5}{3}$ sonority will have to be regarded as being more consonant than a $\frac{6}{3}$ since, according to the theory, a fifth between the outside voices is more consonant than a third between them.

42. Meter itself is a summarization and therefore often does not figure in a parametric evaluation of closure, particularly where rhythms are differentiated (i.e., nonadditive). In this example, 2/4 meter is established chiefly by the harmony: the second-level pattern $\frac{3}{8}$ $\frac{3}{6}$ | $\frac{3}{5}$ $\frac{3}{6}$ creates a regular alternation every quarter note. This regularity is disturbed in measures 3–4, however. Although the listener still carries 2/4 in his head, the music in those bars does not support it. Meyer himself notes that the meter in this piece is often against the patterning (*Explaining Music*, p. 128).

yet recognize with great accuracy as the piece progresses. Although his apprehension of measure 4 may prove faulty in retrospect, his general decision nevertheless is to *summarize* his inferences of the pitch processes in favor of attending to what seems likely to occur in the future of the piece. This means encoding the information on the next higher level in the simplest way possible. Thus, to organize his memory, the listener "chooses" in this example the harmonic closure underneath the G in measure 4 and the melodic closure of the bass line over the unclosed melody of the soprano and the implication of the rhythmic-durational pattern. He "allows" the two closed parameters to override the two nonclosural ones in selecting the structural tones, and this permits him to summarize melodically the G in measure 4 as a closed tone. As we shall see in example 52, on the next higher level he thus structures the first four bars as B–G. And of course he also remembers the same opening B as part of an unclosed, ascending B–C–D–E line.

To be sure, all this is computed so rapidly in our minds that it seems clumsy to talk about it. What the discussion makes clear, however, is that if we are going to have a feasible implication-realization model in which tones are conceived as both open and closed on any given level, we are going to have to know a good deal more about memory—or rather about *forgetting*, since the listener can carry only so many implicative "paths" in his head. Practically speaking, from an analytic-theoretical point of view, we need to formulate some rules of memory because an analysis that enumerates every possible connection between tones can be confusing.[43]

One clear advantage of analyzing generations of implications from parametric processes "upward" instead of from hypothetical rhythmic summarizations "downward" is that arguments about closure and nonclosure can be stipulated in very precise terms. As we just saw in our discussion of the G in measure 4 in example 50, for instance, the weighting of parameters could be formulated in a ratio which would enable us to discuss the degrees of simultaneous closure and nonclosure

---

43. Rules in which discontiguous realizations have to occur at the same durational level as the generating implications go a long way toward cutting down on the number of "paths"—in other words, a "law of hierarchical equivalence." For more on this see Meyer, *Explaining Music*, p. 134 and throughout.

on that pitch. For implications to be strong on any given pitch, parameters would have to be proportionately more open than closed. That is to say, more parametric implications would have to be left unrealized than were realized. This is the case with the soprano E in measure 2. It is closed only harmonically (on the $\frac{3}{5}$ chord), being implicative in every other way. For implications to be weak on any given pitch, parameters would have to be proportionately more closed than open—more parametric implications would have to be realized than unrealized. This would be the case with the cadential soprano G in measure 32. Even if it were performed as an eighth note and therefore kept rhythmically open, the melody, harmony, bass line, and rests would still close it. Parameters could be said to be congruent either when they were all implicative or when they were all closed realizations. Relative non-congruence among parameters could be expressed precisely in terms of ratios. Consequently, realizations could be defined more accurately and so, therefore, could next-level transformations.

Thus, analyzing process from the bottom up—directly from the parameters—enables us to evaluate the function of the formal parts more accurately. This could lead to the development of an authentic theory of form, since form is a result of what happens processively, not vice versa. I have already shown in the parametric analysis of Schumann's piece why measure 1 can be considered a partially closed form and why measures 1–4 can be said to function as a partially closed phrase. A parametric analysis, of course, could be extended to every level of the piece (since the principles of the implication-realization model are recursive), and if the theory is correct we should be able to say why, for instance, the cadential G in the return is more closed than the cadential G in the beginning. Theorists often regard returns as more closed than first presentations of the original material simply *because* they are returns. But this puts the cart (the formal function) before the horse (the process). If returns are really more closed in the function of the form, we should be able to say why on the basis of the parametric process.

Good reasons can be found why the cadential G in measure 28 of the return in Schumann's piece is significantly more closed than the analogous G in measure 4 (or measure 12). These reasons are chiefly har-

monic and melodic, and they have to do not only with the norms of
process established in the piece but also with the functional transformations of these processes as the piece progresses. Through repetition,
the piece establishes intraopus, stylistic norms between descending
melodic lines and the progression toward harmonic closure. In example
50 the correspondence between the falling melodic line (50*a*) and the
harmonic progression (50*d*) in measures 2–4 is heard also in measures
7–8, 10–12, and 15–16. Thus the middle section (measures 17–24),
partly because it partially conforms to this stylistically established
correspondence in the piece, also strongly implies harmonically and
melodically the cadential G in the return (measure 28), an implication

Example 50

borne out by the conformant similarity between measures 19–20, 23–24 and measures 2–3–4 (and 10–11–12) (see example 51). Moreover, as we shall see, this harmonic implication to the $\frac{8}{3}$ sonority in measure 28 occurs on several levels as the transformation of harmonic closure on lower levels takes place.

Some explanation of the analysis shown in example 51 is necessary. The analysis of the harmonic process by means of figured bass symbols (which, in being figured from the bass upward, tend to give structural priority to the outer voices) is based on the historically founded notion that harmonic intervals can be ranked from most stable to least stable, from most consonant to most dissonant, for example, unisions, octaves, and fifths ("perfect" consonances) to thirds and sixths ("imperfect" consonances) to fourths, seconds, and sevenths (dissonances). Thus, given any point within the continuum, a syntactic pattern can imply either a motion toward greater consonance or greater dissonance. Consequently, a harmonic process always carries the possibility of moving toward closure (toward consonance) or nonclosure (toward dissonance). In other words, harmonic patterns, like melodic patterns, are simultaneously open and closed on the same level. Hence, the direction a harmonic pattern is to take becomes manifest only when three or more vertical patterns create a process. In measures 18–21 in example 51*b*, for instance, the $\begin{smallmatrix}&3&d5&3&5\\6&&3&8&3&8\\&&&6&5&8\end{smallmatrix}$ is a process that becomes increasingly consonant until closure is achieved on the octave F♯ (the 8) in measure 21. The harmonic processes on all the levels in example 51 typify motion toward increased consonance.

Harmonic levels in example 51 are created by the initiation and closure of such processes. That is to say, initial and terminal sonorities (symbolized ♪ and ♩) in processes become transformed, creating new implications and realizations on the next level. In the ^{8} $\frac{4}{3}$ $\frac{3}{6}$ process of measures 18–19 (51*f*), for instance, the initial 8 and the terminal $\frac{3}{6}$ are the chords taken to the next level (51*c*). The process ends on the $\frac{3}{6}$ because what follows that sonority (the $\begin{smallmatrix}d5\\3\\6\end{smallmatrix}$ in measure 20) initiates a new process (51*b*). Thus, the reasons behind the derivations of the structural harmonies and the emergence of levels can be easily traced.

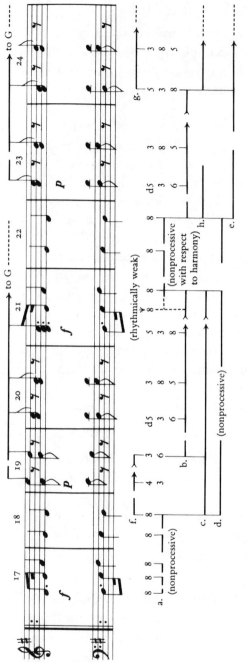

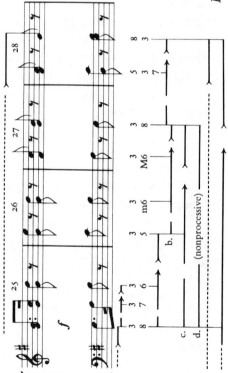

Example 51

Note in example 51 that in the case of textural changes between any two chords, a decrease in the number of voices will always result in an increase toward closure—provided all other harmonic relationships are equal—since the fewer chord voices there are, the fewer harmonic implications there are. Thus, the motion from the $\frac{3}{8}$ on the second beat
 $_5$
in measure 24 (four voices) to the $\frac{3}{8}$ on the downbeat of measure 25 (three voices) is a motion toward closure even though both chords are I's in the position of the third (51*g*). (The "all other things being equal" is an important proviso in the study of textural change for we can easily imagine harmonic processes that would negate any textural rules about the number of chordal voices. For example, $\frac{5}{3}$ to $\frac{8}{5}$ would result in an
 $_3$
increase in closure [5 moves to 8 in the top voice] even though the number of voices is increased; conversely, $\frac{8}{5}$ to $\frac{7}{3}$ would result in
 $_3$
nonclosure even though the number of voices decreases. The point to realize is that the implication-realization model offers a precise way of talking about the effect of textural change on musical structure.)

Finally, note in example 51 that repetition of harmonic intervals is nonprocessive. The low-level octaves in measures 17–18 and 21–22 (51*a*), the high-level octaves connecting measure 18 to measure 21 (51*d*), and the high-level $\frac{3}{8}$s connecting measure 25 with measure 27 (51*d*)—all these are harmonically nonimplicative on the levels of their occurrence (symbolized in the example with "backward" beams, ⅃⅃⅃) in contrast, say, to the somewhat differentiated and therefore processive $\underset{\text{m6}}{}\overset{3}{}\underset{\text{M6}}{}\overset{3}{}$ pattern in measures 26–27 (51*b*). (The reader should recall the summarizing nature of figured bass symbols as outlined in chap. 10, note 41.)

One advantage of such a detailed harmonic analysis is that it offers a more illuminating way of talking about the relationship of pitch structure to form. From a harmonic and melodic point of view, it is clear from the analysis in example 51, for instance, how important the G in measure 28 in the return (beginning in measure 25) is to the implications generated in the middle section (measures 17–24). Moreover, we see that the stability of the G in measure 28 is much greater than the stability of the G in measure 4 because in measure 28 the G is

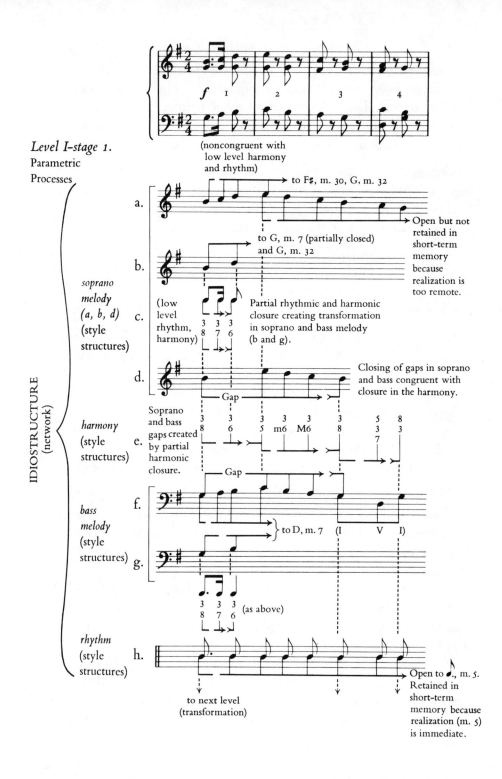

Level I–stage 1.
Parametric
Processes

(noncongruent with
low level harmony
and rhythm)

IDIOSTRUCTURE
(network)

soprano
melody
(a, b, d)
(style
structures)

harmony
(style
structures)

bass
melody
(style
structures)

rhythm
(style
structures)

a.

→ to F♯, m. 30, G, m. 32

Open but not
retained in
short-term
memory
because
realization is
too remote.

b.

to G, m. 7 (partially closed)
and G, m. 32

c.

(low
level
rhythm,
harmony)

3 3 3
8 7 6

Partial rhythmic and harmonic
closure creating transformation
in soprano and bass melody
(b and g).

d.

Gap

Closing of gaps in soprano
and bass congruent with
closure in the harmony.

e.

Soprano
and bass
gaps created
by partial
harmonic
closure.

3   3   3 3   3   3   5 8
8   6   5 m6 M6   8   3 3
                        7

Gap

f.

Gap

to D, m. 7   (I   V   I)

g.

3 3 3
8 7 6 (as above)

h.

Open to ♩., m. 5.
Retained in
short-term
memory because
realization (m. 5)
is immediate.

to next level
(transformation)

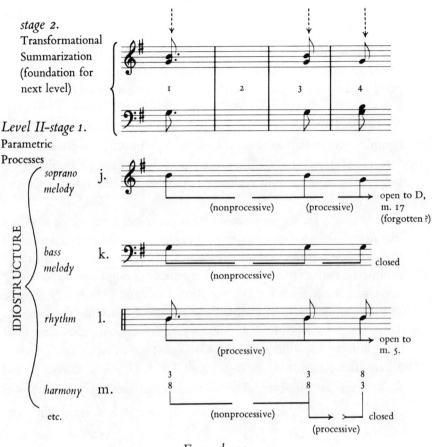

Example 52

the realization of more harmonic implications—three in all (again see example 51). Thus, measures 25–28 are not simply a return of measures 1–4; rather, they function as an implied recurrence, a necessary outcome of the events in the middle section.

There is much more to be said about Schumann's little piece. The surprise motion in measure 29 which takes the D of measures 18 and 22 farther downward to the low C and the long-delayed realization of the F♯–G in the soprano melody's upper register are indeed a child's delight, but my main point here is to show that a processive analysis of the individual parameters can demonstrate how thematic material returning at the end of a piece becomes more closed than when initially presented.

One consequence of analyzing separate parametric processes as a way of discovering form, instead of vice versa, is that a given level becomes a good deal more complex. Specifically, analyses generated by the model I have outlined will be very "network-oriented," since parametric implications are evaluated separately before they are summarized. This complex network can be dealt with by splitting levels into two "stages": (1) the intertwining processes of the parametric implications, and (2) the summarizing realizations that lead to the transformations on the next level.

In example 52, for instance—which combines examples 47, 48, 49 (the first four bars), and 50—stage 1 results from the interaction of all the *style forms* in the various parameters. By style form, I mean those parametric entities in the piece which achieve enough closure to enable us to understand their intrinsic functional coherence without reference to the functionally specific, intraopus context from which they come. Thus, the lines B–C–D–E and E–D–C–B–A–G (*52a*), the triad B–D (*52b*), and the gap–filling B–E–D–C–B (*52d*) are all *melodic* style forms, as are the patterns G–A–B–C, G–C–B–A–G, G–D–G (*52f*), and G–B (*52g*) in the bass. The durational patterns ♩♪ (*50c*) and ♪.♪♪|♪♪♪|♪♪♪|♪. (*52h*) are *rhythmic* style forms, while the patterns $\frac{3}{8}\frac{3}{7}\frac{3}{6}$ (*52c*), $\frac{3}{8}\frac{3}{6}\frac{3}{5,5}\frac{3}{m6}\frac{3}{M6}\frac{3}{8}$, and $\frac{3}{8}\frac{5}{3}\frac{8}{3}$ (*52e*) are *harmonic* style forms.

Combining all the style forms in the various parameters in stage 1 produces a specific functional complex of *style structures* which together create a network of relationships I will call the *idiostructure*. The distinction between style form, style structure, and idiostructure has important ramifications for the study of music and will be discussed shortly. Ideally, if my analysis in example 52 is correct, the idiostructure's representation should capture all those characteristics that make the first four bars of Schumann's piece its unique self, whereas the "style" of the piece will be found in the way the style forms interact specifically as style structures in various parameters, for example, the specific way B–C–D–E is enchained to E–D–C–B–A–G in the soprano melody (example *52a*).

The interaction among parameters leads to the closure of various pitches which creates levels of transformation. For instance, as has been discussed, low-level rhythm and harmony (52*c*) transform the linear patterns of the soprano and the bass melody in measure 1 into triadic patterns (52*b* and *g*); harmony (52*e*) also transforms the continuation of these patterns into gaps (measures 1–3, 52*d* and *f*); the closure of these gaps in measure 3 is underscored by the congruent closure of the harmony (the $\frac{3}{8}$), and so forth. *Transformation* is always a result of closure, the partial or complete realization of parametric implications, while *formation* is always a result of nonclosure, the continuing, unrealized implications of parametric patterns. In example 52, transforming realization is denoted by the broken vertical lines, whereas forming implication is denoted by the absence of vertical lines. Therefore, the fewer the vertical lines, the more processive a passage is.

What is significant about the parametric analysis of example 52, then, is that it shows us the exact *shape* of the phrase. Scanning the analysis up and down, we can see that the beginning of the phrase (the first three beats of the piece) is characterized by relative noncongruence between closure and nonclosure of the parameters. In contrast, the middle of the phrase (beat 2, measure 2, to beat 1, measure 3) is open and ongoing in every parameter (no vertical lines, i.e., no transformations), whereas the end of the phrase (the last measure and a half) is again characterized by some transformation.[44]

---

44. I suggested earlier (p. 147) that whatever was "right" about the poetic feet tradition of analysis could be demonstrated in a parametric analysis of implication and realization. And I also suggested that the figured-bass tradition could be included in the implication-realization model (see n. 41, p. 154). Here we see how the implication-realization model incorporates one other tradition, the notion of "shape" or "wave" in musical rhythm. The concept runs strong throughout the nineteenth century—see, for instance, Wiehmayer's *Musikalische Rhythmik und Metrik*—and it has been kept alive recently by Edward T. Cone in *Musical Form and Musical Performance* (New York: W. W. Norton, 1968), which compares beginnings, middles, and ends of phrases to "the throw, the transit, and the catch" of a ball (see p. 26 ff). Cone denotes such shapes by the symbols ⌐ ⌣ ⌐. The analogy to my discussion of example 52 is clear. Jan LaRue in his *Guidelines for Style Analysis* (New York: W. W. Norton, 1970) also is attracted by the notion of capturing musical shape in analysis—though LaRue prefers the word "Movement" to describe such large-scale motions (while reserving the word "Shape" to refer to form). See pp. 13–17.

Stage 2 in the analysis results from a *summarization* of the transformations in the idiostructure and therefore establishes the foundation for a new level (see the example). The whole operation is recursive. On level II, stage 1, the parameters again create syntactic relationships. In contrast to level I, however, here there is much less "activity." Measures 1–3 by and large are nonprocessive—that is, the repetition of pitch in the soprano and the bass, and the repetition of the $\frac{3}{8}$ sonority in the harmony set up no implication (see example 52*j*, *k*, and *m*). Only the rhythm is processive (52*l*).

In measure 4 on this level, we find the implication of the soprano melody and the durational-rhythmic pattern noncongruent with the closure of the harmony and the static quality of the bass—creating again roughly a ratio of 2:2 between parameters. Once more, the matter of memory arises. Meyer shows the B–G melodic pattern (52*j*) as implying the D in the middle section (again see his analysis in example 46, graph 4). If, however, our reasons on level I for weighting such parametric evaluations toward closure were right, it remains an open question here on level II whether the high-level B–G implication is retained by the listener during the measures that follow.

Finally, note that, despite the detail of the analysis in example 52 and the apparent simplicity of Schumann's phrase—so simple that one would think there would be little room for disagreement—there is *no* emergence of any *Urlinie*-like pattern; neither a 3̂–2̂–1̂ nor a 5̂–4̂–3̂–2̂–1̂—the only possibilities—shows up. The soprano E in measure 2 is not simply a neighboring tone; the descending motion in measures 2–3 is not merely "interval-filling"; and the soprano D in measure 1 is not a prolonging "outside voice" to a 3̂ (the B).

It is true *harmonically* that a I–V–I pattern is created on level I (see 52*f*). And it is also true that in the summarization of level I (stage 2) the third degree (B) figures strongly in the structural representation of the melody of measures 1–3. This only proves, however, what I have implied all along: whatever is "right" about a Schenkerian analysis can be amply demonstrated in an implication-realization model which relies on the individual parameters as the "postulates." And whatever is "wrong" shows up just as clearly.

Eleven
IDIOSTRUCTURE, STYLE FORM, AND STYLE STRUCTURE

LINGUISTICS REVISITED

A S WE HAVE SEEN, THE MAJOR TENET (AND THE MAJOR PROBLEM) OF transformational grammar and Schenkerian theory is the notion that language, musical or otherwise, is a *whole system*. This leads to the belief that linguistic usages at any given time can be described independently of particular statements. In Schenkerian theory, for instance, neighboring-tone structures, passing-tone structures, and so forth, have independent status as transformational structures and are believed to be governed in some sense by rules which are not dependent on context.

In linguistics this belief in independent linguistic usages results on the one hand in a distinction between language (*la langue*) and speech (*la parole*), first made by the Swiss linguist Saussure, and on the other in a similar further distinction between "competence" and "performance," first made by the American, Chomsky. Since many utterances produced by native speakers—their "speech performances"—appear "ill-formed" to "competent" listeners, linguists have envisioned discovering the grammar underlying competence-recognition as a major goal of linguistics,[1] and they have thus spent their time trying to formalize a deductive theory that would separate grammatical sentences of a language from ungrammatical ones in hopes of giving a systematic account of both the grammar of the language and the structure of its "well-formed" sentences. In order to do this, however, much of the data of language has had to be "dematerialized," with the result that

---

1. Although the distinctions between language/speech and competence/performance have often been accepted with little reservation, there has been much argument about which factors make up competence or performance.

the linguistic behavior of any group can be described only in terms of abstract, idealized, highly generalized *norms,* since transformational grammarians operate under the assumption that there exists one set of rules agreed to by all the "performers" in the community. To complement this rationalistic approach, the transformational grammarians have, moreover, formulated a concept of an "ideal speaker."[2]

Critics of transformational grammar have viewed the distinction between competence and performance as a specious fabrication necessitated chiefly by transformational grammar's failure to account for (and generate) many of the accepted, albeit "ill-formed," sentences in a given language. Moreover, the very notion of an "ideal speaker" has been attacked as an absurd concept based on the false premise that there is only one well-defined language, fixed and immutable, which everyone in a given linguistic community speaks.[3] To the critics of transformational grammar, language is not innate but learned, and the observed agreement between speaker and listener is the result of social interaction, not an a priori assumption, since each speaker has his or her own unique idea of the community's spoken language. The critics of transformational grammar conclude then that the study of language should concern itself not with a structural idealization of the language, in which language is stripped of all its peculiar characteristics, but rather with the distinctive and unique structures of native utterances in all their idiosyncratic differentiation, however "incompetent" such utterances may seem to any given outsider. In other words, the critics of transformational grammar argue for discovering rules that govern *idiolects.*

I have discussed here the distinctions the transformational grammarians make between language and speech, competence and performance, and the criticisms of these distinctions, because I think it will help lay to rest one of the great myths perpetrated by the Schenkerians:

2. The concept of an ideal speaker is criticized by Robert M. Schwarcz, "Steps toward a Model of Linguistic Performance: A Preliminary Sketch," *Mechanical Translation* 10 (Sept.–Dec. 1967):39–52. See also Ian Robinson, *The New Grammarians' Funeral.*

3. See, for example, Paul Ziff, *Semantic Analysis* (Ithaca: Cornell University Press, 1960).

namely, that Schenkerian analysis is "about the individual musical art object in all its specificity."[4] If the analogy between Schenkerian theory and transformational grammar is correct, as the neo-Schenkerians maintain—and I believe the evidence demonstrates that the two fields are very similar in philosophical outlook—then it is clear that we cannot seriously contend that Schenkerian analysis deals with the individuality of a work. For, like transformational grammar, Schenkerian theory, with its *Ursatz*-kernel and its assumption of tonal language as a whole system without diachronic implications, accounts for the syntactic structure of a work by idealizing pitch relationships and disembodying them from much of their relevant data—for example, their rhythmic, metric, formal, melodic, and, in some cases, registral characteristics, as we saw in our discussion of examples 11, 12, 18, 22, 23, 25, 28, and 32. No transformational grammarian maintains, for instance, that a structural tree diagram captures the idiolect of, say, a Keats poem; similarly, because Schenkerian theory is so much like transformational grammar in outlook, no Schenkerian should be allowed to perpetuate the illusion that a Schenker graph depicts adequately the structure of, say, a Beethoven symphony. For a Keats poem or a Beethoven symphony is highly idiosyncratic. And the structure of an artwork cannot be reduced to the idealized norms of a synchronically conceived language. As Barbara H. Smith has pointed out, a poem is not a "saying," that is, an utterance, but the representation of one.[5] Similarly, a piece of music cannot be regarded as just another "usage" of the style. Artworks only exhibit style. They are not assimilated by it.

4. Batstone, "Musical Analysis as Phenomenology," pp. 95–96.

5. Barbara Herrnstein Smith, "Poetry as Fiction," *New Literary History* 2, no. 2 (Winter 1971): 271: "For what is central to the concept of the poem as a fictive utterance is not that the speaker is a 'character' distinct from the poet, or that the audience purportedly addressed, the emotions expressed, and the events alluded to are fictional, but that *the speaking, addressing, expressing and alluding are themselves fictive verbal acts*. To be sure, a fictive utterance will often resemble a possible natural utterance very closely, for the distinction is not primarily one of linguistic form. . . . The distinction lies, rather, in a set of conventions shared by poet and reader, according to which certain identifiable linguistic structures are *taken* to be not the verbal acts they resemble, but representations of such acts."

ON STYLE ANALYSIS AND CRITICAL ANALYSIS

Let us lay aside Schenkerian theory for the time being, however, and return to a consideration of a theory of style analysis and critical analysis. Since the real issues at stake concerning Schenkerian analysis are directly involved with these matters, the subject of style and criticism is by no means peripheral either to an understanding of Schenkerian theory or to the concept of an implication-realization model. And since "style" may be conceived as a "language" (*la langue* as distinguished from *la parole*), the subject is germane to our discussion.

The distinction made between style analysis and critical analysis is, of course, somewhat "fictional": style analysis cannot take place without critical judgment, and critical analysis depends upon an understanding of stylistic norms. Each is a necessary part of the other's explanatory context. But the goals of the two methods are diametrically opposed. Style analysis begins with the specific and moves to the general. In critical analysis the strategy is the reverse,[6] as the epistemological hierarchy in figure 7 suggests (each word or line of words

Criticism

global (universal) domain
culture
period of history (era, epoch): time
geographical locale: place
school (conventions)
genre
parametric forms (norms)
composer's *oeuvre*
types of "material" (extraopus)
work itself
particular section, part, motive, etc.
  (intraopus materials)

Style

Fig. 7

6. See Leonard B. Meyer's discussion on critical analysis in *Explaining Music*, chap. 1.

stands for a level; the whole diagram is to be imagined as a kind of hierarchical system, with each "level" implying an area of intellectual and scholarly concentration). Thus, the word "style" can refer to any level of our epistemological hierarchy. Adopting the anthropological view, we may, for instance, speak of the style of a culture, of a period, a school, a genre, a piece, even a particular motive.[7] (When we say something is "styleless," employing the concept as a value judgment, we are, strictly speaking, using the term "style" metaphorically.)

The style analyst serves primarily under the imperatives of historiography (cultural, global, whatever), and his evidence is thus gathered with the intention of its eventual use on the many levels of the epistemological hierarchy. Regardless of the level on which he starts, the style analyst thus looks up the hierarchy. And this stance prevents him from incorporating idiosyncratic information, from including "the secrets of the singular." For to accomplish his historical imperative—the assimilation of information on ever-higher levels—the style analyst must emphasize similarities between things. That is, in order for the style analyst to move from, say, the study of sections or parts of a particular piece to the study of extraopus materials, he must stress the similarities common to both levels. (This is not to say that the style analyst does not seek out and discover differences, but when he does, he is primarily interested in discovering differences between similar *classes* of things on the *same* level, rather than finding unique, intralevel differences—which are more properly the concern of the critic.)

The failure to recognize that the style analyst can emphasize similarities between two levels or within only one has led to a certain confusion about the nature of style analysis itself. Ackerman says, for instance,

> The word style defines a certain currency—distinguishable in the work (or in some portion of the work) of an artist, a place, or a time—and it is inefficient to use it also to define the unique traits of single works of art; uniqueness and currency are incompatible.

7. The anthropological view is expressed by George Kubler in *The Shape of Time* (New Haven: Yale University Press, 1962).

And LaRue says,

> style analysis attempts to discover more the individuality of
> a piece or composer than the conventionality.[8]

Clearly, Ackerman's view is correct only if the style analyst is attempting to make sense out of what is "current" to two manifestly contrasting
levels. Conversely, LaRue's remarks about the "individuality"
(= uniqueness) of a piece are true only if the style analyst remains on
one level, levels being recognizable only when structural differences are
apparent. Hence, there is no "inefficiency" involved when the style
analyst speaks about the unique, differentiated stylistic traits of Beethoven's Fifth Symphony, provided he contrasts them—implicitly or
explicitly—with those of a similar (level-equivalent) class, for example,
with those of the Sixth Symphony. Inefficiency results only if we try
to carry unique, lower-level differences to the next higher level. For
in order to move up to another level in the hierarchy—in order to
talk about the Fifth Symphony in relation to symphonies as a genre—the
style analyst must filter out the differentiated data from the lower level.
The point to remember is that the differences the style analyst locates
are differences between *exemplars*—between constructed classes of
similar things that are hierarchically equivalent, between the typical
features of one sort of thing on one level as opposed to the things
typical of another on the *same* level—whereas the similarities the style
analyst identifies and compares are usually similarities *between* levels.

We recognize the aspect of style partly through repetition and
recurrence (regardless of level). As I argued in examples 44 and 45,
the more recurrent an event is, whether within or outside a work, the
more it will seem to be part of a style. If we ask people, for instance,
to describe a style, they will invariably list all those characteristics of a
repertory on various epistemological levels for which there is ample
statistical evidence (e.g., most favored cadences, progressions, forms,
rhythmic motives, etc.).

Statistical information, by itself, however, is not enough to identify

8. James S. Ackerman, "Style," in *Art and Archeology*, ed. James S. Ackerman and
Rhys Carpenter (Englewood Cliffs, N.J.: Prentice-Hall, 1963), p. 166; Jan LaRue,
Guidelines for Style Analysis, p. 16.

a style. The number of B♭s or the number of II-chords or the number of *sforzandi* in a work are all ad hoc features that interest us only to the extent that they connect with the *style structure* at hand and add to our aesthetic comprehension of the work. In the absence of a structural framework, the distributional effect of a quantitative attribute makes for trivial information.[9] A large number of B♭s in a melody predominately in C major might be an interesting feature in that it may relate negatively to our theoretical notion that C is the diatonic tonal center, but even in this case we would have to examine how each B♭ operated with respect to the intrinsic *structure* of the melody if we wanted to test the validity of, say, some statistical law that dealt with various frequencies of nondiatonic notes and their relation to tonal coherence. Beethoven's music can be distinguished from Bach's by the number of *sforzandi* it contains. But so what? Accurate statistical data is no guarantee of significant stylistic information.

Thus, in order to discover the system of significant traits which defines the stylistic language, the style analyst will abstract from the repertory at hand a lexicon of *style forms*. As we saw in the discussion of example 52, style forms may be defined as those parametric entities which achieve enough closure so we can understand their functional coherence without reference to the specific intraopus contexts from which they come—all those seemingly time-*independent* patterns, large and small, from parameter to parameter, which recur with statistically significant frequency. The vocabulary of extraopus forms from a style may be envisioned collectively as a pool of information, an encompassing circle of "facts" into which all relationships of similarity in the given repertory may be placed. Clustering toward the center of the pool lie those facts of the style for which there exists the greatest evidence—statistically the most recurrent; toward the periphery, those for which there is the least evidence.

9. Despite this fact, graduate students continue to grind out statistical dissertations of this sort. It is worth pointing out that the frequency distribution curve of a particular stylistic trait in a given work may not be comparable to the distribution curve of the extraopus style from which the trait comes and which it seems to exemplify. That is, a given trait may occur *more* frequently in one work and less frequently in another than it occurs in the style in general.

In order to avoid creating an ocean of lifeless facts, devoid of operational significance, and in order not to deny facts their proper habitat, however, the style analyst will attempt to restore the syntactic function of style forms by arranging them in various specific contexts according to their statistically most common functional occurrences. The contexts which result from such arrangement can be called *style structures* in the sense that they are directly tied to and contribute to the structure of real pieces, not just to constructed classes of things, as are style forms. Unlike the description of style forms, the identification of style structures involves ascribing time-*dependent* function to patterns—as we saw, for instance, in example 52, where certain style forms were connected in functionally specific ways, in intraopus relationships.

Ascribing functional significance to statistical information is of course necessary if statistical evidence is to have any kind of meaning beyond feeble explanatory notions like "trends" or "tendencies." We may count the number of chord progressions based on the fifth (style forms) in a piece, but obviously the usefulness of that information as a style characteristic depends on whether the progressions function

One-Level Orientation	*Two-Level Orientation*
1. external generation:	2. internal generation:
extraopus norms mapped onto intraopus norms	intraopus norms compared with extraopus norms
Similarities between Classes (e.g., how Beethoven symphonies are alike)	Differences between Similar Classes (e.g., how Beethoven's Symphony no. 5 differs from all other symphonies in general)
↓	
increase in mode-knowledge (the "way" of style forms)	↓
	increase in code-knowledge (the functional rules of style structures)

Fig. 8. Two methods of style analysis.

initially, medially, or terminally in a structure and whether they operate on low, middle, or high levels. Thus style analysis attempts to discover two things about a structure: (1) its "mode"—the specific way an extraopus structure appears as a style form—and (2) its "code" —the set of specific functional rules under which the form operates as an intraopus structure from one piece to the next.

Accordingly, the style analyst may study the style of a piece from two vantage points. If he intends to remain on only one level of the epistemological hierarchy—that is, if he intends to study only, say, a particular genre or a particular school—he will analyze pieces "externally," by reducing them to known style forms via a process of matching copy (the work) to extraopus models. But if he wants to make use of this information on other levels—if, say, he wants to discover the relationship of a genre to a school—he will analyze pieces "internally" by reducing them to known, intraopus style structures. (Or he might attempt to discover new internal style structures.) The external approach results in a more refined knowledge of "mode"; the internal, with its emphasis on function, results in a more refined knowledge of "code." All this may be seen more clearly in figure 8.

(In general, historians that deal at the global, cultural, epochal, geographical, or institutional levels tend to be concerned mostly with modes—and therefore diachronics—whereas historians that deal at the level of genres, parametric forms, composers' *oeuvre*, types of material, or individual works tend to be concerned mostly with codes—and therefore synchronics. Traditionally, the former group of scholars leans toward ethnomusicology as a discipline; the latter, toward style history.)

The particular style of a piece will thus result from the interaction between the "external" and the "internal," between the time-independent style forms and the time-dependent style structures, between the mode and the code, between the extraopus and the intraopus norms. The fixed relationship between these two poles at any level in a work will therefore account for that complex of things we call style.

Style analysis may thus emphasize either an "external" or an "internal" approach. In order to facilitate comparisons between events on the same level, a style analyst may map external style forms onto a given piece. Or, in order to make comparisons between epistemological levels—how one composer's piece in a specific genre differs from the genre of the style in general—he may analyze internally, attempting to discover specific function by reducing the piece according to known style structures.

The style analyst, of course, may find it necessary to construct new style structures on the basis of the "interior" evidence, when known style-structure reductions seem inadequate in the analysis and explanation and revision of past codes seem warranted. Thus research in style structures often results in an increase in the repository of possible style forms. Accordingly, research in style forms attempts to systematize these results.

The distinction made between external and internal approaches is naturally somewhat mythical. In reality the style analyst relies on feedback between style forms and style structures in order to establish his explanatory facts. He rarely is content to view things from only one level.

Regardless of whether the approach is internal or external, however, if the style analyst wants to make his work historically useful he must be pragmatically willing to ignore many anomalies, even important ones. He must strip away many interesting details in favor of what is directly relevant to his task. And the higher he ascends in the epistemological hierarchy—from the study of the works of one composer to the study of a genre or a period—the more he must generalize. That is to say, as in all hierarchical progressions, codification demands economy. Each ascending step requires a "rewriting" and restructuring of style information from lower levels to higher. In short, the very posture the style analyst assumes and the imperatives that motivate his stance necessitate that he eventually idealize his information.[10]

No one should be able to appreciate the work of style analysts more than the critic. For the critic augments his intuition and imagination by relying on style analysis to define the idiosyncratic, to ferret out "default cases" in individual works. The main difference between the style analyst and the critic is that the critic never turns his back on

10. This is why studies on the global domain are so abstract and metaphysical. The change from the concrete to the abstract is largely a matter of abandoning codes in favor of modes—or dynamic structures in favor of static forms.

the idiosyncratic elements of the work. The critic thrives on unique detail. He focuses on the function of specific intraopus relationships. Forms without content concern him only indirectly. It is true that in studying a work the critic makes use of his knowledge about the composer's other works, the genre to which the specific work seems related, the period it exemplifies, the apparent cultural influences, and so forth— indeed true criticism is impossible without *all* such considerations.[11] But, in contrast to the style analyst, the critic faces the work looking downward from the top of the epistemological hierarchy.

His interest in history is instrumental, for his analytical imperative literally emanates from the work itself. He avoids glossing over details for the sake of a style-structure reduction. Nor is he primarily interested in discovering the general rules of the style the piece exemplifies (though these are clearly germane to his explanation). Rather, he believes that the work writes *its own* rules—is a law unto itself, as we say—that it establishes its own intrinsic method of operation, its own idiosyntax. In short, the critic's attention is directed toward the *idiostructural aspects* of the work so he may understand how they enter into *unique* structural relationships with *other* structural levels in the epistemological hierarchy.

Distinguishing Idiostructures from THE Structure

This is a good place to point out that the idiostructure must not be confused with THE structure of a work. THE structure of a work can never be precisely pinpointed because it lies in the midst of an aesthetic triangle created by the artist who composes the work, the performer who brings the work to life, and the listener whose imagination completes the work.[12] Since the aesthetic beliefs of the performer and the listener will converge differently each time the work is brought into existence, THE structure remains a virtual entity. It cannot be found in the notes on the printed page or in the individual disposition of either

11. See Edward T. Cone's review of *Explaining Music* by Leonard B. Meyer in *Journal of the American Musicological Society* 27 (Summer 1974):335–38. As Ackerman says, "Each work of art can be considered a repository of experiences entering from every direction in the artist's surroundings" ("Style," p. 177).

12. For an excellent discussion of this with regard to reading, see Wolfgang Iser, *The Implied Reader* (Baltimore: Johns Hopkins University Press, 1974), chap. 11.

the performer or the listener. "The" structure, on the other hand, is something tangible and finite with which we theorists can deal via the idiostructure and the style structure (implications, realizations, and nonrealizations).

Earlier I suggested that style may be imagined as a large circular pool with the most frequently recurring forms at the center and the least frequent at the periphery. If we imagine THE structures of works as "triangles" (brought into active existence by the composer's music, the performance, and the listener) containing convergent (though ever-changing) aesthetic points of view operating within the stylistic circle, we can see that style functions as a kind of *environment*. To the theorist its value is thus primarily pragmatic: it serves as a practical source of models of implication and realization. To the listener its value is didactic: it conditions his expectations and modifies his knowledge about the familiar. The more a piece confirms his expectations—the more the triangle lies close to the center of the circle—the more purposely didactic a piece will seem and the more boring he will find it. In order to bring the triarchic relationship into existence, a work must therefore leave some expectations unfulfilled. Thus, in important respects all pieces of music are unclosed. Because of this, great works never lie completely within the stylistic circle; nor do they lie completely without. Rather, they constantly remake the periphery as the aesthetic of the triarchy changes. Hence, the stylistic circle is a construct whose synchronic center can be identified but whose diachronic edges are perpetually being altered.

Although neither the idiostructure nor the style structure by itself is THE structure of a work, the idiostructure is the critical nucleus upon which structural relationships are made, including those of style. An explanation of "the" structure of a work thus always entails a consideration of both idiostructure and style structure. However, the idiostructure and the style structure are never the same thing and therefore should not be confused in analysis.[13]

13. On the importance of distinguishing the structure of a piece from its style, see Meyer, *Explaining Music*, chap. 1; William Thomson, "The Problem of Music Analysis and Universals," *College Music Symposium* 6 (Fall 1966): 89–107; and Edward T. Cone, "Analysis Today," *Musical Quarterly* 46 (April 1960):172–88.

In the sense that all works diverge from the style, constantly modifying our expectations, it is the individual work that has empirical reality, not the style. Thus, in order to establish a knowledge of style, we must work from individual works "inward"—toward the synchronic center—just as we did in example 52, where the analysis of the individual parameters led us first to recognize the networked idiostructure of the phrase, then to understand how the various style structures contributed to it, and eventually to identify the different style forms.

DISTINGUISHING STYLE STRUCTURE FROM IDIOSTRUCTURE

In the relatively new discipline of historical musicology, there has been in the past a necessary and understandable emphasis on style analysis. The result, however, has been detrimental to critical analysis and in the long run has led to a lack of emphasis on genuine theory.[14] It is well to remember that general theoretical principles are derived from answering specific questions within a limited framework; that genuine theory is more likely to be derived from the activity of criticism than from style analysis. In general, the broader one's analytical goals, the more one tends to rely on the mode of description (inductive reasoning) rather than on real analytical explanation. Scientists are more aware of this than musicologists:

> Science developed only when men began to refrain from asking general questions such as: What is matter made of? How was the universe created? What is the essence of life? Instead, they asked limited questions, such as: How does an object fall? How does water flow in a tube? Thus, in place of asking general questions and receiving limited answers, they asked limited questions and found general answers. It remains a great miracle that this process succeeded, and that the answerable questions became gradually more and more universal.[15]

14. This is not the situation, incidentally, in related fields. Methods of criticism, for instance, are slightly more advanced in literature and the fine arts than they are in music, primarily, one suspects, because the referential content is greater.

15. Victor F. Weisskopf, "The Significance of Science," *Science Magazine* 176 (April 1972):143. I am grateful to Leonard B. Meyer for pointing this article out to me.

If we apply techniques of style analysis to a work and reduce it to its style structures, we will certainly understand it much better; but what we will understand better is the style aspect of the piece, not its idiosyncratic "content." To understand idiosyncratic content we need to derive the idiostructure, and in order to do that we need authentic theories of critical analysis. However, because every piece displays both idiostructural and style-structural aspects, and because these aspects are interdependent, analytical theory must obviously be able to account for both. Indeed, we may measure the adequacy of any theory by its ability to explain both aspects with a single unified set of postulates.

Since style structure and idiostructure are inextricably intertwined, how can we distinguish them? The answer is that because style structures—as the norms of a piece, a composer's works, a genre, a school, a geographical locale, a period of history, or whatever—are characterized primarily by stability,[16] their identity can be located by attending to closure. For a style structure to be established, it must achieve some degree of equilibrium in a given context. This equilibrium may be achieved monoparametrically, for example, the ♩♪ rhythmic pattern in example 52c, or transformationally, for example, the occurrence of congruent closure in several parameters that weaken nonclosure in another (see the creation of the gap pattern in measures 1–2 in examples 52d and f). In short, for a structure to become part of a composer's style or the style of his school, his geographical locale, or such, it must possess enough closural features so that other composers can reproduce it. A structure acts as a style structure because it "works" in a particular context, and, if it is capable of being imitated, it becomes further established and continues to "work."[17] The mimetic process

16. See Ackerman, "Style," pp. 164–65, 169.

17. A point made by E. D. Hirsch, Jr., in "Stylistics and Synonymity," *Critical Inquiry* 1 (March 1975): 576. At some point of statistical recurrence, a style structure becomes a *sign*; that is, it comes to symbolize all the previous functional uses of it in accordance with the closural characteristics of the convention. See Nelson Goodman, "The Status of Style," *Critical Inquiry* 1, no. 4 (June 1975):808. Elsewhere (p. 806) Goodman says, "Exemplification involves reference by what possesses to the property possessed, and thus that exemplification though obviously different from denotation (or description or representation) is no less a species of reference."

depends on abstraction.[18] But we can abstract for purposes of imitation only if we emphasize the closural aspects of a structure over the nonclosural ones. Style is therefore identified by stability and closure.

The idiostructure, on the other hand, is defined chiefly by nonclosure. That is, within a piece idiostructure will often be exemplified by those things that keep the motive, phrase, or section ongoing and processive, and style structure will be exemplified by those things that create articulation and disjunction between events. I have discussed how the style analyst may consider his field from "external" (style forms) or "internal" (style structures) vantage points. Similarly, the critic may look at the idiostructure from two viewpoints. He may regard the totality of events in a piece in terms of the network structure it creates. Or he may look at any part of the network of a piece in terms of its idiostructural aspect. The two viewpoints are obviously complementary, just as those of the style analyst are. Which one the critic emphasizes depends on the type of work under consideration. In a work that is heavily stylistic in orientation, the critic will normally be interested only in explaining certain idiostructural aspects, whereas in a highly original work he will necessarily have to consider complex structural networks in order to arrive at a satisfactory explanation. In a general sense, the idiostructural aspect and the style structural aspect are simply extensions of the idea that tones are simultaneously open and closed on any given level.

AN EXAMPLE

Let us examine again how style structures become transformed to an idiostructural realization—to a unique network of structures. We have already discussed the theme in the second key area of the first movement of Beethoven's Fifth Symphony in connection with Schenker's optimization of the harmonic parameter and his neglect of the triadic implications in the melody, and we may now reconsider the melody with respect to both style-structural and idiostructural aspects.

Since the first four bars of Beethoven's theme create a formal phrase which can result only from closure, we may take these bars as the

18. Ackerman, "Style," p. 165: "Style is not discovered but created by abstracting certain features from works of art."

formation of a level. And since style structure is also characterized by closure, the identity of the style structures within this level can be recognized. A few of these may be discussed. Melodically, the first four bars of Beethoven's theme, for example, may be broken down into three little style structures (see example 53): the B♮–E♮ gap structure with the descending fill (D–C–B♮), the D–E♮–F linear structure, and the B♮–D–F triad. Any one of these by itself is a common style form in tonal music with varying degrees of implication, and in functional contexts like Beethoven's melody and countless other melodies each

Example 53

operates as a style structure. Taken as a whole, of course, the particular functional combination chosen by Beethoven recurs in other places as well, and as such the three motives together may also be called a style structure, albeit at a higher level. In the old popular song "Aura Lee," for instance, the gap of the fourth, the linear pattern, and the triad function similarly (example 54). In the four-bar motive from Beethoven's theme (example 53), all the style structures function to close the melodic pattern, though not uniformly: the gap-filled B♮–E♮ (with a return to the initial B♮) is more closed than both the triad B♮–D–F and the linear pattern D–E♮–F.

Example 54. George R. Poulton, "Aura Lee" (text omitted)

From the idiostructural aspect, however, we find all these same melodic structures acting to keep the motive open and ongoing. The initial gap filling from B♭–E♭ downward, for instance, is interrupted with the interpolation of the upward E♭–F, and the final note of the gap fill (B♭) is weakened because it falls not on the first beat of measure 4, as expected, but on the second. (The reader may experience the weakened closure in Beethoven's melody by comparing example 55—"as it might have been"—with the original melody in example 53.) Indeed, though *rhythmically* a style structure, the repeated Cs in Beethoven's melody (measures 3–4, example 53), coming as they do after the upwardly mobile D–E♭–F to renew the descent from the same D in measure 2, infuse the whole four bars with a lyrical effect that would otherwise be lacking. Further, the linear D–E♭–F animates the B♭–D–F triadic structure on the metric beats (measures 1–3), strengthening the nonclosure which impels the pattern onward toward its eventual realization. Any one of these things taken "externally," of course—the repetition, the weak-beat ending, the interruption of the gap, the linear animation of the triad, and so forth—would exemplify style

Example 55

forms; and when taken together, "internally" in terms of closural function, they exemplify the style structure of these four bars. From a nonclosural, processive point of view, however, they contribute unmistakably to the idiostructure of the four-bar motive.

Perhaps the easiest way to comprehend the idiostructure of a work is to construct a shadowgraph of its unrealized implications. I have argued and emphasized throughout that the structure of a work is a result of its implications, its realizations, *and* its nonrealizations. In other words, behind the actualized events of every work, there exists a "structure" of *unrealized* implications which contribute to the "depth" of the piece and to the richness of our experience with it. In example 56,

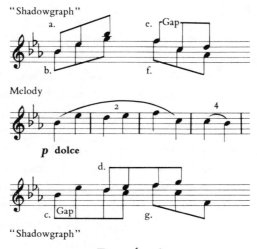

Example 56

for instance, the initial B♭–E♭ of Beethoven's melody implies a continuation to the octave above (graph a), a triadic continuation (b), and a gap (c)—all three being known melodic forms in the style. On the D in measure 2, the filling in of the gap is started, only to be immediately interrupted by the D–E♭–F reversal. The implied continuation of that pattern up to G (graph d) is itself broken off by the leap down to C, which sets up three new implications (graphs e, f, g). Thus, *denial* of implication is always an important part of the idiostructural aspect in the sense that denial always sets up unexpected implications.

At any point in composing the melody, Beethoven had to make a choice about which implication to realize. Similarly, during a rehearsal the conductor and the orchestra would have to choose which implications they would emphasize (the multiplicity of implications being by no means equiprobable). Finally, during a performance the listener, according to his imagination, intelligence, and learning in the style, would respond in retrospect to these choice points and envision their meaning in prospect in a unique and ineffable way. (Thus the interaction among these three "participants" depends not so much on expectation as on its continual modification.) It is for this reason, as we have seen, that THE structure of a work is always indeterminate and configurational—the result of the triarchy among composer, performer, and listener. Be that as it may, the shadowgraph technique—"what might have been"—offers an important means of discovering the idiostructure of works. Though the opening melodic style structure of Beethoven's melody and "Aura Lee" are highly similar, for instance, a comparison between their shadowgraphs would show in a forceful manner how radically different their idiostructures are.

I have already discussed in detail the idiostructural realization of the B♭–D–F triad on the high B♭ in measure 32 and need not review that process (see example 14). Suffice it to say here that the idiostructural realization of this triadic pattern—its delayed realization (a delay, as we recall, intensified by a highly motivated ascending bass) and its peculiar interlocking with the other triads—is possible only because on a lower level the patterns close as style structures. That is, as a closed style structure, the B♭–D–F (measures 1–3) permits the *formation* of an unclosed idiostructural implication on a higher level (example 57). Style always lays the groundwork on which the next idiostructure builds. The signif*ied* style structure becomes on a higher level a signify*ing* idiostructure.[19] What is structur*al* becomes structur*ing*.

For example, the linear pattern D–E♭–F (measures 2–3) that begins as a style structure in a major key later becomes part of the idiostructure as the ascending implication is transformed through a change of mode

19. The "signified-signifying" dualism was first put forth by the Swiss linguist Saussure. As my colleague Eugene K. Wolf has pointed out, the parallel German terms are *Form* and *Formung*.

Example 57

(example 58). The change of mode in measure 13 (to F minor), followed by a modulation to A♭ major (measure 17), has a quieting effect on the upward mobility of both the D–E♭–F and the higher-level B♭–D–F triad in the early bars because the change of mode from measure 13 onward, as I pointed out earlier, is not recognized at first for what it is: a long delay to the high B♭ (see example 58). Rather, the listener at first has to deal with the prospect that the serious turn of events may be irrevocable—that the initial ascent and its promise of release and fulfillment may never be realized. The repeated E♭–F–G♭ pattern in measures 21–22 then comes as a hopeful sign in that it renews the earlier ascent and converges the earlier D–E♭–F and the D♭–E♭–F lines while portending the realization of the B♭ in measure 32. But the release of the tension is anything but sudden, since relentless repetitions of the melodic line, a new minor mode (B♭ minor) in measures 21–31, a rising bass line, and a long crescendo delay the culminating melodic B♭ for eleven bars.

Of such linear and triadic processes, then, is the idiostructure of Beethoven's melody made. Thus we can easily understand why one of the most difficult problems facing music theorists is the accurate symbolization of these kinds of implicative, idiostructural relationships.

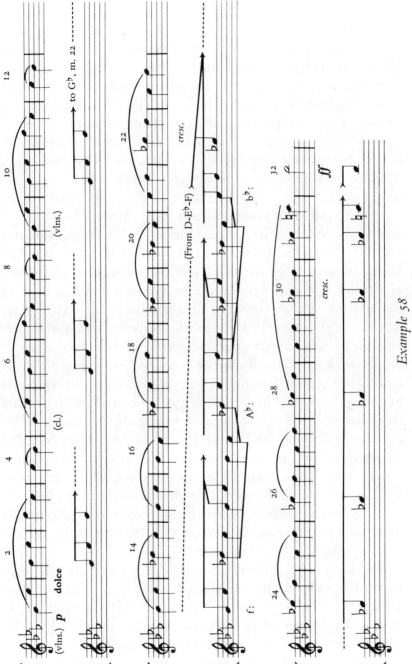

Example 58

The closural relationships of style structures seem, in contrast, much easier to represent. Idiostructural symbolizations, such as those found in examples 14 and 58, are important, of course, not only because they show critical aspects of structure that are lost when only known style-structure reductions are invoked in the analysis, but also because they indicate to style analysts the source of style structure. We can never know whether our style-structure reductions are correct unless we can describe how idiostructures are achieved, since, as I have emphasized, style structures emerge from the closure of idiostructures.

STYLE STRUCTURES AND THE LISTENER

It is not difficult to see how the listener puts style information to use. For style forms, as style-structure realizations shorn of intraopus functional meaning, are stored in the listener's memory as a repository of potential *implications*—as unactualized *prospective* meanings, ready to be put to use. Our perceptual faculties cause us to interpret what we hear in a new context in relation to what we know from past realizations and to evaluate what we expect in terms of implications. Thus the listener uses a style form in either of two ways: (1) by using the implication aspect of the style form (i.e., the style-structure aspect) in prospect to evaluate strength of implication in the new context; or (2) by using the realization aspect of it in retrospect to measure the extent to which the new context matches the old (i.e., its formal synonymity). The listener always calls upon his knowledge of the style in order to deduce relevant information about the intraopus context. At the same time, he relies on inductive reasoning to deal with the deviations from the norm. In prospect, deduction allows him to invoke the relevant models of implication. Simultaneously in retrospect, he inductively evaluates his comprehension of the realization.

We have heard the melody of so many pieces in tonal style begin with a 3–4–5 motion, for instance, that when we hear measure 1 of Schumann's "Soldier's March" (example 59a) we instinctively "know" in prospect where the melody is going: the 3–4–5 (B–C–D) will move either on to the eighth degree (G, a triadic continuation at a higher level), or back to the fourth degree (to C, beginning a gap fill on the next level), or on to the sixth degree (to E, a continuation pattern on the same level). At the same time, we have also heard countless tonal pieces begin with the ♫ ♪ rhythm. Thus, the combination of these two style structures (B–C–D in the soprano and the ♫ ♪ rhythm) enables us to evaluate which of the three implications is the strongest and which is the weakest. For the ♫ ♪ rhythm, as we saw, transforms the B–C–D pattern to B–D (example 59*a*). Therefore, calling upon his knowledge of the style as it appears in, say, the other three excerpts of example 59, the listener would deduce about the beginning of example 59*a* that the motion to the octave (as in the piece of example 59*b*) or the motion back to the fourth degree (59*c*) would be more likely than an ascending linear continuation. For the linear continuation of the pitch pattern (B–C–D to E) to be strongly implicative, the rhythm would also have to have been continuing on that level—that is to say, additive, as in example 59*d*.[20] Accordingly, the motion to E in measure 2 of example 59*a* is the least likely realization, and because of that, its occurrence is all the more effective (this explains, perhaps, why performers invariably stress the downbeat in measure 2 of Schumann's piece). Thus, our knowledge of, say, the style structures in examples 59*b*, *c*, and *d* would enable us to evaluate in prospect the strength of the melodic implication in measure 1 of example 59*a*. At the same time, the actual intraopus melodic realization that occurs in measures 1–2 of Schumann's piece would retrospectively be evaluated in terms of the comparative differences between it and the relevant style structures known to the listener.

Assuming an *active* predisposition on the part of the listener, that is, a selective propensity to structure new information, what is required to trigger his expectations is (in part) a sufficient degree of functional synonymity between his prior knowledge stored in the form of style forms and the style structure that occurs in the new context. Although we do not know the conditions for enough functional synonymity to activate expectation, it is clear that *structured* statistical information plays an important part, since on the whole those structural events which frequently recur in the style are more easily remembered and

---

20. Examples 59*b* and *d* also have the bass following in parallel tenths, just like examples 47*a–c*.

Example 59. (a) *Schumann's "Soldier's March"*; (b) *Handel*, Siroe ("*Non vi piacque inguisti Dei*"); (c) *Mozart's Symphony no. 35, Trio*; (d) *Dvořák's Symphony no. 8, II.*

more readily triggered than nonstructured, isolated, nonrecurring events. One expects also that these structural events must in some respect be isomorphic to our basic mental processes. Otherwise no veridicality—reinforcing feedback—would occur. Style, then, operates as a mechanism for memory and an important vehicle for comprehension.

At any given moment, of course, idiostructural and style-structural aspects are usually interlocked in such a way as to give rise to new levels. Because of this, the equilibration achieved between nonclosure and closure is rarely perfect. Between levels, nonuniform noncongruence is the rule. One parameter of a piece may be processive and idiosyncratic while another may be highly conventional and style-bound. Furthermore, individual pieces obviously vary in the degree to which they are idiostructural or style structural. The theme in the second key area of the first movement of Beethoven's Fifth Symphony (example 14), for instance, is of great originality and impact; Schumann's "Soldier's March" (the melody reproduced in full in example 49) is much less so. Some pieces, like nursery-rhyme tunes, seem to be mostly a redundant concatenation of one style structure enchained to another. Others, like Stockhausen's *Momente*, are wildly idiosyncratic. Overemphasis on either aspect in a composition can be a liability. If a piece is so style structural in orientation that it leaves nothing to the imagination, we quickly grow bored. If a piece is so idiostructural that it leaves practically everything to the imagination, we feel put upon and become irritated. Great works fall somewhere between these two extremes. The listener must be cognitively engaged—the work must "activate" the listener's knowledge of the style; and he must be aesthetically rewarded for his efforts—the piece must deviate sufficiently to produce new reactions on the part of the listener.

Within any given system, style-structural aspects tend to become increasingly dominant as we ascend the hierarchy. The reason for this is that in any hierarchical system, each level must be somewhat more closed than the level preceding it. As we saw in example 52, Level II was much less "active" than Level I. This gradual increase in closure is in fact a necessary condition for the emergence of levels. Parametric congruence with respect to closure increased during the course of the phrase in example 52 (recall the growing incidence of vertical lines between examples 52*d*, *e*, *f*, and *h*) until eventually a summarization resulted (example 52, stage 2). Thus it seems logical that the more levels a piece has (the greater the "arch"), the more style will dominate the top of the hierarchy. This principle is also a direct result of our memory, since the most economical way to cope with large spans of time is to hang musical events on the archetypal trellis we erect on the basis of our past experience of the style. If we could construct a physical model of a piece in the same way scientists construct models of a DNA molecule, the structure would probably appear heavily networked on the lower levels and more treelike on the higher.[21] Peel away the idiostructural network and what remained would be the summarizing tree.

SCHENKERISM AND ITS HARMONIC STYLE STRUCTURES

With this introduction to a basic theory about style structures and idiostructures, we are now in a position to understand that Schenkerian analytical reductions are primarily *style structure reductions*. All of Schenker's transformational structures exemplify harmonic style structures—finite in number and presumably governed by immutable rules within the system. The nonclosural, idiostructural network is almost completely left out. Even though idiostructural aspects can be found in Schenkerian analyses—mainly harmonic ones—the theory must of necessity obscure them, since all the events of a piece are purposely assimilated into an analytical tree. It could hardly be otherwise. For any theory that operates like a transformational grammar system has to emphasize the closural aspects of a piece in order to become operational.

A style is like a language.[22] But the syntactic structure of a language, necessarily idealized and abstracted, simply cannot capture the inherently rich structure of the idiolect. Style functions internally in a particular work as an element of reference enabling the emergence of higher-level idiostructures; or it functions externally as a symbol of any one of the various levels suggested in our epistemological framework (p. 170). But it cannot, by itself, account for the unique complexity of an

21. Recall that in a Schenkerian analysis, just the opposite was true. Lower levels were analyzed as trees. Only the *Anstieg* and the various forms of the *Ursatz* stretch across every branch of the tree at the highest level.

22. Meyer Schapiro, "Style," in *Aesthetics Today*, ed. Morris Philipson (Cleveland: World Publishing Company, 1961), p. 86. Syntax can most profitably be regarded as style on a very high level. Thus, the continuum between syntax and style is like the continuum between space and time—that is, a matter of relativity.

individual work. Generation of structure from style rules can never lead to a critical explanation. Style-structure analysis is to music what linguistics is to literature or iconology is to art.[23]

Although it is clear that the transformational grammar approach—high-level generation of structure from a known style form (like the *Ursatz*)—is a very good way of deriving style structures and putting them into a functional framework, the style structures displayed in Schenkerian analyses are of a particularly limited kind. Since harmony is the optimized parameter, exercising control over all the other parameters, the style structures in Schenkerian analyses primarily exemplify the voice leading of the style. We have already seen in the first four bars of Beethoven's melody from the first movement of the Fifth Symphony, for instance, that Schenker's reduction is blatantly harmonic. Schenker, it will be recalled, conceived measures 2–3 as a series of motions over a dominant which lead to the $\frac{5}{3}$ over the tonic in measure 4 (see again example 12).

The *melodic* style structures in the first four bars, however, which were just discussed (example 53)—the gap filling from B♭–E♭ down to B♭, the linear D–E♭–F, and the B♭–D–F—do not even appear in Schenker's analysis.[24] Furthermore, like melody, the *rhythmic* style structure of ♪♩♩♩|♩ in the bass in measure 4 (example 17) is also reduced to a harmonic style structure (the V–I cadence, see example 12), though clearly the rhythmic motive functions decisively as a style structure to increase the closure of the tonic in measure 4. Nor does the 2/4 *meter* in Beethoven's melody—another style structure—figure in Schenker's harmonic reduction. Yet meter emphasizes melodic closure on the B♭–D–F downbeats in measures 1–2–3. Thus melodic, rhythmic, and metric style in Beethoven's melody are assimilated in Schenker's

---

23. I have elaborated here on some points made by E. H. Gombrich in his article, "Style," *International Encyclopedia of the Social Sciences*, 15:353–60.

24. Though in all fairness, if Schenker had displayed all the details, the D–E♭–F would have appeared, but only as a voice-leading passing-tone structure to an "outside" voice; what I have called the gap-filling motion would have been reduced as a horizontalization of the B♭–E♭ interval of a fourth—the B♭ being a voice of the tonic chord.

analysis to serve under the control of harmonic voice leading in tonal style.

One might defend Schenkerian analysis by contending that the Beethoven theme is so idiosyncratic that no systematic account or accurate symbolization of its structure is possible. In other words, one might argue that Schenkerian analysis is applicable only to works that are heavily stylistic—where we know from empirical evidence what progressions and voice-leading forms are most typical (mean), most frequent (mode), or most representative (median). In such a case, Schenkerian theory would be useful in critical analysis as an anomaly-identifier: any aspect for which we can find no statistical support would be an anomaly and therefore not stylistic, and thus could be consigned to the idiogram.

The difficulty with this argument—and theorists who embrace the transformational approach are fond of it—is that it conceives the idio-structure as a default case where function is viewed as a kind of negative operation. This is obviously at variance with our experience. Artworks are perceived as positive cases, and in fact we usually feel most negative about works that are wholly derivative, which are manifestly stylistic and therefore unoriginal—characterized by repetition and redundancy within and by academic imitation and pedantic conventionality without.

Thus, because Schenkerian analysis relies primarily on the voice-leading style structures of harmony to reduce tonal pieces to structural levels, important aspects of style (melodic, rhythmic, metric, etc.) are ignored. For instance, in example 60, which almost any competent listener would recognize as "very representative" and "very typical" of late baroque style, a Schenkerian type of analysis distorts the melody in order to assimilate the passage on the middleground level into an arhythmicized, voice-leading style structure beginning on an octave and followed by parallel tenths (60*b*).[25]

Thus Salzer would have us believe that the F in the melody in measure 2 follows as a natural consequence of a typical passing-tone motion from the E on beat 3 (over the C♯ in the bass). Actually, however, the

25. The example is from Salzer, *Structural Hearing*, 2:68. Note that Salzer does maintain melodic register in his first-level reduction.

Example 60. After Salzer (C. P. E. Bach, Fantasia, *measures 1–2)*

F in measure 2 would have followed directly from that E only if beats 3 and 4 in measure 1 had been written differently—along the line of least resistance—as shown in example 61*a* (a shadowgraph of "what might have been"). In that case, the E on beat 3 (measure 1) would have been connected to the F on beat 1 in measure 2 as the opening D on beat 1 in measure 1 is connected to the E—by gaps with a partial fill (cf. graph c with graph d). Because this does not happen, the F in measure 2 thus functions somewhat surprisingly as a terminal note in an E–C♯–A–F triad (graph e). In contrast, in Salzer's analysis (example 60) the C♯ and the A function only as "inside voices" to the preceding E—the A being prolonged by the neighboring tone B♭ (N). Consequently the F in measure 2, though obviously following the B♭–A–G on the second half of beat 4, is beamed back to the E (see example 60*a*).

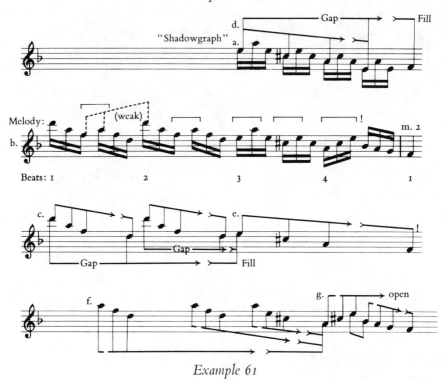

Example 61

This simplistic, voice-leading reduction, however, causes Salzer to omit completely one of the most significant changes in the melody, the ascending A–C♯–E on beat 4. For if we look at the beginning of the melody, we will see that on every preceding beat there is a latent tendency for the triadic motion to ascend (see the brackets in example 61*b*), a tendency that is accelerated on beat 3. Thus, though beats 1–3 set up a stylistic norm of denial that suggests that the ascending tendency can be disregarded in the mind of the listener, the A–C♯–E on beat 4 comes as a significant idiostructural change. Its significance is that it functions to obscure and delay, albeit momentarily, the overriding descent, so that the renewal of that descent with the B♭–A–G on the last half of beat 4 irrevocably connects the F to the E–C♯–A that precedes it (again see example 61*e* and *g*). None of this shows up in Salzer's voice-leading reduction. And we could not look to his analysis to tell us how the melody functions either as a style structure or as an idiostructure in its own right. Notice, for instance, how different the closural patterns (style structures) and nonclosural patterns (idiostructures) in the analysis of example 61 are from those given by Salzer in example 60.

There is no question that the Schenkerian reduction of melody and rhythm to the voice leading of harmonic style structures has to be regarded as an analytical misconception of the first order. Let us take another, more complex, example—Schenker's analysis of the first eight bars of the Sarabande from Bach's Third Suite for Unaccompanied Cello (example 62). Beginning at the top of the tree, we can see how the basic structure, the $\hat{8}$–$\hat{7}$–$\hat{6}$–$\hat{5}$ *Urlinie* over the I–V, generates the analysis (level a).[26] On each succeeding lower level, the basic structure is filled out and elaborated upon. Measures 1–6 create a harmonic motion from the I to the VI$_5^6$–V/V–V (level b–^{6} $_5^7$), the V/V being analyzed as a neighboring-tone structure (N), while the governing melodic motion is the $\hat{8}$ to the $\hat{7}$. On level c, we observe more of the details. The voice-leading progression from the I in measure 1 now goes to the I^6 in measure 5 which precedes the VI$_5^6$ (Schenker's figures in parentheses refer to the intervals over an imaginary prolongation of the tonic). And on the foreground level (d) we can see the specific prolonging motion from measure 1 to the V$_5^6$ in measures 3–4 and the I^6 in measure 5. Let us concentrate on just the first five bars, paying particular attention to measures 3 and 4.

Laying aside the problems of the *Urlinie*—the $\hat{7}$ which comes out of the sixteenth-note motion on the third beat of measure 6 in the music seems farfetched—I can find little to disagree about in the foreground of measures 1–2. The harmonic background is very clear in the cello's double stops, and a parametric analysis of the melody and the rhythm according to the implications and realizations (examples 63*a*, *h*, and *j*) supports Schenker's analysis of the descending C–B–B♭–A in the

---

26. The example is originally from Schenker, *Das Meisterwerk in der Musik*, 2, appendix, 6. Schenker's comments regarding the analysis have been translated by Hedi Siegel in "The Sarabande of J. S. Bach's Suite No. 3 for Unaccompanied Violoncello," in *The Music Forum*, ed. William J. Mitchell and Felix Salzer (New York: Columbia University Press, 1970), 2:274–82.

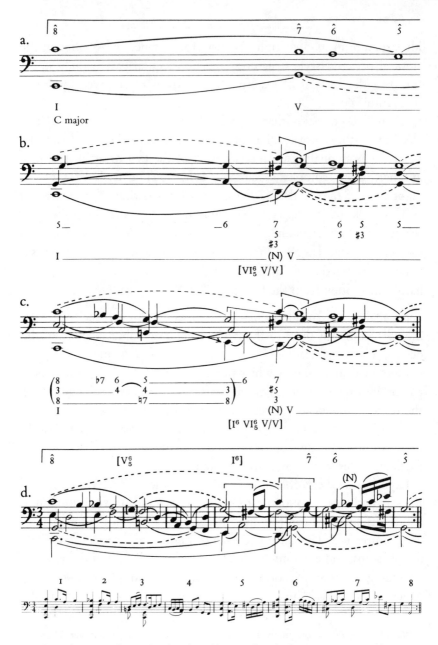

Example 62. After Schenker (Bach's Sarabande from Suite no. 3 for Unaccompanied Cello, measures 1–8).

Example 63

melody (cf. measures 1–2 of example 63*b* with Schenker's analysis in example 62*d*). In measure 3, however, the first problem arises. Schenker is aware that the descending C–B–B♭–A line preceding measure 3 implies a G, and he is aware that that G is delayed until measure 5 (see the dotted slur connecting the bracketed G in measure 3 to the stemmed G in measure 5 in example 62*d*). What he cannot see, however, is that the G of measure 5 is also strongly implied by the D–E–F melodic motion in measure 3, a gap-filling motion which by its very repetition and rhythmic process points forcefully to measure 5 (see the descending A–D and F–D gaps in example 63*c*, and particularly note in measure 3 in example 63*h*, *j*, and *k* how the rhythmic process transforms and contributes to the melodic implication of the F to the G despite the C-harmony on beat 2).

In contrast, Schenker sees,the D–E–F patterns in measure 3 as simply prolongations of the V_5^6 (see example 62*d*). In Schenker's view the F, as the dissonant tone over the prolonged dominant, cannot imply the G in measure 5 but must function as the suspended diminished fifth (the "seventh") of the $_5^6$-chord. That is, the F, as the diminished fifth over the B in the bass, must go to an *E*, not a G. (To Schenker, the E in the music in measure 3 on the third beat would either fill the F–D–F interval, despite the fact that the E is the resolution of the dissonant F over the I chord, or else the last F would simply be an incomplete neighbor to the E.) There is no E in measure 4; so where is the resolution of the prolonged F? This kind of problem is typical and comes up regularly in analysis when one is trying to reduce everything to voice-leading principles. Schenker's incredible solution is to construe the F in measure 3 as part of a prolongational arpeggiation of the first inversion dominant seventh—F, D (measure 3), B, G (measure 4)—leading finally to a "resolution" of the F on the low E in measure 5. (See example 62*d*; the octave transfer is most clearly seen in example 62*c*: note the arrow.)

Such a preposterous analysis cannot help but lead to other problems. In order to make measures 3–4 a prolongation of the V_5^6, Schenker has to verticalize the sixteenth-note motion in measure 4 (C–B–C–A) to $_A^C$ so that $_A^C$ can be seen to function as a passing motion from the D in measure 3 to the B in measure 4 (see example 62*d*). In the Schenkerian scheme, then, we have to accept D–C–B and B–A–G—not to mention

F–D–B—as melodic voices (see the slurs in measures 3–4 in the example) when, in fact, no such manifest melodic lines exist in the actual music.

In an implication-realization model, however, we need not ignore the contiguous relationships on the printed page in order to understand the music. The sixteenth notes in measure 4 are part of an F–C–A triadic pattern (example 63*d*) that becomes gap-implicative on the next level (example 63*e*). F–C–A becomes a descending F–A gap leading directly to the B on beat 2 in measure 4 and finally to the C in measure 5 (63*e*). Moreover, the rhythmic process insures the contiguous connection of the A to the B (see example 63*h*, measure 4). That is, the sixteenth notes' drive to the second beat of measure 4 guarantees that the connection from the A to the B is straightforward and direct. The relationship needs no harmonic mediation or distorting verticalization to be understood.

I have argued that a Schenkerian analysis is primarily a reduction according to harmonic style structures and that style structures in other parameters are often ignored. The F–A–B–C gap-filling pattern, for instance (example 63*e*), is a *melodic* style structure, which does not appear in Schenker's analysis. Neither does the *rhythmic* style structure, the ♩♪♪♪ ♪ of measure 3, figure in. It has also been emphasized that a Schenkerian analysis is inadequate in analyzing idiostructures. The most processive part of measures 1–6 in the Sarabande, for instance, takes place in measures 3–4. Yet the complex network of activity shown in example 63 becomes in Schenker's analysis part of a treelike prolongation of a dominant seventh. To be sure, Schenker's analysis tells us a good deal about the harmonic structure of Bach's piece; the mapping of the *Ursatz* and *Urlinie* onto the music and the generation of the various tonal levels are in many ways instructive. But where harmony is not the dominant parameter, as in measures 3–4, the analysis is seriously inadequate—even misleading. We simply cannot allow voice leading to assimilate melody and rhythm.

The conclusion, then, is that Schenkerian theory can be put to good use as a means of style analysis where (and only where) harmony is the dominant parameter and the closural aspects of tonal harmonic style predominate. But that is saying a lot: I can think of no other analytical system that can claim that much. For this reason, and because Schen-kerian analysis often *does* generate good harmonic style structures, it should not be discarded in toto, as some anti-Schenkerians have argued.[27] Schenker's analysis of the First Prelude in Book I of Bach's *Well-tempered Clavier*, for instance, is instructive in many ways for just these reasons (see the analysis in *Fünf Urlinie-Tafeln*):[28] harmonic implications in this piece are significantly stronger than the implica-tions in other parameters. That is, Schenker's analysis of the structure of Bach's prelude is useful because idiostructural aspects are all but buried by the heavy overlay of baroque clavier style (e.g., arpeggiated chords, motivic repetition, "normal" harmonic progressions, etc.). Melody and rhythm seem to serve mostly at the pleasure of the harmonic voice leading.

Where harmony is not the dominant parameter of the style, however, and where idiosyncratic elements are present in great strength, Schen-kerian analysis is of limited value. William Mitchell's Schenkerian analysis of Wagner's *Tristan Prelude* is deficient, in my view, precisely because Wagner's music is so idiosyncratic and style-*transforming*.[29] Mitchell, for instance, adds Wagner's concert ending to the overture so that he can view the "entire work as a unified, articulated structure" in A major-minor.[30] Thus, in Schenkerian fashion, all the motion in the flat keys from measures 74 to 83—which in the opera pave the way for the opening scene in *C minor*—become flatted submediant (F) and neopolitan (B♭) prolongations in A major. The point, of course, is not to deny the function of the keys of F and B♭ in A major in the concert version, but rather to recognize that Wagner saw them functioning *both* ways *simultaneously*. That is, regardless of whether one is listening to the overture as a concert piece or as the prelude to the opera, measures 74–83 have strong implications to the flat side—to C minor.

27. E.g., Michael Mann, "Schenker's Contribution."

28. Heinrich Schenker, *Five Graphic Music Analyses* (New York: Dover Publica-tions, 1969).

29. William J. Mitchell, "The Tristan Prelude: Techniques and Structure," in *Music Forum*, ed. William J. Mitchell and Felix Salzer (New York: Columbia Uni-versity Press, 1967), 1:162–203.

30. Ibid., p. 162.

And these implications cannot be completely assimilated into some hypothetical unified whole. The events of Wagner's overture are simply too idiosyncratic to be selected and organized under one key like A major. Indeed, the resistance of the overture to supersummation by any *Ursatz*-like tonal structure is literally the source of its power.

To repeat: Schenkerian analysis can tell us a good deal about the style structures of tonal harmonic language and their function in particular pieces, but not about idiostructures. In this respect Schenkerian analysis is like transformational grammar, which can teach us a lot about a given language but little about the nature of individual utterances insofar as they do not conform to or exemplify the ideal of good form as defined by the theory. And we should recall once again that we can never know *that* something is in fact a style structure unless we know *how* it is derived from the idiostructure in the first place.

MUSIC VERSUS THE STUDY OF LANGUAGE

In this connection, let us briefly review some crucial differences between music and language. One important but obvious difference is that language is used for ordinary social discourse and music is not. This is not to deny that music has important social functions. Clearly it does.[31] But because music is an art, its communicative function is radically different from that of normal language. Recorded music, for instance, is often used as a background for chatter at a party, but we never *literally use* "talk" as a "setting" for any social function.[32]

Many examples could be cited illustrating the weakness of the analogy between music (or any of the arts) and ordinary language, but the point to be stressed here is that, because of the ordinary social use to which language is put, a linguist's interest in conventions is vitally different from a music theorist's interest in style structures. A sociolinguist may be interested in grammar in order to understand the rules that govern how two speakers communicate with *each other*. But since in music our

---

31. It is, of course, these very functions in *both* language and music which the transformational grammar approach ignores.

32. Though movies and plays do use "talk" as a "setting," they cannot be classified as ordinary social discourse, since, like music, they are art forms, and our response to them is more or less tacit.

"response" to what is "spoken" is more or less tacit (though certainly not passive), our interest in style conventions is directly tied to the experience of a specific artwork. In art we do not learn style structures in order to "participate" in ordinary "discourse." We learn them in order to participate in a specific aesthetic experience. Similarly, a performer learns conventions not in order to put them to use *as* conventions, but in order to integrate them into that uniquely specific expression that belongs to an artwork. A linguist can easily imagine utterances without reference to real people, but a theorist can hardly conceive of style structures apart from specific musical acts. Put another way, although a good case can be made and has been made for someone or something definitely "speaking" in music,[33] the concept of an "ideal speaker," which may be a valid rationale in transformational grammar, makes no sense whatever in music. Theorists can, and sometimes do, make a case for an "ideal *listener*," but they never posit an ideal speaker.

In Schenkerian philosophy, however, the *Ursatz* is conceived as an ideal utterance. Consequently as in transformational grammar, in the idealistic, rationalistic approach of Schenkerian analysis the actual utterance of an artwork is treated as a neutral object exemplifying the significations the observer attaches to the transformations.[34] That is, the Schenkerian analyst does not see the meaning of the artwork as inextricably linked to its extra- and intraopus diachrony. For instance, the stylistic history of the artwork and its effect on style change, its unfulfilled implications for the "future," both within and without the piece, and the ineffable meaning of the "eternal now" that obtains between performer and listener—all these are of no virtual significance in the Schenkerian transformational approach. Schenkerian transformations are seen taxonomically to be operating under the laws of a pure syntax. All those things the grammar cannot take care of are eliminated. Rhythmic, metric, and specific registral considerations are completely assimilated into the analysis because, unabsorbed, they

33. See Edward T. Cone, *The Composer's Voice* (Berkeley: University of California Press, 1974), an interesting and suggestive study.

34. See Thomas Clifton, "Some Comparisons between Intuitive and Scientific Descriptions of Music," *Journal of Music Theory* 19 (Spring 1975):66–111.

"pollute" the assumed systematics of the harmonic style.[35] The music of Bach, Handel, Mozart, Haydn, Beethoven, and Brahms is conceived as part of the same synchronic system—diatonic tonality. And the system is treated as a whole so that the coherence of pieces can be derived deterministically by analyzing them according to a finite number of tonal transformations. Thus the more any given piece exemplifies the tonal transformations (the style structures)—harmonic or otherwise—*the less an analysis of it depends on the time element.* This is true both historically (I have already pointed out that the synchronic view of Schenkerian theory by its very nature has to ignore the diachronic aspect) and within the piece itself: Schenkerian analysis with its treelike generations cannot deal with the structural networks created by the "unabsorbed," nonadjacent realizations of time-*dependent* implications in the idiostructure.

To return, however, to the main point. Music is an art. And because it does not function as a means of communication in ordinary social discourse, listeners or theorists of music do not have the same kind of interest in style structures that grammarians have in transformations. Musical style structures offer a way of comprehending real pieces, not ideal utterances. That is, listeners and theorists view the rules of grammar not as the absolute constraints of a given system but as a means of identifying idiosyncratic deviations from the norm. A class of style structures, like the various versions of the *Ursatz*, is plainly a mental construct. Schenker to the contrary, such structures do not occur in nature. Thus a style structure cannot be regarded as a proper representative "species" because the *general* signification of a style structure is ultimately related directly to the *specific* piece (or pieces) from which it comes. The general notions we bring to bear on a piece of music are bound up with a unique idiostructure.

Another crucial difference between music and linguistics is that in music the criteria for what constitutes well-formed "utterances" are determined by *internal context*, that is to say, by the *closure* achieved or

---

35. I remind the reader that in order to make the grammar work, things are added as well—for example, *Urlinie*-tones and bass-roots, which literally do not occur in the music in any register.

implied by the idiostructure. This is in sharp contrast to transformational grammar, where criteria are determined by *external conventions*.[36] In linguistics these conventions are used to derive rules which will generate a finite number of transformations that can be mapped onto sentences in order to give a systematic account of the differences between the grammatical and the ungrammatical. Likewise in Schenker: harmonic style structures (conventions) are used to deduce rules to generate voice-leading transformations that can be used to obtain various levels of structure from the *Ursatz* down through the middleground and foreground. And like transformational grammarians, Schenker is also interested in separating the grammatical from the ungrammatical, but for quite a different reason: Schenker wants to use his theory not only as an analytical method but also as a system of aesthetics—as a way of separating good pieces (those well formed according to the theory) from bad pieces (the ill formed).

Since, as Schenker proclaims, all content in art is determined by considering the relation of the *Urlinie* to the *Bassbrechung*[37]—without a goal, there is no content[38]—and since coherence is foreordained by nature in conjunction with the *Ursatz*,[39] it follows for Schenker that if one cannot find the *Ursatz*, the piece is incoherent and has no background. As in transformational grammar, where assumptions about language (= style) are partially defined according to what does *not* belong (like mathematical sets), so in Schenkerian theory any work which does not exemplify the transformational rules is automatically tagged as a bad piece, as being ill-formed[40]—despite the fact that Schenkerians have never been able to formulate the criterial attributes of tonal style (see p. 135).

Most aestheticians would take the opposite position, arguing that the closer a work is to the style—that is, the more it exemplifies the rules, the more it belongs to the statistical center—the less the chances

36. Boretz, "Meta-Variations," p. 55.

37. *Der Freie Satz*, p. 45.

38. Ibid., p. 29.

39. *Das Meisterwerk in der Musik*, pp. 500–12. (Schenker, 3:15–21).

40. See, for instance, in *Das Meisterwerk* Schenker's criticisms of Stravinsky (p. 213 ff.) and Wagner (p. 242). (Schenker, 2:38 ff., 54).

are that it will be aesthetically satisfying. Nursery-rhyme tunes can be "Schenkerized" with little trouble because they exemplify statistically the heart of tonal style, but their being well formed hardly makes them aesthetically valuable. For aesthetic content in artworks depends to some extent on originality, on the innovation of new, intraopus "modes" and "codes," on an internalized assimilation of the style, instead of on a complete dependence on the old and hackneyed.

Aesthetic value results when idiostructural elements and style-structural elements are fused in such a way as to elicit a continuing and profound reaction from the listener. No doubt tonal composers rely on models. The studies of manuscripts (e.g., those concerned with Beethoven's sketches) prove this conclusively. And we know how important the acquisition of theoretical rules is for a composer's learning of a given style. *But it simply does not follow that works can be reduced on higher levels to these models*—voice-leading, contrapuntal, harmonic, formal, or otherwise. Style structures make up only part of the explanation of a work; the simultaneous idiostructure must also be considered.

Style rules, after all, are not constraints in the true sense of the word, in the sense of obligatory norms that fully determine the structure of a work. If they were, historians and aestheticians and music theorists could all operate as scientists. A breaking of the rules of *Praxis* is not necessarily an aesthetic error. Like a great speech, a great musical work establishes its own unique, inalienable laws which may be so convincing as to eventually establish a new "language"—the innovation of a new style. In short, the aesthetic authority of a work does not come from its compliance with external style rules. Our sense of its significance emanates from the internal structure of the work itself.

Finally, let us remember that, in contrast to language, the meaning of music is primarily syntactic, not semantic. In music, denotation—for example, the playback of the recording of a nightingale in Respighi's *Pines of Rome* or the jingle of sleighbells in LeRoy Anderson's *Sleigh Ride*—constitutes only a small portion of the overall meaning. Furthermore, like all the arts, the relationship of music to the world is that of a sustained metaphor. That is, the syntactic relationships in musical structures suggest a comparison with structured experiences in the world, but no more. Because of this constant analogy from art to life, an artwork's dependence on style conventions is thus greatly loosened.[41] And, unlike language, where syntactic meaning is heavily dependent on denotation and semantic structure, in music the syntactic reference of a style structure—its likeness (or difference) in meaning in relation to other style structures—is ultimately dependent on how it functions in a specific relation with the idiostructure.

41. Henri Zerner, "Master of Arts," review of *Words and Pictures: On the Literal and the Symbolic in the Illustration of a Text* by Meyer Schapiro, in *New York Review of Books,* 14 November, 1974, pp. 39–40.

Twelve
CONCLUSION

IN THIS BOOK MANY OF THE PROBLEMS SURROUNDING SCHENKERIAN theory have been examined. I have argued that Schenkerian theory will not pass muster as either a formal or an informal axiomatic method, and that the affirmation of the *Ursatz* as a high-level (background) structure and its rationalistic use as a method of generating lower-level structures are mistaken. Because the actual structures derived and the structure of the method of derivation cannot be distinguished, Schenkerians are unable to give convincing closural principles—that is, genuine rules of *construction*. This would perhaps have less damaging consequences were tonality truly a synchronic system with a finite number of invariant rules. But, as we have seen, in music the assumption of a synchronic system is untenable. An important part of music has to do with diachronic meaning, a virtual concept of implications apart from their specific realizations.

Since the chief unitary principle of Schenkerian analysis lies in the application of the *Ursatz*, where the functional meaning of a part is known in advance, Schenkerians cannot avoid committing the error of asserting that the deterministic wholes are prior to the parts. In a temporal art, this means that a "predetermined future" (the later strata) establishes the syntactic meaning of the present, whether within or without the piece. Such "finalism," however, does violence to a piece because it denies to the parts the inherent, self-regulating, independent status they clearly have. And further, this "finalism" leads to a complete disregard of any virtual prospective meaning where both *transforming potential* and *nonrealization of implications* of the parts exist as real possibilities. The disregard of prospective meaning, apart from the preformed *Ursatz* and the assumption of a finite number of voice-leading transformations operating within a whole system called diatonic tonality, is, of course, responsible for the idealized, diluted, impoverished, and often simply erroneous explanations of artworks that Schenkerian analysis offers.

Further, Schenkerian analysis, as we have seen, requires that the harmonic (voice-leading) parameter be weighted over all the other parameters. Since the the theory is synchronically built to accommodate any kind of transformation, the analysis assimilates all parameters according to the voice-leading rules of tonal harmony. Melodic, metric, rhythmic, and registral facts are ignored except when they adventitiously coincide with the supersummative aims of the theory. The same can be said of form. Because Schenker believes that form on lower levels is generated from pitch-levels *above*—although the converse is more nearly true—he necessarily has to disregard much of the formal tradition of analysis.[1] Moreover, favoring certain kinds of idealized harmonic norms over formal or rhythmic norms requires Schenker to reduce all pieces to treelike structures. As in the approach of transformational grammar, levels are thus completely decomposed and a "systems approach" analysis results instead of a "hierarchical network" analysis.

Finally, the question of virtual implication within a piece or virtual stylistic formation without never arises in Schenkerian theory. There is nothing in the analytical results to indicate how a given piece transforms (assimilates) the style system. Similarly, the question of how the systematic elements of the assumed style came into being, and the extent to which presystematic elements are still operative in it, simply never arises. No room exists for what I have called a two-way assimilation-accommodation view. Although Schenkerian synchronics and the Hegelian view of history go hand in hand—the *Ursatz* is to analysis what the *Zeitgeist* is to historiography[2]—we have to discover how and why goals come to function as such both in history and in individual works. This cannot be done unless the concept of transformation is complemented by a virtual concept of implication. We must adopt a

1. E.g., the poetic feet tradition.
2. For a view of the flaws of this insofar as style is concerned, see Schapiro, "Style."

"telenomic" view in music without becoming dupes to teleology. For the signifying implication and the signified realization are two inseparable, complementary aspects of our temporal experience. Any illuminating music theory must take both aspects into account *simultaneously*. The idea that an organizational "basis" like diatonic tonality ordered by a "structure of structures" (the *Ursatz*)[3] contains everything in advance should be abandoned. Instead, we must search for the general principles of hierarchical *construction* that govern various parameters on various levels.

The implication-realization model sketched throughout this essay offers, I believe, one way of doing this. If we recognize that tonality is not a synchronic system but a historical style—and in the face of everything we know about history I do not see how even the Schenkerians can deny this—it follows that our idea of transformational operations must be reformulated. Because we are not able to distinguish clearly between invariant laws and variable rules, it should be obvious that we must regard with considerable skepticism any notion of a standard set of tonally syntactic transformations.

But by creating a theory of prospective formation—pattern generation—which deals with the processes of construction inherent in idiostructures, it should be possible to identify the transformational aspects of individual works. By thus integrating the concept of formation with transformation—implication with realization—it may be possible to explain processes of development and growth and to discover the transforming *potential* of individual works as they contribute to historical change. An implication-realization model would also provide a method of evaluating Schenkerian reductions, since whatever is systematic in the style—harmonic or otherwise—is ultimately based on recurrences of realized implications. A feasible model would be illuminating in that it would necessarily require us to coordinate—theoretically, methodologically, and analytically—the relationship of structure to transforming potential. The concept of generation would then become genuinely operational in prospect as well as retrospect. Formation would replace preformation. Construction and structuralism would be united.

3. Or serialism ordered by a tone row.

In an implication-realization model, style forms—schemes based on statistical recurrences—would be conceived as forming anterior pools of *implicative* resources on which the idiostructure (and the style structure) would draw. In the actual piece, of course, only some implications would be present. And only some, not all, of these would be realized. Thus the structure of work would be composed of the realizations of implications presented *against* the background of specific implications *and* specific nonrealizations which the idiostructure and the style structure simultaneously invoke—instead of simply a rearrangement of patterns belonging to a standard list of transformations, as we find in the Schenkerian model. As in microphysics, where the temporal "acts" of particles are studied by the "tracings" they leave, so behind each piece of music would lie a "shadowgraph" of unrealized implications whose *implied* (unrealized) *structure* would contribute to the richness and depth of the actual realizations of the idiostructure and the style structure.

Because in the implication-realization model a specific realization in the idiostructure would not need to be a priori an exemplar of the system, the way new contexts transformed the style could be studied. An implication-realization model would thus enable us to attempt an "ideal" theoretical approach: to balance the diachronic output (the form*ing* implications and the transform*ing* potential of the idiostructure) with the synchronic inputs (the form*ed* realizations which become the basis of the style).

Doubtless an implication-realization approach would introduce an element of uncertainty into analysis that is not found in the standard transformational model as conceived by the neo-Schenkerians. For instance, in making provision for the historicostylistic view in the analytical methodology, we would find that the analytical results of an implication-realization model would not be internally verifiable. That is why it would be necessary to go "outside" and "enrich" the model in some way in order to add elements of formalization. That this is necessary should come as no surprise, however, for we have long known that rules of inference must be strengthened by appealing to theories of a higher rank.

I argue that we should attempt to formalize an implication-realization model within the context of certain psychological theories that bear directly on the problems of perception and structure. For the construction and the forming of inferences about initial gap patterns (essentially, I am referring to preparatory "sets"), we could rely on certain formalized covariation principles suggested in hypothesis theories and set dynamics in cognitive psychology.[4] To evaluate the continuation and realizations of processes, we could employ selected principles of pattern perception from Gestalt psychology—for example, the Gestalt law of "good continuation" discussed earlier (chap. 10, note 38). Finally, certain principles of hierarchy theory could be invoked in order to circumvent the fallacies of Gestaltism.

The great problem facing us in the formulation of an implication-realization model—as I see it—is the lack of a good psychological theory on memory, particularly as it pertains to syntactic systems. To date, most psychological studies on memory have been concerned only with the memory of various kinds of randomized patterns. Psychologists choose such material for running their empirical tests in order to minimize the role of learning so that they may have some assurance that they are evaluating man's inherent cognitive structures. So far, however, these studies are of little use to music theorists. It may be that in attempting to formulate the rules of implication and realization we can suggest alternative ways for cognitive psychologists to study the operation of memory in syntactic systems.

On the other hand, from a purely methodological point of view, many psychological theories are illuminating and suggestive with regard to music theory because to be internally consistent they have had to meet head-on the epistemological problem of the synchronic/diachronic dualism. Moreover, the external invariant laws taken from certain psychological theories would have the benefit of being abstract enough to allow for concrete applications in musical contexts yet would be "loose" enough to be theoretically elaborated upon. The aim from the beginning would be to create a theoretical synthesis rich enough to deal analytically with both the synchronic and the diachronic aspects of music. The analytical methodology would be built upon an array of external formal concepts that would, when properly linked with an implication-realization theory, be internally coherent.

4. For a summary of these, see Allport, *Theories of Perception*, chaps. 15 and 16.

The details of such a program are beyond the scope and aim of this book.[5] And it should be emphasized that the program itself—the concept of an implication-realization model and the analytical alternatives I have discussed in light of such a model—would not be possible without the accomplishments of Heinrich Schenker and his followers. On the other hand, only by recognizing the fatal defects of Schenkerism and moving beyond the limitations of the transformational model will it be possible to create an adequate theory of music, one that will enable us to write truly explanatory analyses and truly illuminating criticism—perhaps even the first history of artworks and their musical structures.

5. My forthcoming book, *The Melodic Structure of Tonal Music*, will attempt to make explicit the principles of the implication-realization model.

WORKS CITED

Ackerman, James S. "Style." In *Art and Archeology*, edited by James S. Ackerman and Rhys Carpenter. Englewood Cliffs, N.J.: Prentice-Hall, 1963.

Allport, Floyd H. *Theories of Perception and the Concept of Structure*. New York: John Wiley and Sons, 1955.

Babbitt, Milton. Review of *Structural Hearing*, by Felix Salzer, *Journal of the American Musicological Society* 5 (1952):260–65.

———. "The Structure and Function of Musical Theory: I." *College Music Symposium* 5 (1965):49–60.

Batstone, Philip. "Musical Analysis as Phenomenology." *Perspectives of New Music* 8 (1969):94–110.

Beach, David. "A Schenker Bibliography." *Journal of Music Theory* 13 (1969):3–37.

Bent, I. D. "Current Methods in Stylistic Analysis, Summary of Remarks." In *Report of the Eleventh Congress, 1972*, International Musicological Society. Vol. 1. Copenhagen: Wilhelm Hansen, 1974.

Boretz, Benjamin. "Meta-Variations: Studies in the Foundations of Musical Thought (I)." *Perspectives of New Music* 8 (1969):1–74.

Bruner, J. S.; Goodnow, J. J.; and Austin, G. A. *A Study of Thinking*. New York: Science Editions, 1959.

Bunge, Mario. "The Metaphysics, Epistemology and Methodology of Levels." In *Hierarchical Structures*, edited by L. L. Whyte, Albert G. Wilson, and Donna Wilson. New York: American Elsevier, 1969.

Chomsky, Noam. *Syntactic Structures*. The Hague: Mouton and Co., 1957.

Clifton, Thomas. "An Application of Goethe's Concept of *Steigerung* to the Morphology of Diminution." *Journal of Music Theory* 14 (1970):165–89.

———. "Some Comparisons between Intuitive and Scientific Descriptions of Music." *Journal of Music Theory* 19 (1975):66–111.

Cohen, Morris R., and Nagel, Ernest. *An Introduction to Logic and Scientific Method.* New York: Harcourt, Brace and Co., 1934.

Cone, Edward T. "Analysis Today." *Musical Quarterly* 46 (1960):172–88.

———. *The Composer's Voice.* Berkeley: University of California Press, 1974.

———. *Musical Form and Musical Performance.* New York: W. W. Norton, 1968.

———. Review of *Explaining Music,* by Leonard B. Meyer. *Journal of the American Musicological Society* 27 (1974):335–38.

Cooper, Grosvenor, and Meyer, Leonard B. *The Rhythmic Structure of Music.* Chicago: University of Chicago Press, 1960.

Daniskas, John, *Grondslagen voor de analytische Vormleer der Musiek.* Rotterdam: W. L. and J. Brusse, 1948.

Federhofer, Helmut. *Beiträge zur musikalischen Gestaltanalyse.* Vienna: Akademische Druck- und Verlagsanstalt, 1950.

Forbes, Elliot, ed. *Ludwig van Beethoven: Symphony No. 5 in C Minor.* New York: W. W. Norton, 1971.

Forte, Allen. *Contemporary Tone-Structures.* New York: Bureau of Publications, Teachers College, Columbia University, 1955.

———. "Schenker's Conception of Musical Structure." *Journal of Music Theory* 4 (1959):1–30.

———. *Tonal Harmony in Concept and Practice.* New York: Holt, Rinehart and Winston, 1962.

Gombrich, E. H. *Art and Illusion.* Princeton: Princeton University Press, 1960.

———. "Style." *International Encyclopedia of the Social Sciences.* 15:353–60.

Goodman, Nelson. "On Likeness of Meaning." Reprinted in *Semantics and the Philosophy of Language,* edited by Leonard Linsky. Urbana: University of Illinois Press, 1952.

———. "The Status of Style." *Critical Inquiry* 1 (June):799–811.

Hamblin, C. L. *Fallacies.* London: Methuen and Co., 1970.

Harris, Roy. *Synonymy and Linguistic Analysis.* Oxford: Blackwell, 1973.

Hartmann, Heinrich. "Heinrich Schenker und Karl Marx." *Oesterreichische Musikzeitschrift* 7 (1952):46–52.

Henneberg, Gudrun. *Theorien zur Rhythmik und Metrik.* Tutzing: Hans Schneider, 1974.

Hesse, Mary. "Models and Analogy in Science." *The Encyclopedia of Philosophy.* Reprint ed. 5:354–59.

Hirsch, E. D., Jr. "Stylistics and Synonymity." *Critical Inquiry* 1 (March):559–79.

Humphreys, Willard C. *Anomalies and Scientific Theories*. San Francisco: Freeman, Cooper and Co., 1968.

Jonas, Oswald. *Einführung in die Lehre Heinrich Schenkers*. Vienna: Universal Edition, 1972.

Kalib, Sylvan. "Thirteen Essays from the Three Yearbooks 'Das Meisterwerk in der Musik' by Heinrich Schenker: An Annotated Translation." Ph.D. diss., Northwestern University, 1973.

Kassler, Michael. "A Trinity of Essays." Ph.D. diss., Princeton University, 1967.

Katz, Adele T. "Heinrich Schenker's Method of Analysis." *Musical Quarterly* 21 (1935): 311–29.

————. *Challenge to Musical Tradition*. New York: Alfred Knopf, 1945.

Koch, Heinrich Cristoph. *Versuch einer Anleitung zur Composition* (1782–93).

Komar, Arthur J. *Theory of Suspensions*. Princeton: Princeton University Press, 1971.

Krueger, T. Howard. "'Der Freie Satz' by Heinrich Schenker: A Complete Translation and Re-editing." Ph.D. diss., State University of Iowa, 1960.

Kubler, George. *The Shape of Time*. New Haven: Yale University Press, 1962.

Kuhn, Thomas S. *The Structure of Scientific Revolutions*. Chicago: University of Chicago Press, 1962.

Langer, Susanne K. *Feeling and Form*. New York: Charles Scribner's Sons, 1953.

LaRue, Jan. *Guidelines for Style Analysis*. New York: W. W. Norton, 1970.

Laske, Otto. "In Search of a Generative Grammar for Music." *Perspectives of New Music* 12 (1973): 351–78.

Lussy, Mathis. *Le Rythme musical*. 3d ed. Paris: Librarie Fischbacher, 1897.

Mann, Michael. "Schenker's Contribution to Music Theory." *Music Review* 10 (1949): 3–26.

Mattheson, Johann. *Der vollkommene Capellmeister* (1739).

Meyer, Leonard B. *Emotion and Meaning in Music*. Chicago: University of Chicago Press, 1956.

————. *Music, the Arts, and Ideas*. Chicago: University of Chicago Press, 1967.

————. *Explaining Music: Essays and Explorations*. Berkeley: University of California Press, 1973.

Mill, John Stuart. *A System of Logic Ratiocinative and Inductive*. Toronto: University of Toronto Press, 1973.

Mitchell, William J. *Elementary Harmony*. Englewood Cliffs, N.J.: Prentice-Hall, 1964.

Mitchell, William J. "The Tristan Prelude: Techniques and Structure." In *The Music Forum*, edited by William J. Mitchell and Felix Salzer, vol. 1. New York: Columbia University Press, 1967.

———, and Salzer, Felix. *The Music Forum*. 3 vols. to date. New York: Columbia University Press, 1967–

Morgan, Robert P. "The Delayed Structural Downbeat and Its Effect on Tonal and Rhythmic Structure of Sonata Form Recapitulation." Ph.D. diss., Princeton University, 1969.

Narmour, Eugene. "The Melodic Structure of Tonal Music: A Theoretical Study." Ph.D. diss., University of Chicago, 1974.

Parsons, Charles. "Foundations of Mathematics." *The Encyclopedia of Philosophy*. Reprint ed. 5:188–213.

Pattee, Howard H. "Physical Conditions for Primitive Functional Hierarchies." In *Hierarchical Structures*, edited by L. L. Whyte, Albert G. Wilson, and Donna Wilson. New York: American Elsevier, 1969.

———. "Unsolved Problems and Potential Applications of Hierarchy Theory." In *Hierarchy Theory*, edited by Howard H. Patee. New York: George Braziller, 1973.

Piaget, Jean. *Structuralism*. Translated by Chaninah Maschler. New York: Harper and Row, 1971.

Pierce, Anne Alexandra. "The Analysis of Rhythm in Tonal Music." Ph.D. diss., Brandeis University, 1968.

Popper, Karl R. *The Logic of Scientific Discovery*. New York: Basic Books, 1959.

———. *Conjectures and Refutations: The Growth of Scientific Knowledge*. London: Routledge and Kegan Paul, 1963.

Rameau, Jean-Philippe. *Treatise on Harmony*. Translated by Philip Gossett. New York: Dover Publications, 1971.

Regener, Eric. "Layered Music-Theoretical Systems." *Perspectives of New Music* 6 (1967):52–62.

Reicha, Antoine (*sic*). *Traité de mélodie*. 2d ed. Paris: A. Farrenc, 1832.

Riemann, Hugo. *System der musikalischen Rhythmik und Metrik*. Leipzig: Breitkopf and Härtel, 1903.

Riepel, Joseph. *Anfangsgründe zur musikalischen Setzkunst* (1754).

Riezler-Stettin, Walter. "Die Urlinie." *Die Musik* 22 (1930):502–10.

Robinson, Ian. *The New Grammarians' Funeral*. Cambridge: Cambridge University Press, 1975.

Rosen, Charles. *The Classical Style*. New York: W. W. Norton, 1972.

Salzer, Felix. *Structural Hearing*. New York: Dover Publications, 1962.

Salzer, Felix, and Schachter, Carl. *Counterpoint in Composition*. New York: McGraw-Hill, 1969.

Schapiro, Meyer. "Style." In *Aesthetics Today*, edited by Morris Philipson. Cleveland: World Publishing Company, 1961.

Scheibe, Johann Adolph. *Der critsche musicus* (1737–40).

Schenker, Heinrich. *Beethoven Fünfte Sinfonie*. Edited by Karl Heinz Füssl and H. C. Robbins Landon, Vienna: Universal Edition, 1969.

———. *Five Graphic Music Analyses*. New York: Dover Publications, 1969.

———. *Der Freie Satz*. Rev. ed. Vienna: Universal Edition, 1956.

———. *Harmonielehre*. Berlin: J. G. Cotta'sche Buchhandlung Nachfolgen, 1906.

———. *Harmony*. Translated by E. M. Borgese. Chicago: University of Chicago Press, 1954.

———. *Kontrapunkt*. 2 vols. Vienna: Universal Edition, 1910 and 1922.

———. *Das Meisterwerk in der Musik*. 3 vols. Munich: Drei Masken Verlag, 1925, 1926, 1930.

———. *Der Tonwille*. Vienna: A Gutmann Verlag, 1921–24.

Schünemann, Georg, ed. *Beethoven: Fünfte Symphonie nach der Handschrift im Besitz der preussischen Staatsbibliothek*. Berlin: Maximilian-Verlag Max Staercke, 1942.

Schwarcz, Robert M. "Steps toward a Model of Linguistic Performance: A Preliminary Sketch." *Mechanical Translation* 10 (1967):39–52.

Seidel, Wilhelm. *Über Rhythmustheorien der Neuzeit*. Munich: Francke Verlag, 1975.

Serwer, Howard. "New Linguistic Theory and Old Music Theory." In *Report of the Eleventh Congress 1972*, International Musicological Society. Vol. 2. Copenhagen: Wilhelm Hansen, 1974.

Simon, Herbert A. *The Sciences of the Artificial*. Cambridge: M.I.T. Press, 1969.

Slatin, Sonia. "The Theories of Heinrich Schenker in Perspective." Ph.D. diss., Columbia University, 1967.

Smith, Barbara Herrnstein. "Poetry as Fiction." *New Literary History* 2 (1971):259–81.

Smither, Howard E. "Theories of Rhythm in the Nineteenth and Twentieth Centuries, with a Contribution to the Theory of Rhythm for the Study of Twentieth-Century Music." Ph.D. diss., Cornell University, 1960.

Thomson, William. "The Problem of Music Analysis and Universals." *College Music Symposium* 6 (1966):89–107.

Treitler, Leo. "Methods, Style, Analysis." In *Report of the Eleventh Congress 1972*, International Musicological Society. Vol. 1. Copenhagen:Wilhelm Hansen, 1974.

Vendler, Z. "Summary: Linguistics and the *A Priori*." In *Philosophy and Linguistics*, edited by Colin Lyas. New York: Macmillan, 1971.

Warfield, Gerald. *Layer Analysis*. New York: David McKay, 1976.

Weber, Gottfried. *Versuch einer geordneten Theorie der Tonsetzkunst*. 3d ed. Mainz, 1830–32.

Weiss, Paul A. "The Living System: Determinism Stratified." In *Beyond Reductionism*, edited by Arthur Koestler and J. R. Smythies. Boston: Beacon Press, 1969.

Weisskopf, Victor F. "The Significance of Science." *Science* 176 (April 1972):138–46.

Weizenbaum, Joseph. *Computer Power and Human Reason: From Judgment to Calculation*. San Francisco: W. H. Freeman and Co., 1976.

Wells, Rulon. "Innate Knowledge." In *Language and Philosophy*, edited by Sidney Hook. New York: New York University Press, 1969.

Westergaard, Peter. *An Introduction to Tonal Theory*. New York: W. W. Norton, 1975.

Westphal, Rudolph. *Allgemeine Theorie der musikalischen Rhythmik*. Leipzig: Breitkopf and Härtel, 1903.

Whitehead, A. N., and Russell, Bertrand. *Principia Mathematica*. Vol. 1. Cambridge: Cambridge University Press, 1957.

Wiehmayer, Theodor. *Musikalische Rhythmik und Metrik*. Magdeburg: Heinrichshofen Verlag, 1917.

Winograd, Terry. "Linguistics and the Computer Analysis of Tonal Harmony." *Journal of Music Theory* 12 (1968):2–49.

Woodger, J. H. *The Axiomatic Method in Biology*. Cambridge: Cambridge University Press. 1937.

Yeston, Maury. *The Stratification of Musical Rhythm*. New Haven: Yale University Press, 1976.

Zerner, Henri. Review of *Words and Pictures: On the Literal and the Symbolic in the Illustration of a Text*, by Meyer Schapiro. *New York Review of Books*, November 1974, pp. 37–42.

Ziff, Paul. *Semantic Analysis*. Ithaca: Cornell University Press, 1960.

Zuckerkandl, Victor. "Schenker System." In *Harvard Dictionary of Music*, 2d ed. Edited by Willi Apel. Cambridge: Belknap Press, 1969.

INDEX

Ackerman, James, 171, 180 n, 181 n

Acoustics, 4 n, 26 n. See also *Klang*; Overtone series

Aesthetics: and internal musical content, 207; and Schenkerian concepts, 38 n, 206; and structure, 177–78, 191; and stylistic rules, 206–7; and value, 207

Allport, Floyd H., 33 n, 125 n, 213 n

Anomalies: and analytical rules, 115, 141; Schenkerian concept of, and style, 194

Anstieg (ascent), 96

Anthropology and style analysis, 171

A priori fallacy: defined, 26 n; in Schenkerism, 15–19 passim, 24, 26, 28–29, 57. See also Apriorism; Fallacies

Apriorism: chess as model of, 114–15, 119; and distortion of temporal meanings in music, 119; and Gestaltism, 40; and linguistics, 115; in Schenkerian generation of structure, 123–24 (fig. 5). See also A priori fallacy; Fallacies

Artworks: empirical reality of, 179, 194; relation to style, 169, 179, 208; Schenkerian treatment of, 169, 204, 205, 206; and transformational grammar, 169, 204

Assimilation-accommodation problem: and history, 45, 47; in Schenkerian theory, 41–46 (fig. 1), 58, 96, 204, 210

Associationism: and Gestaltism, 33; in roman numeral analysis, 1; and structuralism, 137

"Aura Lee," 182–83 (ex. 54), 185

Ausfaltung (unfolding), 5 n, 154 n

Auskomponierungen (prolongations): as artificial creations, 13; distinguishing concept from structure, 26, 42; relation to *Ursatz*, 5–7 (ex. 2); translation of, 5 n. See also Schenkerian method

Austin, G. A., 135 n

Auswechslung (exchange), 5–6 type, 130, 132–33 (ex. 45)

Axial melodic structures, 22–23 (ex. 5). See also Neighboring-tone structures

Axiom: *Klang* as, 19, 28; not equivalent to high-level structure in music analysis, 27; in music vs. mathematics, 27; poetic foot accent as, 139; *Urlinie* as, 20; *Ursatz* as, 12–25 passim, 41, 57, 120. See also Axiomatics

Axiomatics: difficulty with, in music theory, 13–26 passim; distinguished from natural deduction system, 108; informal definition of, 19; and linguistics, 18, 21, 115; and mathematics, 14; neo-Schenkerian view of, and the

History (*continued*)

historians' use of Schenkerian analysis, 45, 47; and implication-realization model, 40, 127–29 (ex. 44), 130–34 (ex. 45), 209–11; and music theory, 134–36; and Schenkerism, 34, 35, 37–40, 42, 45, 47, 121, 204, 210; and style analysis, 171, 179; and concept of transformation, 130–34 (ex. 45). *See also* Synchronic/diachronic dualism

Höherlegung (ascending octave transfer), 7, 81 (ex. 25). *See also* Octave transfer; Register

Horizontalisierung (horizontalization), 5, 73–75 (ex. 22). See also *Klang*; Voice leading

Hoyt, Reed, 144 n

Humphreys, Willard C., 115 n

Idealism, 4, 13, 31, 204

Idiostructure: and aesthetic value, 207; and closure and nonclosure, 181, 191; defined, 164, 181; and denial of implication, 184; distinguished from ineffable structure, 177–79; examples of, 164 (ex. 52), 183–88 (exs. 56, 57, 58); and formation, 185; and hierarchical levels, 191–92; relation to style forms, 212; and shadowgraph technique, 184–85 (ex. 56), 195–97 (ex. 61); style as basis for, 192, 194; style structure derived from, 178, 203; not supersumed in analysis, 203, 205; and symbolization of, 184, 185, 186, 187; and syntactic reference, 208

Implication: general concepts, 122–25, 127, 137, 205; and conformance, 61–63 (ex. 15), 69–70 (ex. 19), 89 (ex. 31); and denial of realizations, 64–65, 125, 126, 127, 184, 209–10; and diachronic meaning, 209–12, 213;

evaluating strength of, 126, 127, 189–90 (ex. 59); harmonic, 146 (ex. 48c), 154 n, 157–58 (ex. 50d), 159–63 (ex. 51), 162–63 (ex. 52e and 52m); metric, 155 n; multiple, not subsumed by realization, 122, 123–25 (fig. 6), 203; and network structures, 127; parametric dependence upon, 126, 127; and generation, 142–66; parametric generation of, contrasted with poetic feet generation of, 142–45 (ex. 46); rhythmic, 91–92 (ex. 34a), 128–29 (ex. 44e and h), 146 (ex. 48c), 148–53 (ex. 49), 158 (ex. 50c), 162–63 (ex. 52h and l), 197, 199–201 (ex. 63); and Schenkerian theory, 52–53, 118, 119, 120, 121, 192, 210, 211; and shadowgraph technique, 63–64 (ex. 16), 184–85 (ex. 56), 195–97 (ex. 61); style as partial basis for, 123, 127, 135, 185; style transformation and realizations of, 128–29 (ex. 44), 130–34 (ex. 45), 210. *See also* Formation; Gap-filling realizations; Implication-realization model, analytical concepts; Implication-realization model, general topics; Linear realizations; Shadowgraph technique; Triadic realizations; Transformation; Voice leading

Implication-realization model, analytical concepts. *See also* Formation; Implication; Implication-realization model, general topics; Realizations; Transformation

—closure and nonclosure: assessment of, 94 (ex. 36); descriptions of, 156–57; simultaneous presence of, on same level, 126, 145–46 (exs. 47, 48), 147 n

—form: 120, 125, 157–63 (exs. 50, 51)

—harmony: examples of transformation, 146 (ex. 48c), 154–56, 158 (ex. 50d), 159–63 (ex. 51); and figured bass,

"irregular" progressions and, 53–54 (ex. 9); as optimized parameter, 41, 48, 89 (ex. 31), 94, 95 n, 210; origin of free composition from *Stufen*, 45; and overtone series, 3–4, 36–37; problems of transformation, 48–57 (exs. 6–11); relationships of, distinguished from counterpoint, 52; status of dissonance, 9, 43–44; status of intervals in, 44; verticalizing horizontal relationships in, 73–75 (ex. 22), 200–201 (ex. 62)

—melody: distortion of relationships in, 194–95 (ex. 60), 198–201 (ex. 62); as horizontalization of harmonic voice leading, 8, 9, 44, 58–86 passim; omission of relationships in, 7 n, 8 n, 69–73 (ex. 18), 200–201 (ex. 62), 205 n; origin of, 44; and polyphonic problem, 73–83 (exs. 22–25, 27), 198, 200–201 (ex. 62); reduction of, to counterpoint, 44; status of intervals in, 44; verticalizations of, 200–201 (ex. 62)

—register: not explicit factor in analytical reduction, 10; independence and potential of, ignored, 44, 81–86 (exs. 25–30), 88, 89

—rhythm: and analytical symbology of method, 90–91 (ex. 32), 91–93 (ex. 34), 95 n, 200–201 (ex. 62); derivation and reduction to counterpoint, 44, 64; not explicit factor in analytical reduction, 10; Schenkerian studies of, 64 n; and time factor, 47, 87, 104–5

—structural levels: concept of, 5–6 (ex. 2), 29 n, 43, 105; derivation of, 8–9 (ex. 2), 44, 50, 93 (ex. 32), 96, 98, 100–102, 105, 123; generation of, 45–46 (fig. 1), 123–24 (fig. 5), 192, 201, 205, 210; rules of transformation

of, 48–54; separation of, 100–103, 104

—voice leading: as dominating parameter, 210; emphasis on, 5–7; importance of, 11; and melody, 77–80 (ex. 24); as misconception with regard to melody and rhythm, 197–201 (exs. 62, 63); reduction of melody to, 8–9, 44, 58–86 passim; rules of, useful in defining tonality, 17

Schenkerism, general topics: as aesthetic system, 38 n, 206; biological metaphor, 35–40, 70, 105; concept of delay in, 119–20; concept of formation in, 108, 119, 120, 123–24 (fig. 5), 210; concept of history in, 34, 35, 37–40, 42, 45–47, 121, 204, 210; concept of implication in, 52–53, 118, 119, 120, 121, 192, 210, 211; concept of structure in, 26, 42, 211, 212; concept of tonality in, 36, 37, 38, 42, 43; concept of tonal space in, 7 n, 12–13, 83 n; concept and treatment of artworks in, 169, 204, 205, 206; concept of unity in, 32, 32 n, 98; and conformance, 88–89 (ex. 31); derivation of counterpoint, 44; and formal analysis, 104; general problems of, summarized, 209–11; and nature, 3–4, 13, 40; and retrospective and prospective relationships in, 51–53 (ex. 8), 55–57 (ex. 11); and rules, 12–13, 42, 48–54, 110, 116–19 (ex. 43), 120–21, 204; as static system, 42 n; and style, 47, 210; and style structures, 193, 194–95 (ex. 60), 201 (ex. 62), 193–94, 201–2 (ex. 62); symbology deficient, 10, 22–23 (ex. 4), 51–52 (ex. 8), 55–57 (ex. 11), 68–73 (ex. 18), 107 n; and transformations, 12–13, 36, 37, 116–20 (ex. 43), 122, 123, 192, 204–5. *See also* Schenkerian method; Schenkerism as intellectual discipline; *Urlinie*; *Ursatz*